LEGENDARY
COMICS

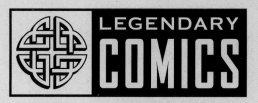

PRESENTS

Thr Lit Wis

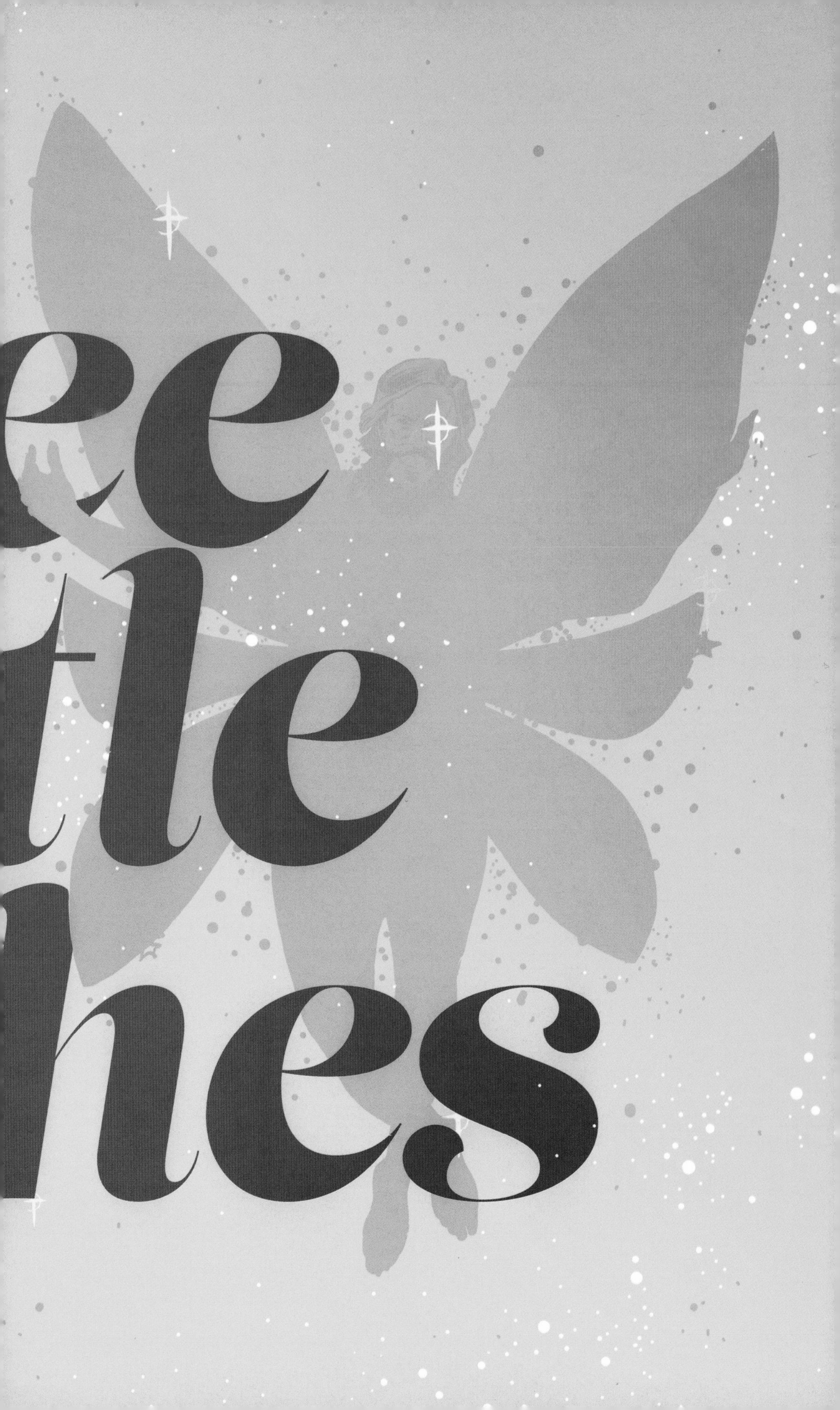
ee
tle
hes

CREATOR & WRITER
PAUL CORNELL

ART & COVER
STEVE YEOWELL

COLORS
PIPPA BOWLAND

LOGO
KATIE AGUILAR

LETTERING
SIMON BOWLAND

COVER & INTERIOR DESIGN
DAVID CURTIS

PRE-PRESS
CONLEY PRESLER

EDITOR
NIKITA KANNEKANTI

SPECIAL THANKS

P.J. HOLDEN

ROB WILLIAMS

SARAH JARVIS

LEGENDARY MARKETING

JOSHUA GRODE
CHIEF EXECUTIVE OFFICER

RONALD HOHAUSER
CHIEF FINANCIAL OFFICER

KRISTINA HOLLIMAN
SVP, BUSINESS & LEGAL AFFAIRS

MARY PARENT
VICE CHAIRMAN OF WORLDWIDE PRODUCTION

BARNABY LEGG
SVP, CREATIVE STRATEGY

REBECCA RUSH
DIRECTOR, BUSINESS & LEGAL AFFAIRS

CHRIS ALBRECHT
MANAGING DIRECTOR, LEGENDARY TELEVISION

MIKE ROSS
EVP, BUSINESS & LEGAL AFFAIRS

BAYAN LAIRD
SVP, BUSINESS & LEGAL AFFAIRS

ROBERT NAPTON SENIOR VICE PRESIDENT AND PUBLISHER

NIKITA KANNEKANTI SENIOR EDITOR

SARA HASKELL DIRECTOR, PUBLISHING MARKETING & SALES

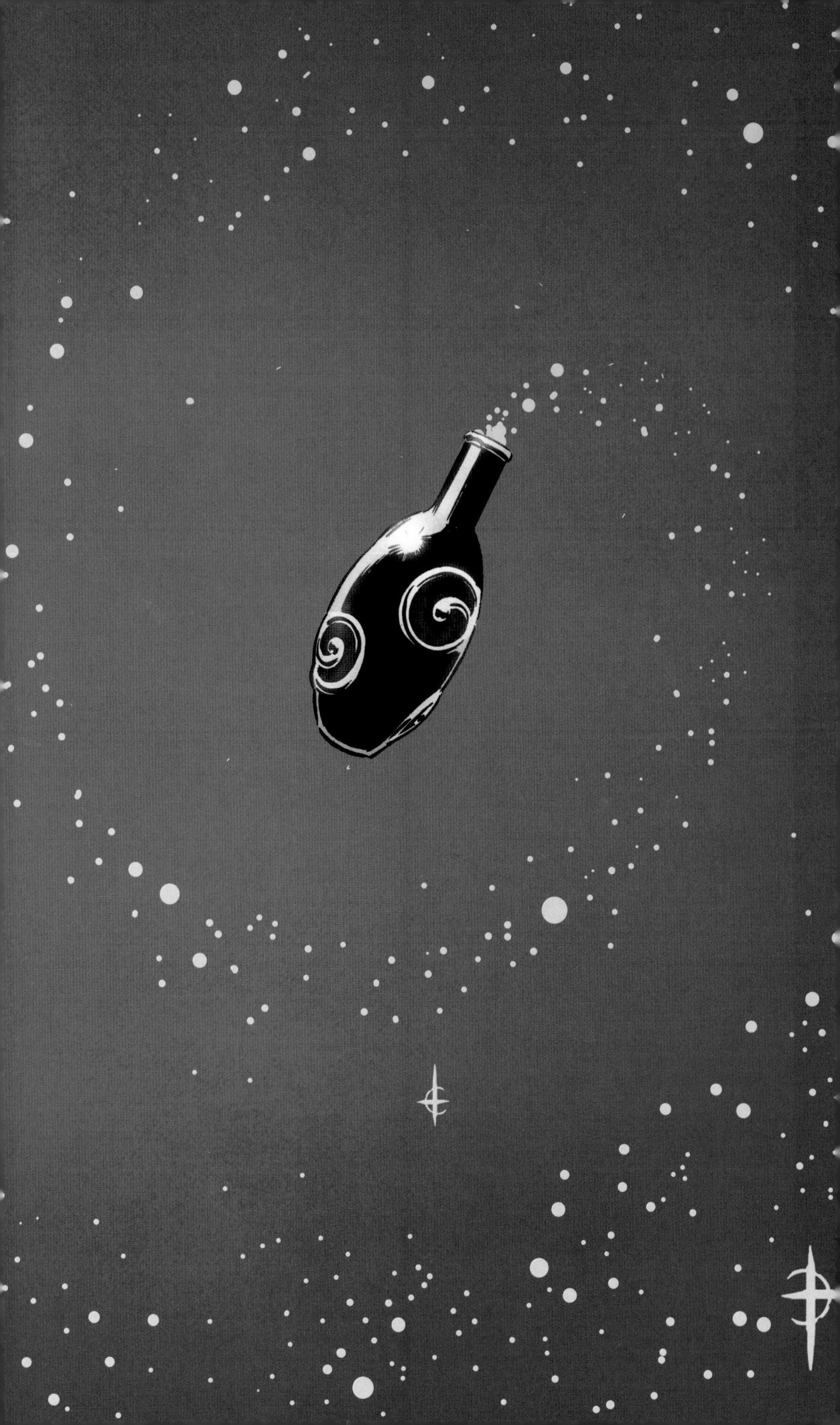

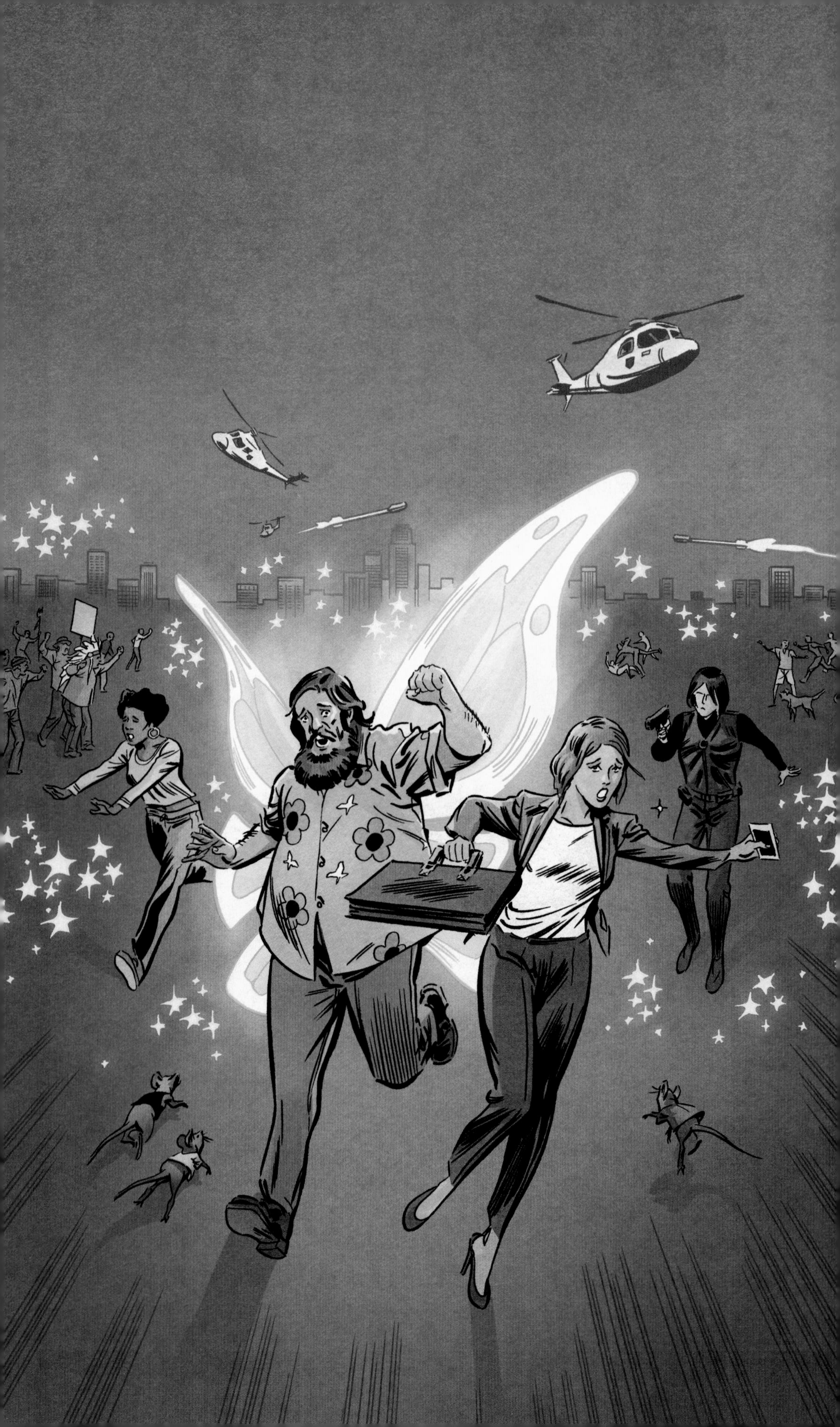

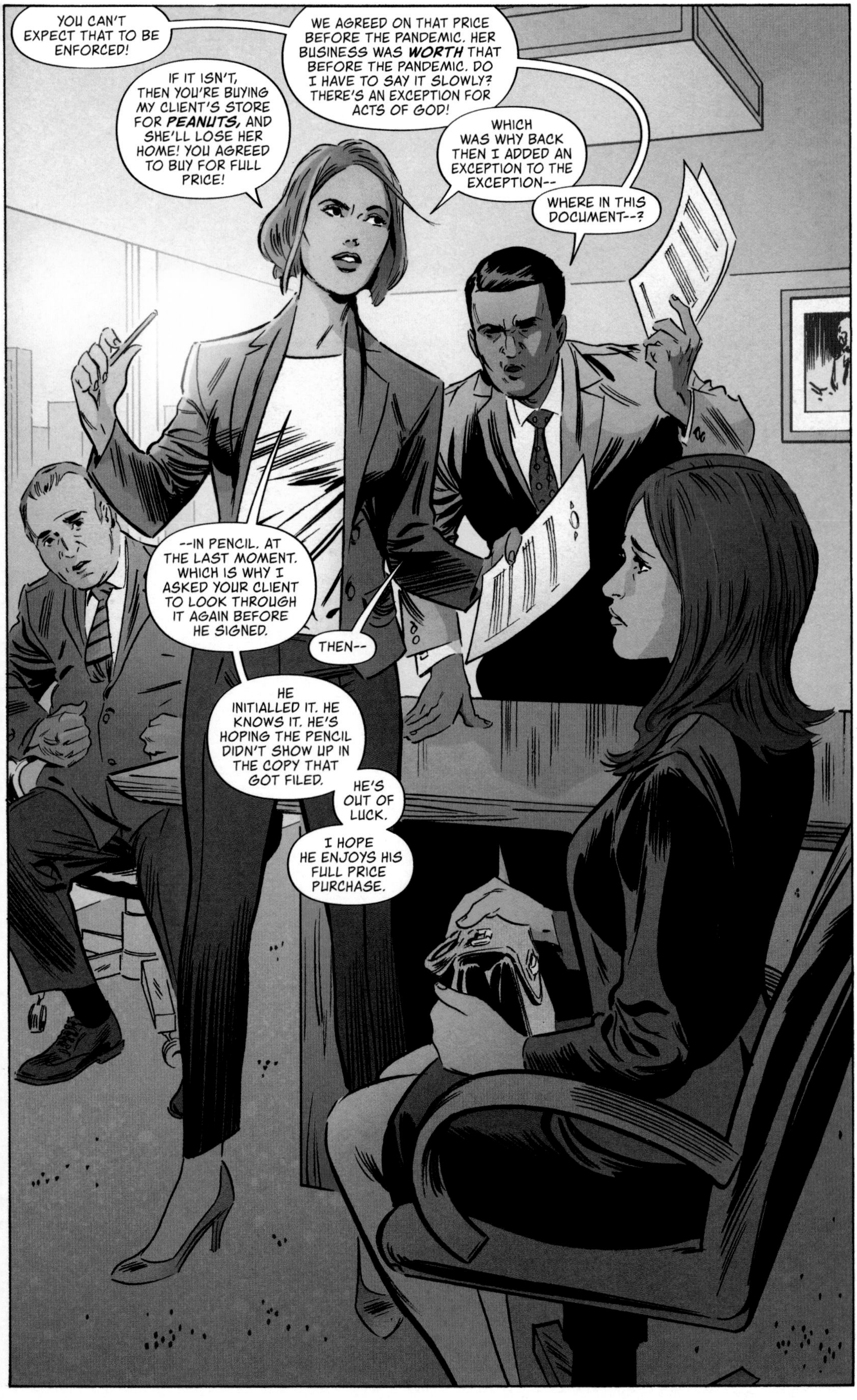
YOU CAN'T EXPECT THAT TO BE ENFORCED!
WE AGREED ON THAT PRICE BEFORE THE PANDEMIC. HER BUSINESS WAS **WORTH** THAT BEFORE THE PANDEMIC. DO I HAVE TO SAY IT SLOWLY? THERE'S AN EXCEPTION FOR ACTS OF GOD!
IF IT ISN'T, THEN YOU'RE BUYING MY CLIENT'S STORE FOR **PEANUTS,** AND SHE'LL LOSE HER HOME! YOU AGREED TO BUY FOR FULL PRICE!
WHICH WAS WHY BACK THEN I ADDED AN EXCEPTION TO THE EXCEPTION--
WHERE IN THIS DOCUMENT--?
--IN PENCIL. AT THE LAST MOMENT. WHICH IS WHY I ASKED YOUR CLIENT TO LOOK THROUGH IT AGAIN BEFORE HE SIGNED.
THEN--
HE INITIALLED IT. HE KNOWS IT. HE'S HOPING THE PENCIL DIDN'T SHOW UP IN THE COPY THAT GOT FILED.
HE'S OUT OF LUCK.
I HOPE HE ENJOYS HIS FULL PRICE PURCHASE.

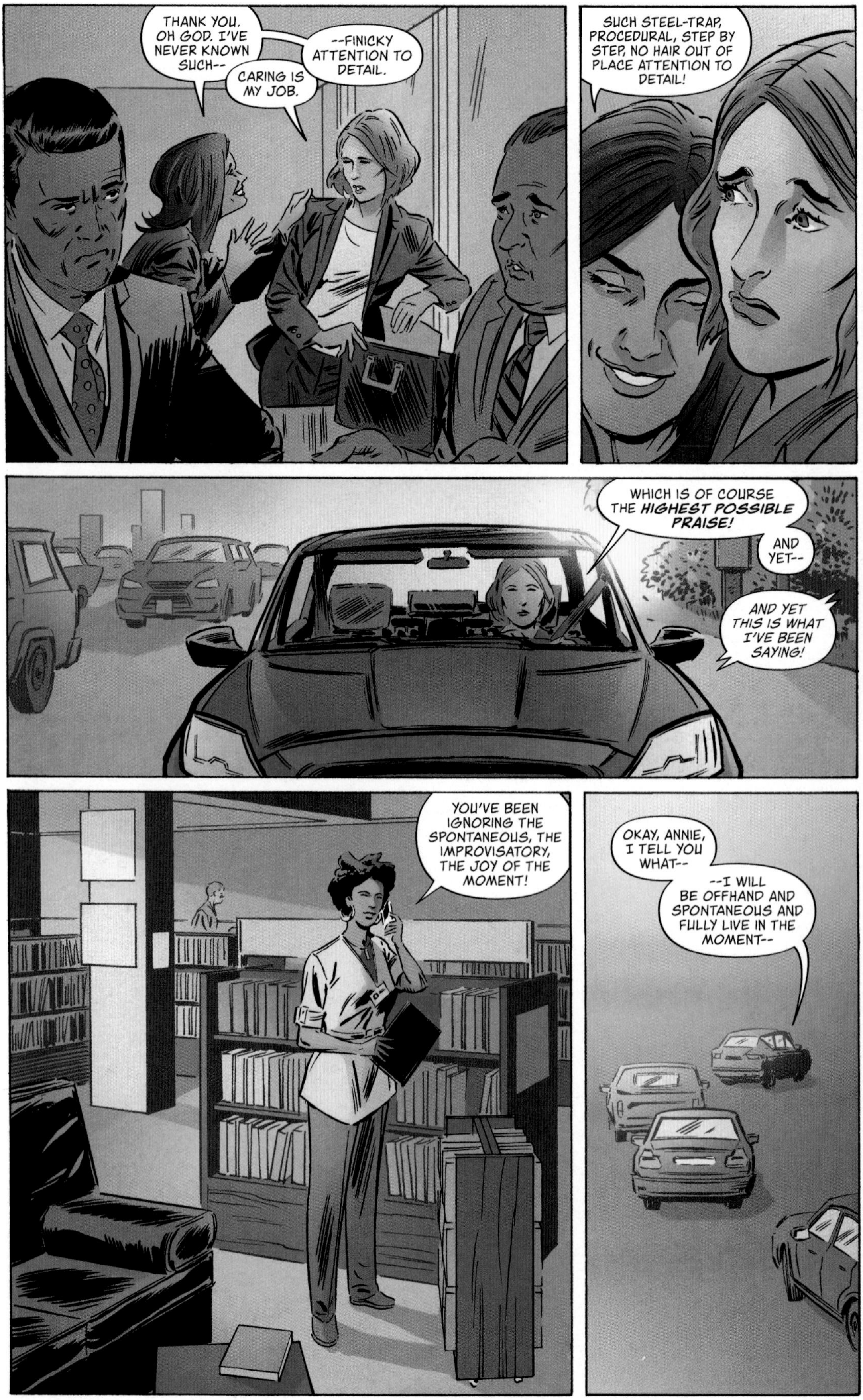

THANK YOU. OH GOD. I'VE NEVER KNOWN SUCH--
CARING IS MY JOB.
--FINICKY ATTENTION TO DETAIL.
SUCH STEEL-TRAP, PROCEDURAL, STEP BY STEP, NO HAIR OUT OF PLACE ATTENTION TO DETAIL!
WHICH IS OF COURSE THE ***HIGHEST POSSIBLE PRAISE!***
AND YET--
AND YET THIS IS WHAT I'VE BEEN SAYING!
YOU'VE BEEN IGNORING THE SPONTANEOUS, THE IMPROVISATORY, THE JOY OF THE MOMENT!
OKAY, ANNIE, I TELL YOU WHAT--
--I WILL BE OFFHAND AND SPONTANEOUS AND FULLY LIVE IN THE MOMENT--

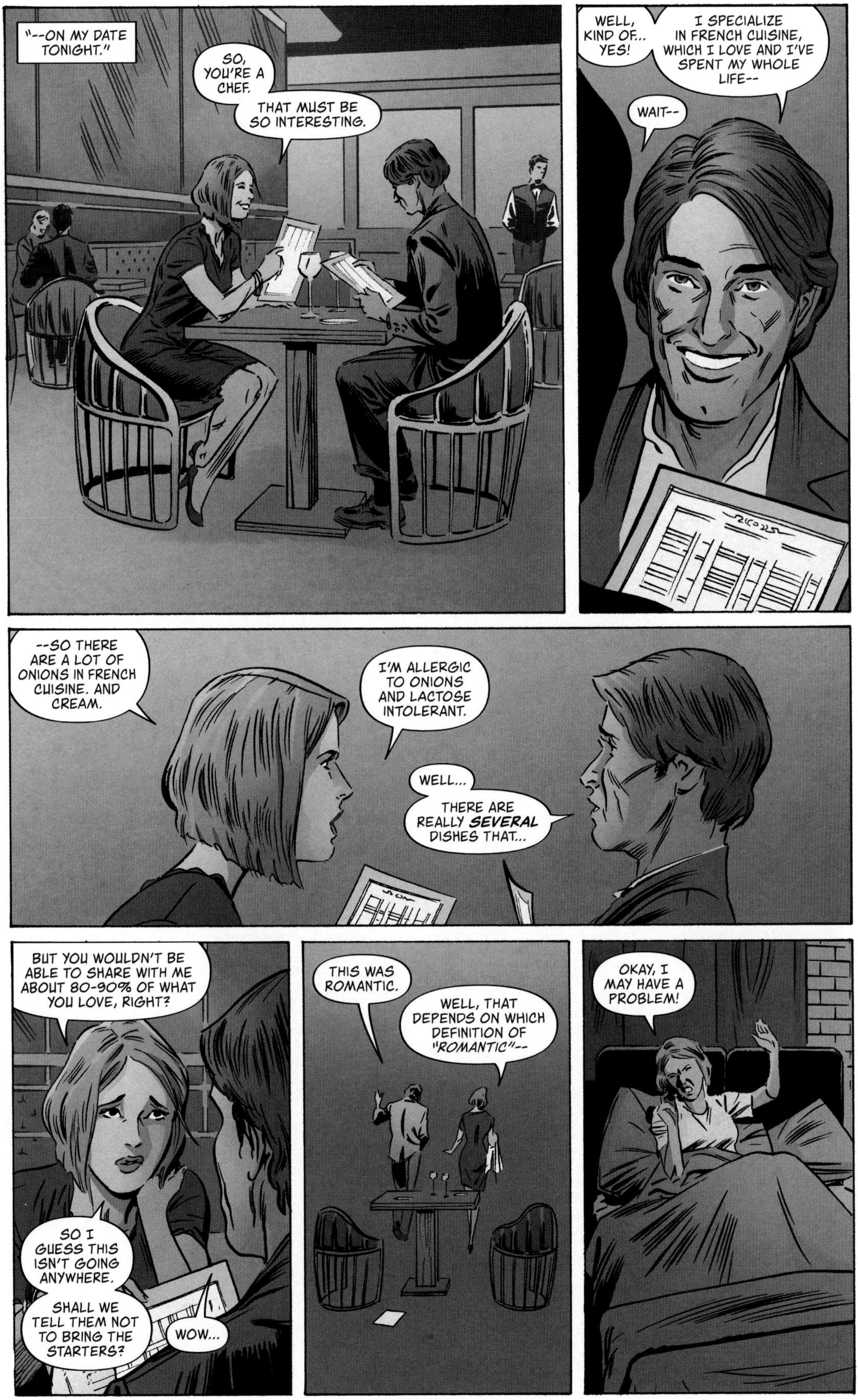

"--ON MY DATE TONIGHT."
SO, YOU'RE A CHEF.
THAT MUST BE SO INTERESTING.
WELL, KIND OF... YES!
I SPECIALIZE IN FRENCH CUISINE, WHICH I LOVE AND I'VE SPENT MY WHOLE LIFE--
WAIT--
--SO THERE ARE A LOT OF ONIONS IN FRENCH CUISINE. AND CREAM.
I'M ALLERGIC TO ONIONS AND LACTOSE INTOLERANT.
WELL...
THERE ARE REALLY **SEVERAL** DISHES THAT...
BUT YOU WOULDN'T BE ABLE TO SHARE WITH ME ABOUT 80-90% OF WHAT YOU LOVE, RIGHT?
SO I GUESS THIS ISN'T GOING ANYWHERE.
SHALL WE TELL THEM NOT TO BRING THE STARTERS?
WOW...
THIS WAS ROMANTIC.
WELL, THAT DEPENDS ON WHICH DEFINITION OF *"ROMANTIC"*--
OKAY, I MAY HAVE A PROBLEM!

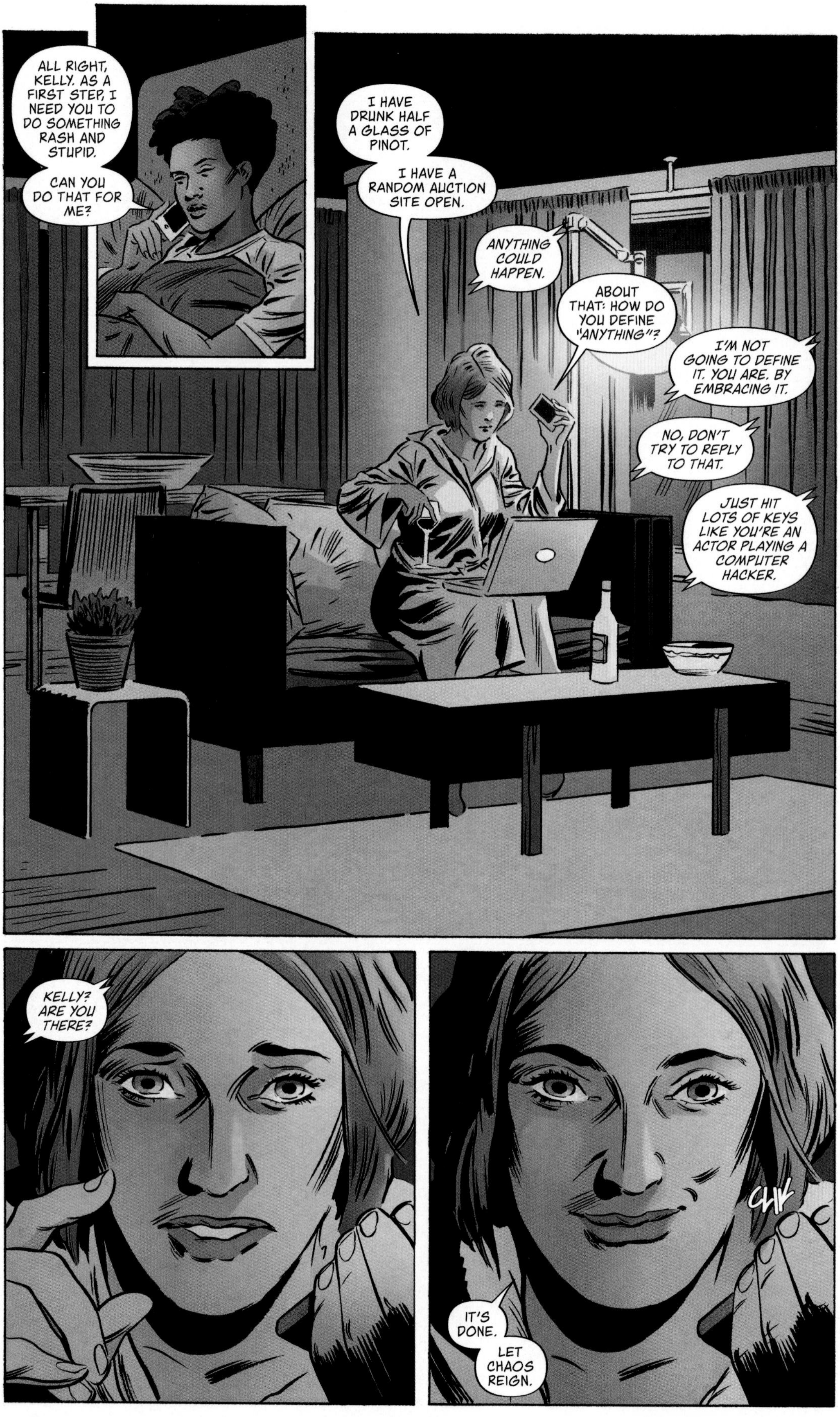
ALL RIGHT, KELLY. AS A FIRST STEP, I NEED YOU TO DO SOMETHING RASH AND STUPID.
CAN YOU DO THAT FOR ME?
I HAVE DRUNK HALF A GLASS OF PINOT.
I HAVE A RANDOM AUCTION SITE OPEN.
ANYTHING COULD HAPPEN.
ABOUT THAT: HOW DO YOU DEFINE "ANYTHING"?
I'M NOT GOING TO DEFINE IT. YOU ARE. BY EMBRACING IT.
NO, DON'T TRY TO REPLY TO THAT.
JUST HIT LOTS OF KEYS LIKE YOU'RE AN ACTOR PLAYING A COMPUTER HACKER.
KELLY? ARE YOU THERE?
CLIK
IT'S DONE.
LET CHAOS REIGN.

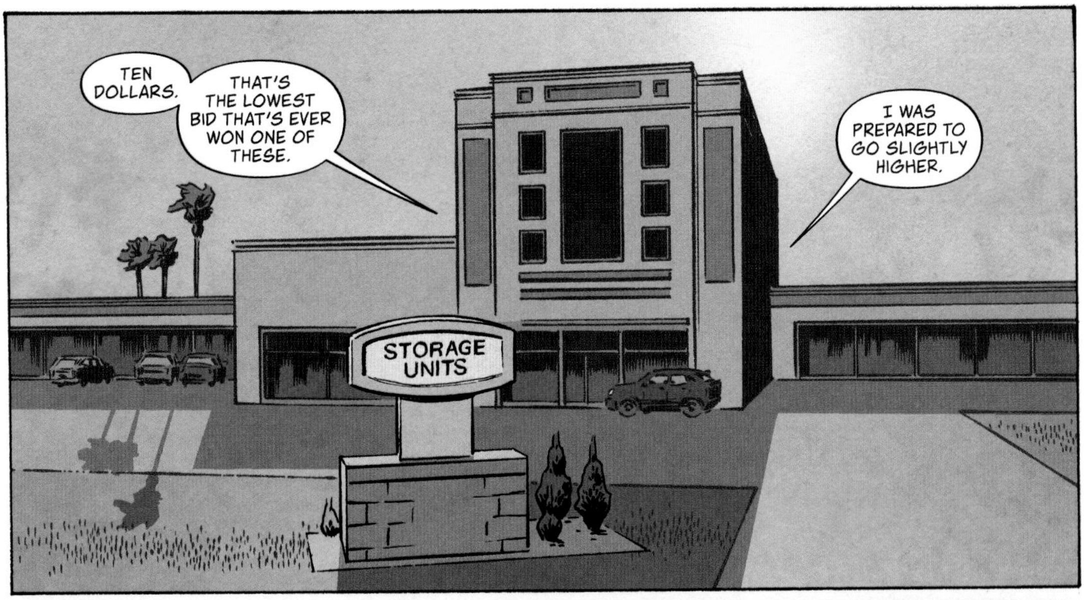
TEN DOLLARS.
THAT'S THE LOWEST BID THAT'S EVER WON ONE OF THESE.
I WAS PREPARED TO GO SLIGHTLY HIGHER.
STORAGE UNITS

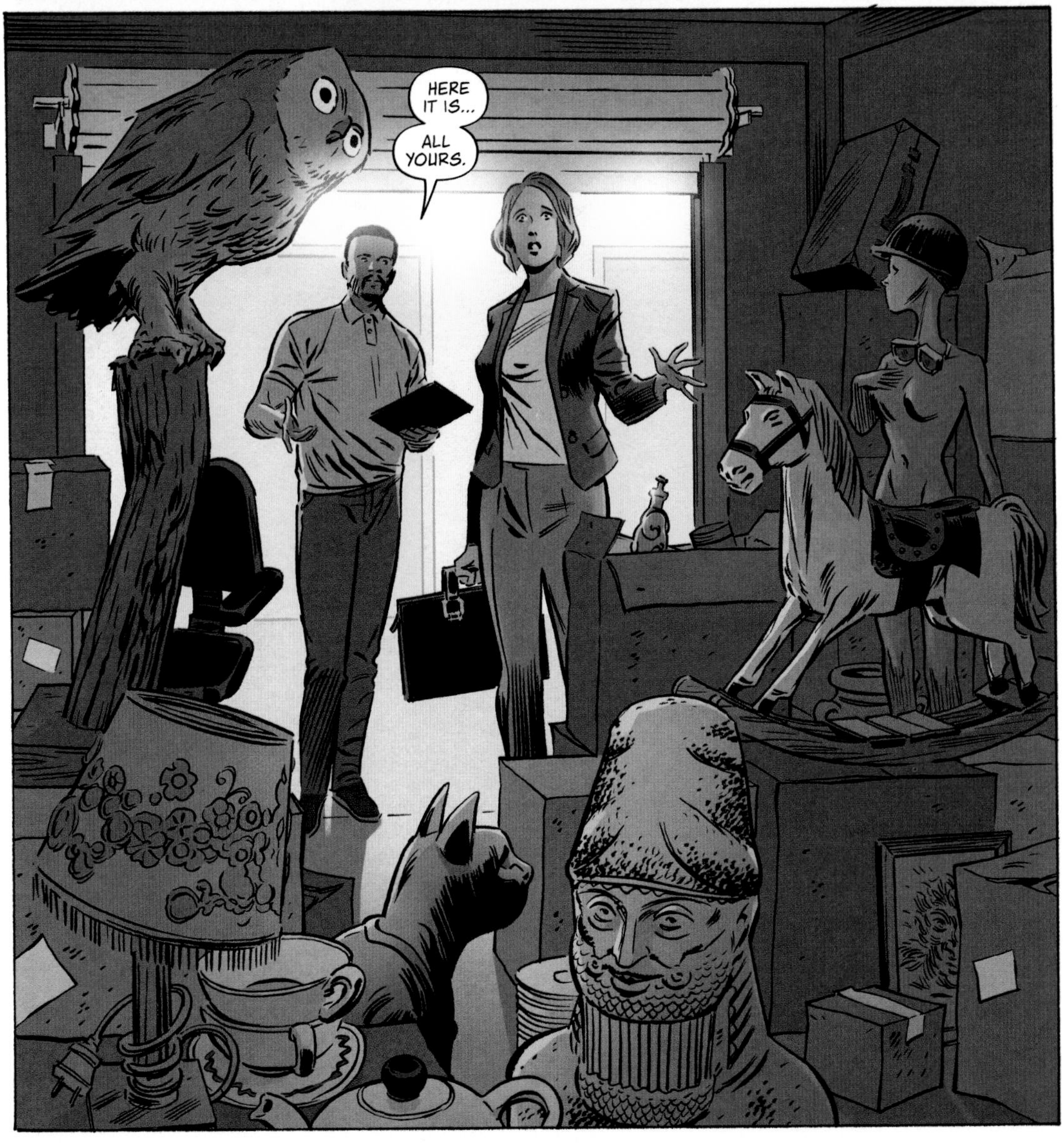
HERE IT IS...
ALL YOURS.

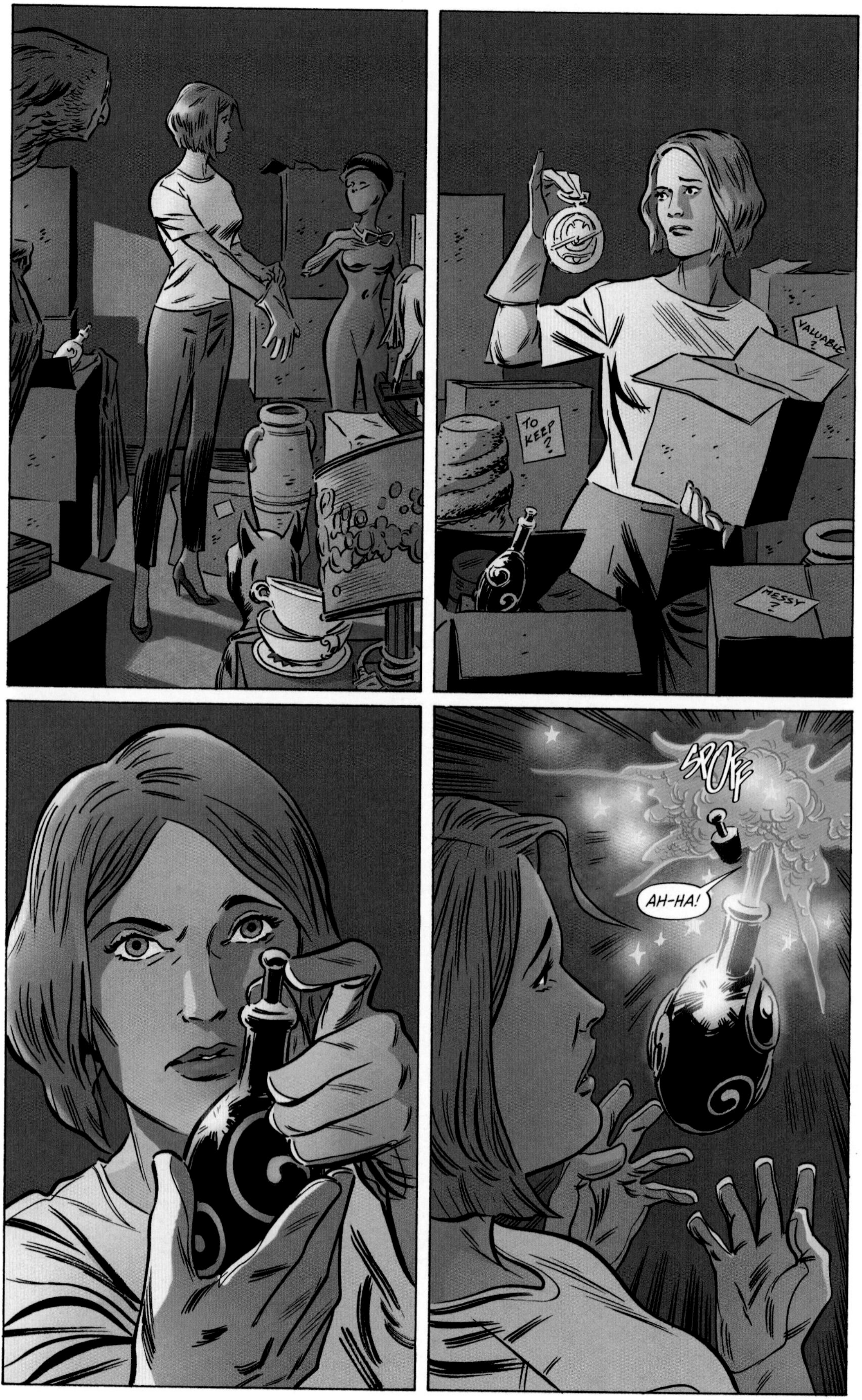
VALUABLE ?
TO KEEP ?
MESSY ?
SPOFF
AH-HA!

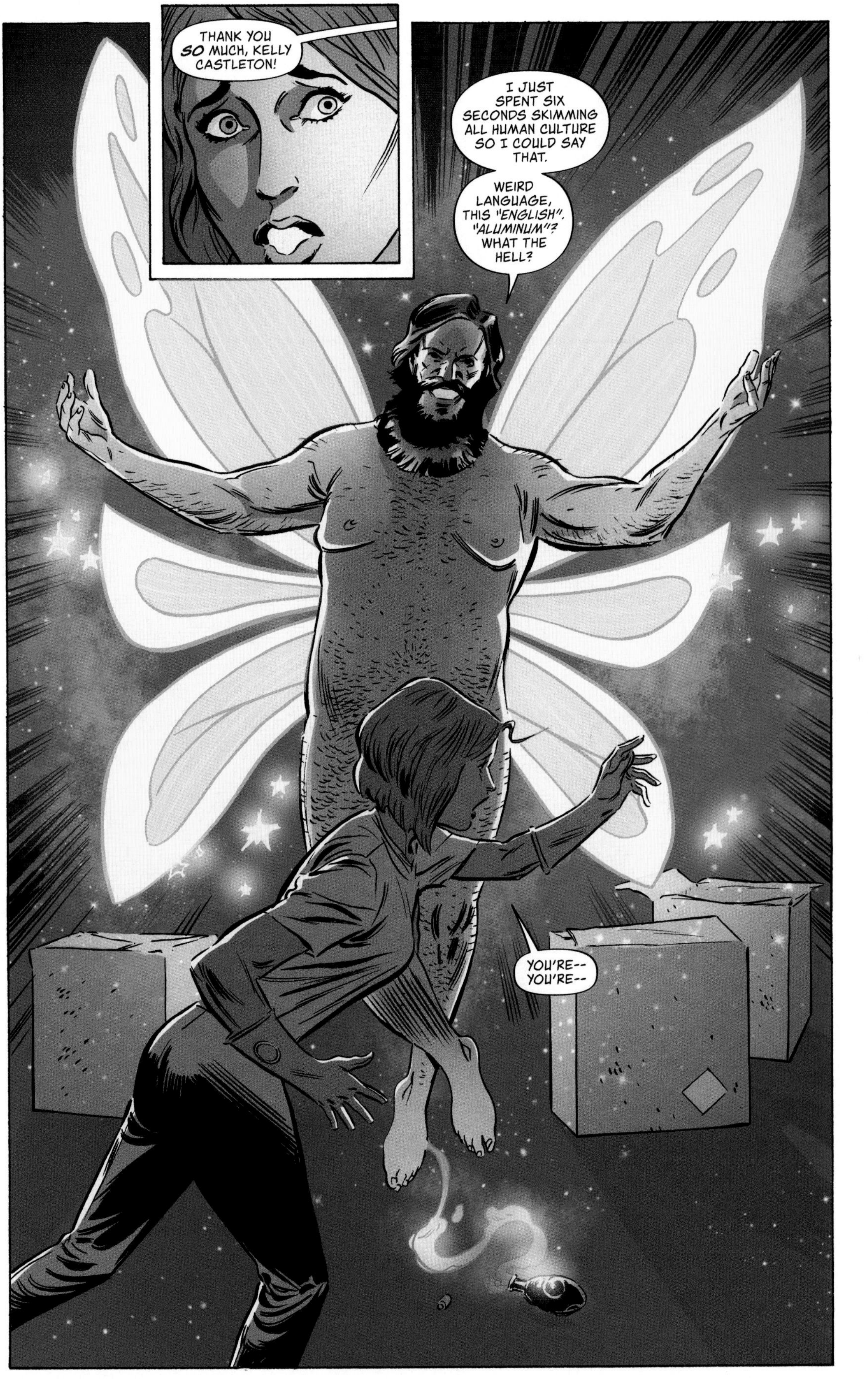
THANK YOU SO MUCH, KELLY CASTLETON!
I JUST SPENT SIX SECONDS SKIMMING ALL HUMAN CULTURE SO I COULD SAY THAT.
WEIRD LANGUAGE, THIS "ENGLISH". "ALUMINUM"? WHAT THE HELL?
YOU'RE-- YOU'RE--

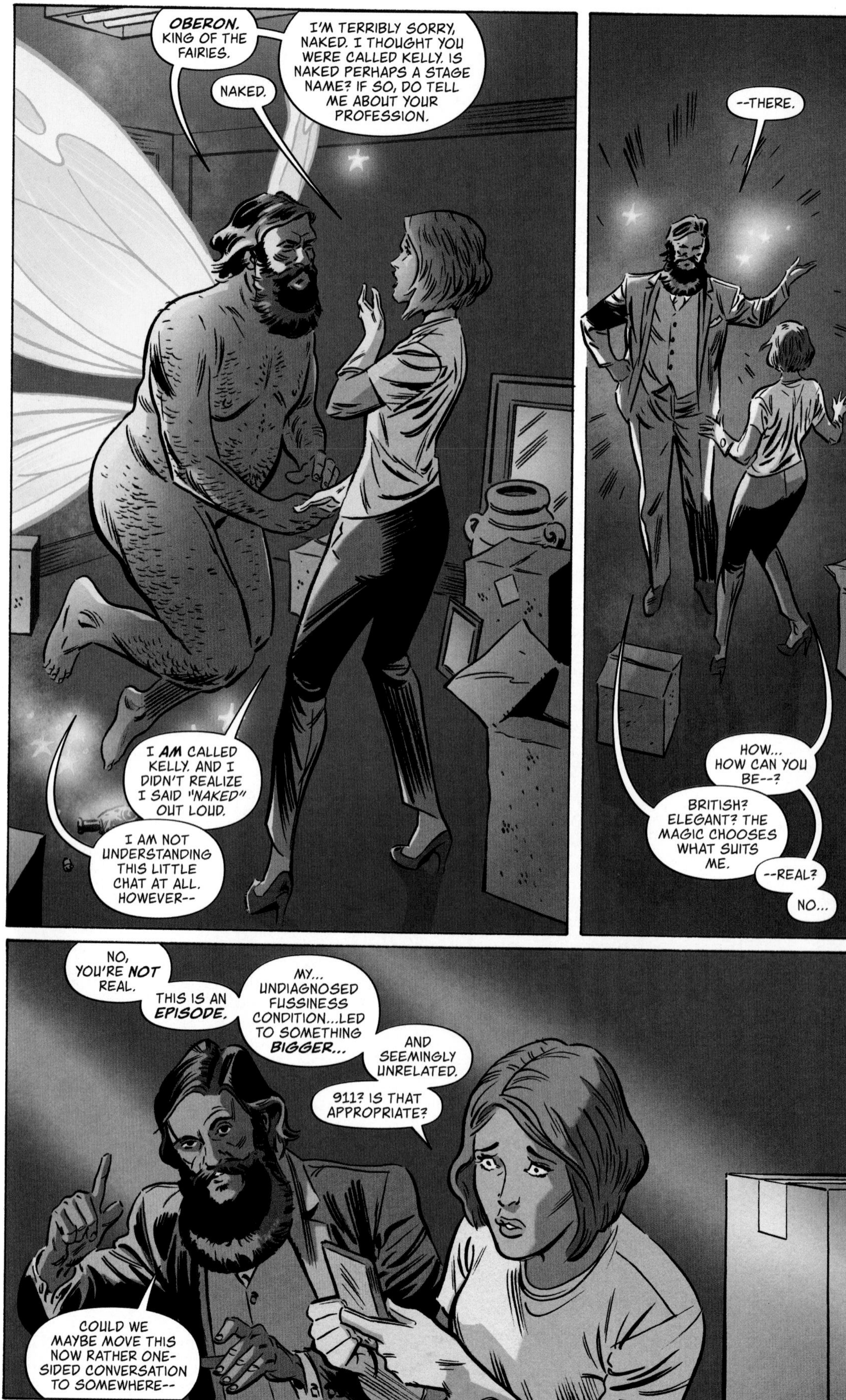

OBERON. KING OF THE FAIRIES.
NAKED.
I'M TERRIBLY SORRY, NAKED. I THOUGHT YOU WERE CALLED KELLY. IS NAKED PERHAPS A STAGE NAME? IF SO, DO TELL ME ABOUT YOUR PROFESSION.
I AM CALLED KELLY. AND I DIDN'T REALIZE I SAID "NAKED" OUT LOUD.
I AM NOT UNDERSTANDING THIS LITTLE CHAT AT ALL. HOWEVER--
--THERE.
HOW... HOW CAN YOU BE--?
BRITISH? ELEGANT? THE MAGIC CHOOSES WHAT SUITS ME.
--REAL?
NO...
NO, YOU'RE NOT REAL.
THIS IS AN EPISODE.
MY... UNDIAGNOSED FUSSINESS CONDITION...LED TO SOMETHING BIGGER...
AND SEEMINGLY UNRELATED.
911? IS THAT APPROPRIATE?
COULD WE MAYBE MOVE THIS NOW RATHER ONE-SIDED CONVERSATION TO SOMEWHERE--

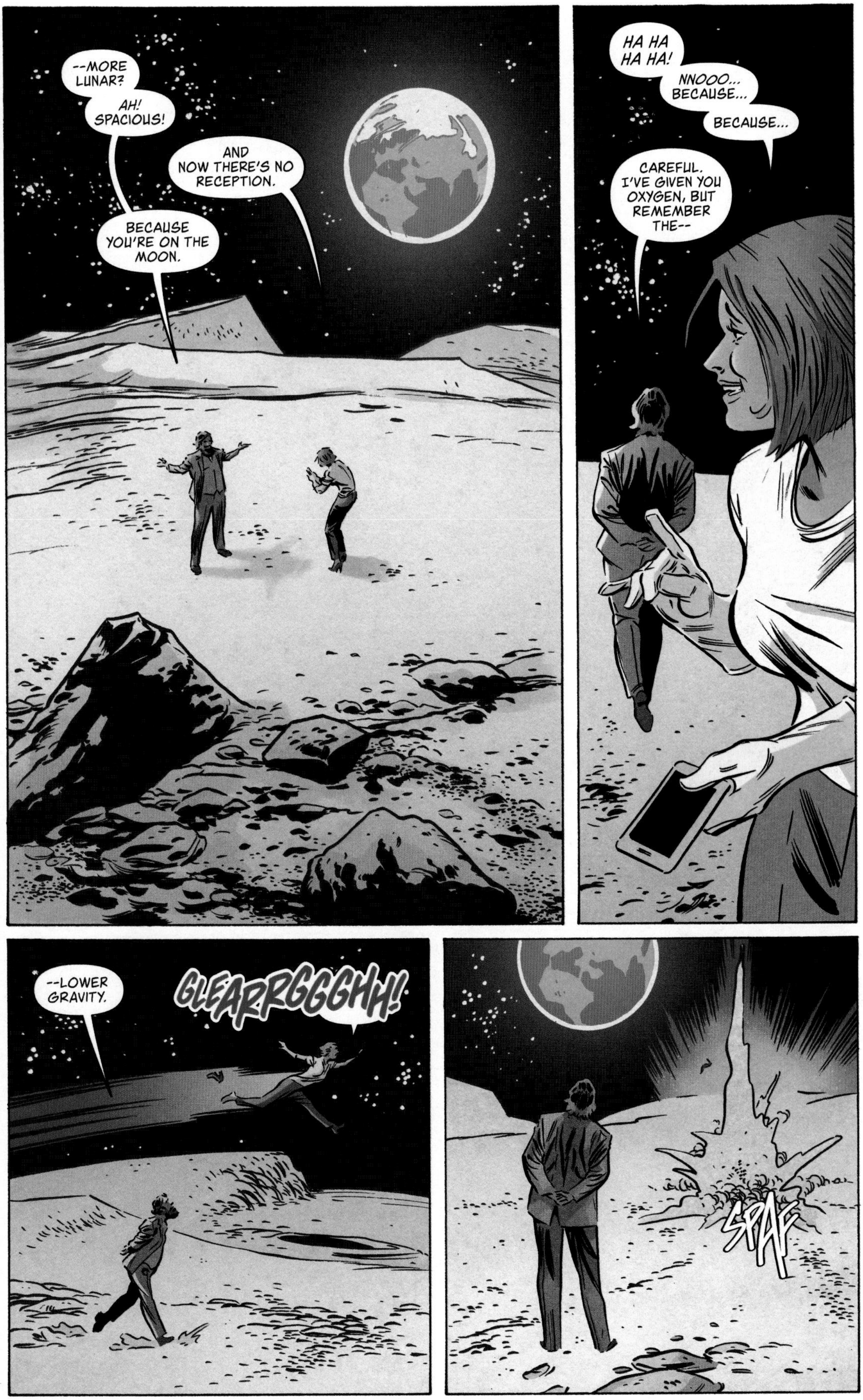
--MORE LUNAR?
AH! SPACIOUS!
AND NOW THERE'S NO RECEPTION.
BECAUSE YOU'RE ON THE MOON.
HA HA HA HA!
NNOOO... BECAUSE...
BECAUSE...
CAREFUL. I'VE GIVEN YOU OXYGEN, BUT REMEMBER THE--
--LOWER GRAVITY.
GLEARRGGGHH!
SPAF

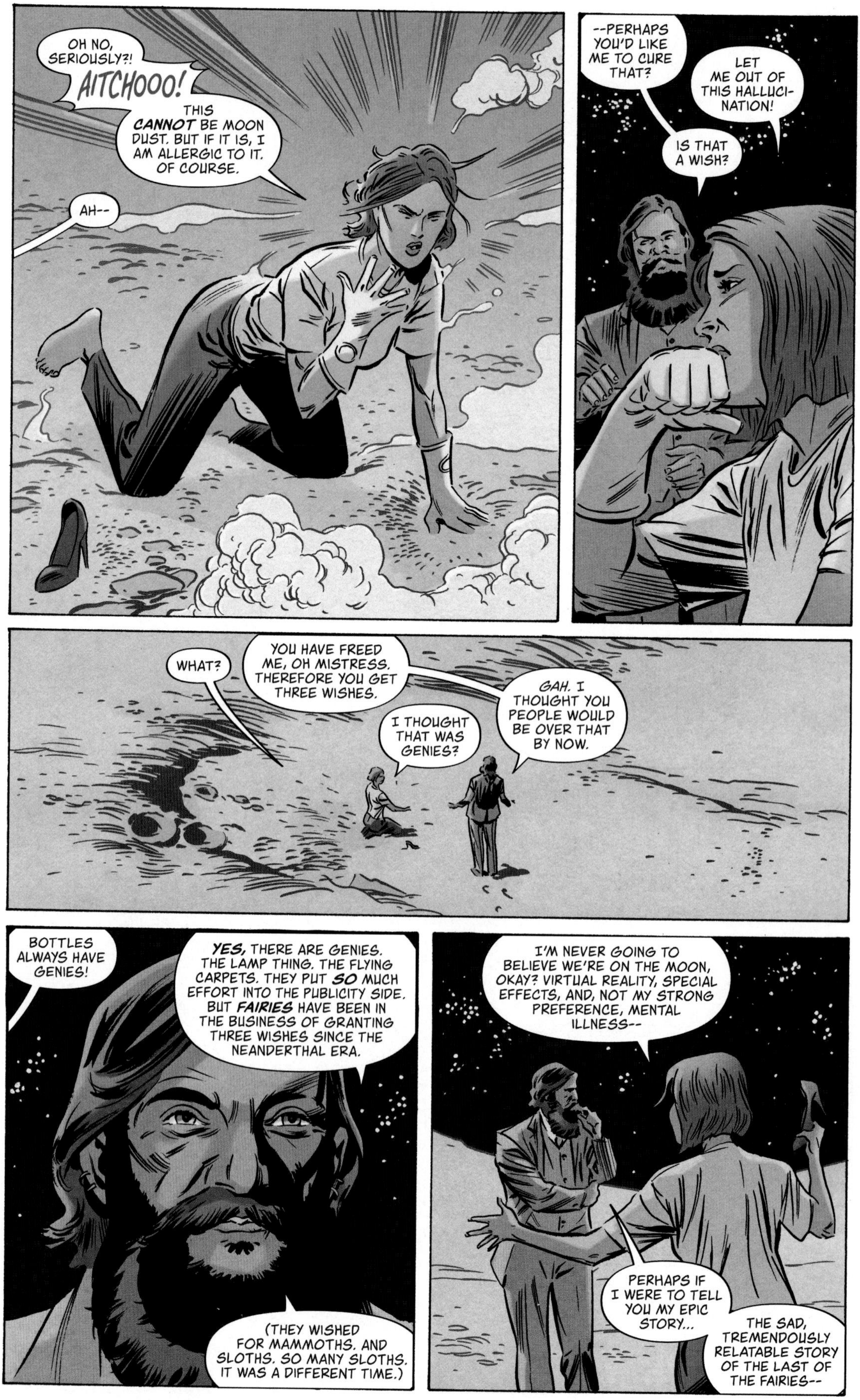
OH NO, SERIOUSLY?!
AITCHOOO!
THIS CANNOT BE MOON DUST. BUT IF IT IS, I AM ALLERGIC TO IT. OF COURSE.
AH--
--PERHAPS YOU'D LIKE ME TO CURE THAT?
LET ME OUT OF THIS HALLUCI-NATION!
IS THAT A WISH?
WHAT?
YOU HAVE FREED ME, OH MISTRESS. THEREFORE YOU GET THREE WISHES.
I THOUGHT THAT WAS GENIES?
GAH. I THOUGHT YOU PEOPLE WOULD BE OVER THAT BY NOW.
BOTTLES ALWAYS HAVE GENIES!
YES, THERE ARE GENIES. THE LAMP THING. THE FLYING CARPETS. THEY PUT SO MUCH EFFORT INTO THE PUBLICITY SIDE. BUT FAIRIES HAVE BEEN IN THE BUSINESS OF GRANTING THREE WISHES SINCE THE NEANDERTHAL ERA.
(THEY WISHED FOR MAMMOTHS. AND SLOTHS. SO MANY SLOTHS. IT WAS A DIFFERENT TIME.)
I'M NEVER GOING TO BELIEVE WE'RE ON THE MOON, OKAY? VIRTUAL REALITY, SPECIAL EFFECTS, AND, NOT MY STRONG PREFERENCE, MENTAL ILLNESS--
PERHAPS IF I WERE TO TELL YOU MY EPIC STORY...
THE SAD, TREMENDOUSLY RELATABLE STORY OF THE LAST OF THE FAIRIES--

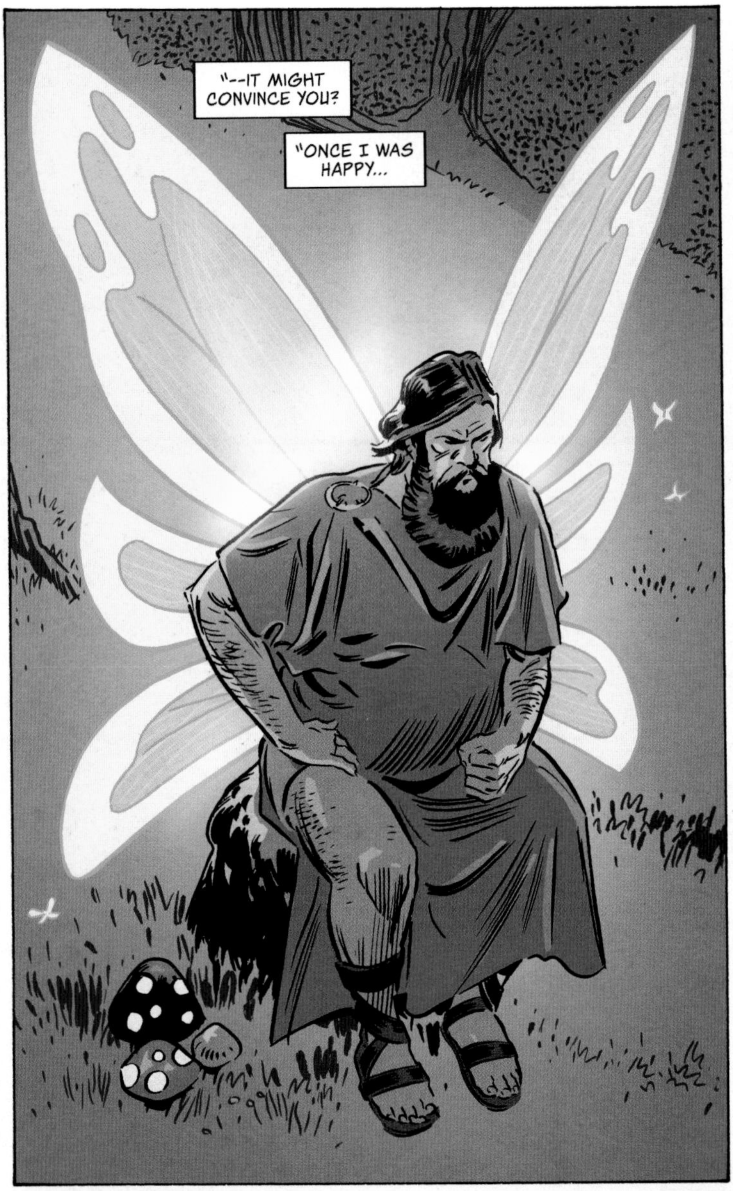
"--IT MIGHT CONVINCE YOU?
"ONCE I WAS HAPPY...

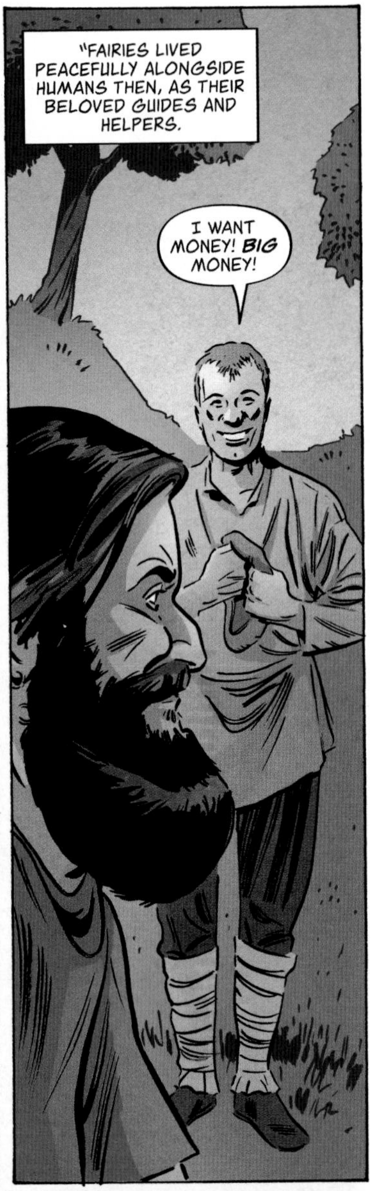
"FAIRIES LIVED PEACEFULLY ALONGSIDE HUMANS THEN, AS THEIR BELOVED GUIDES AND HELPERS.
I WANT MONEY! BIG MONEY!

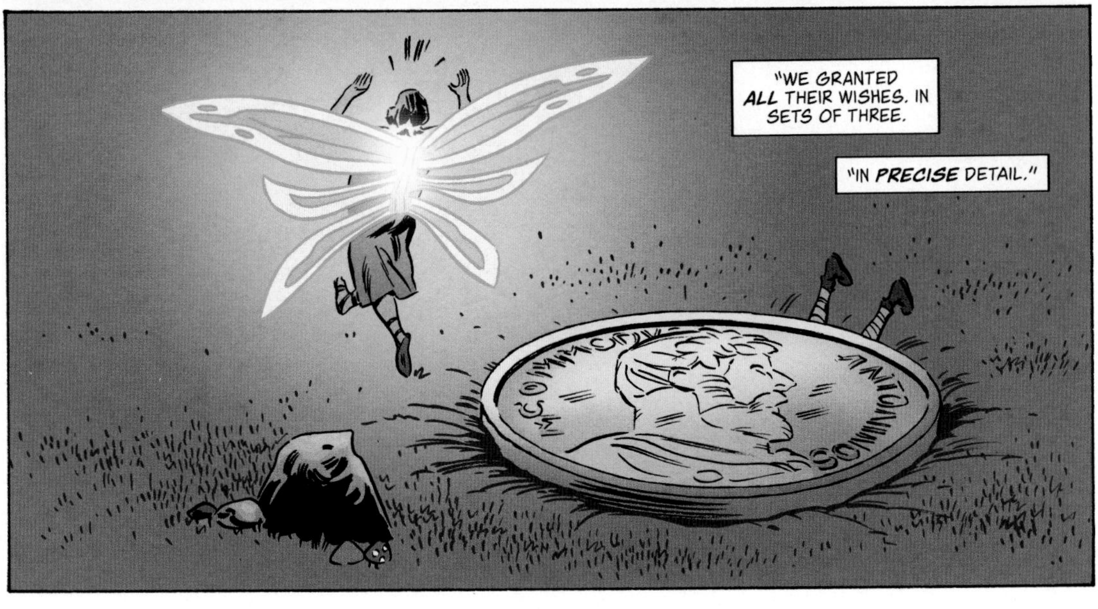
"WE GRANTED ALL THEIR WISHES. IN SETS OF THREE.
"IN PRECISE DETAIL."

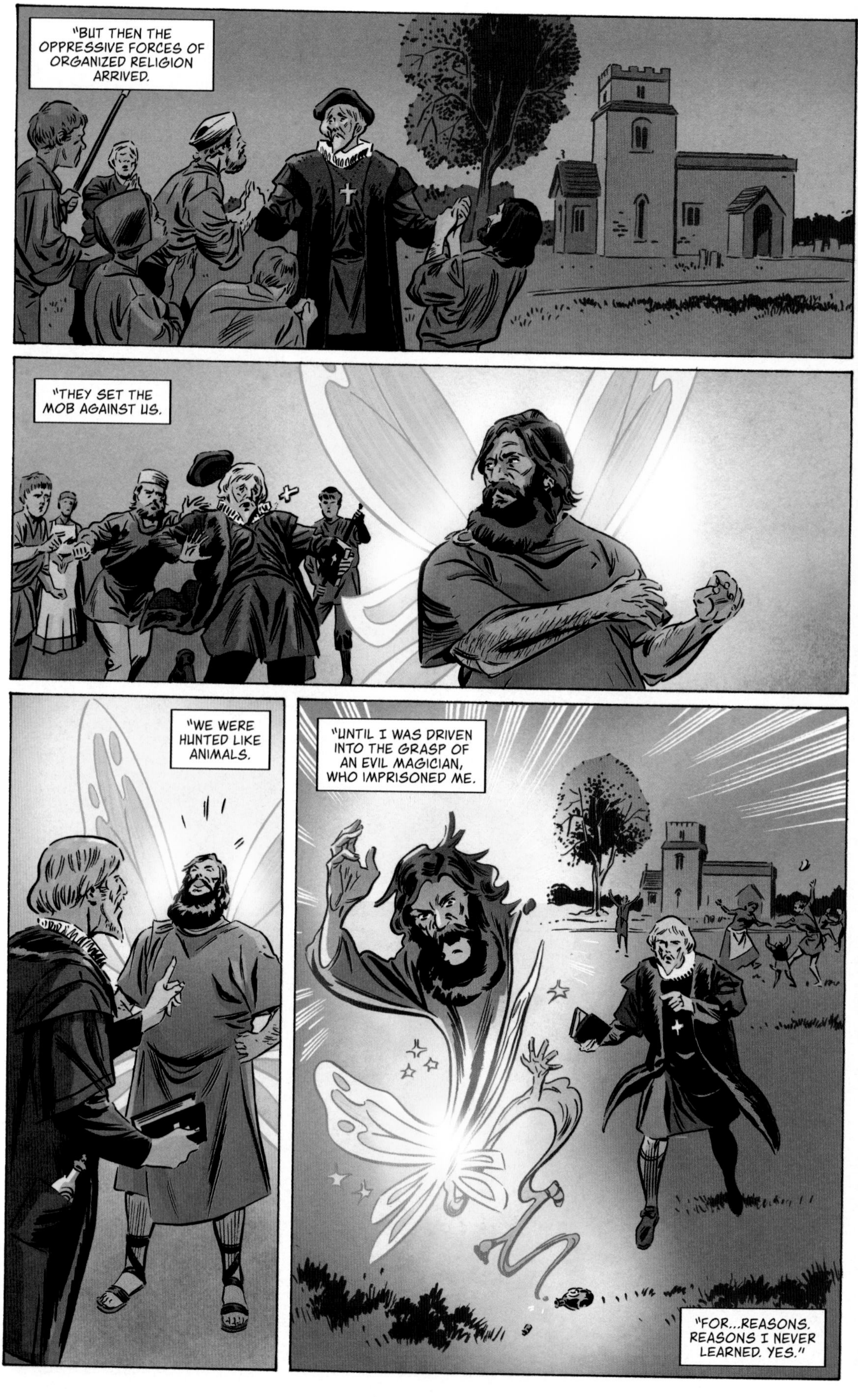
"BUT THEN THE OPPRESSIVE FORCES OF ORGANIZED RELIGION ARRIVED.
"THEY SET THE MOB AGAINST US.
"WE WERE HUNTED LIKE ANIMALS.
"UNTIL I WAS DRIVEN INTO THE GRASP OF AN EVIL MAGICIAN, WHO IMPRISONED ME.
"FOR...REASONS. REASONS I NEVER LEARNED. YES."

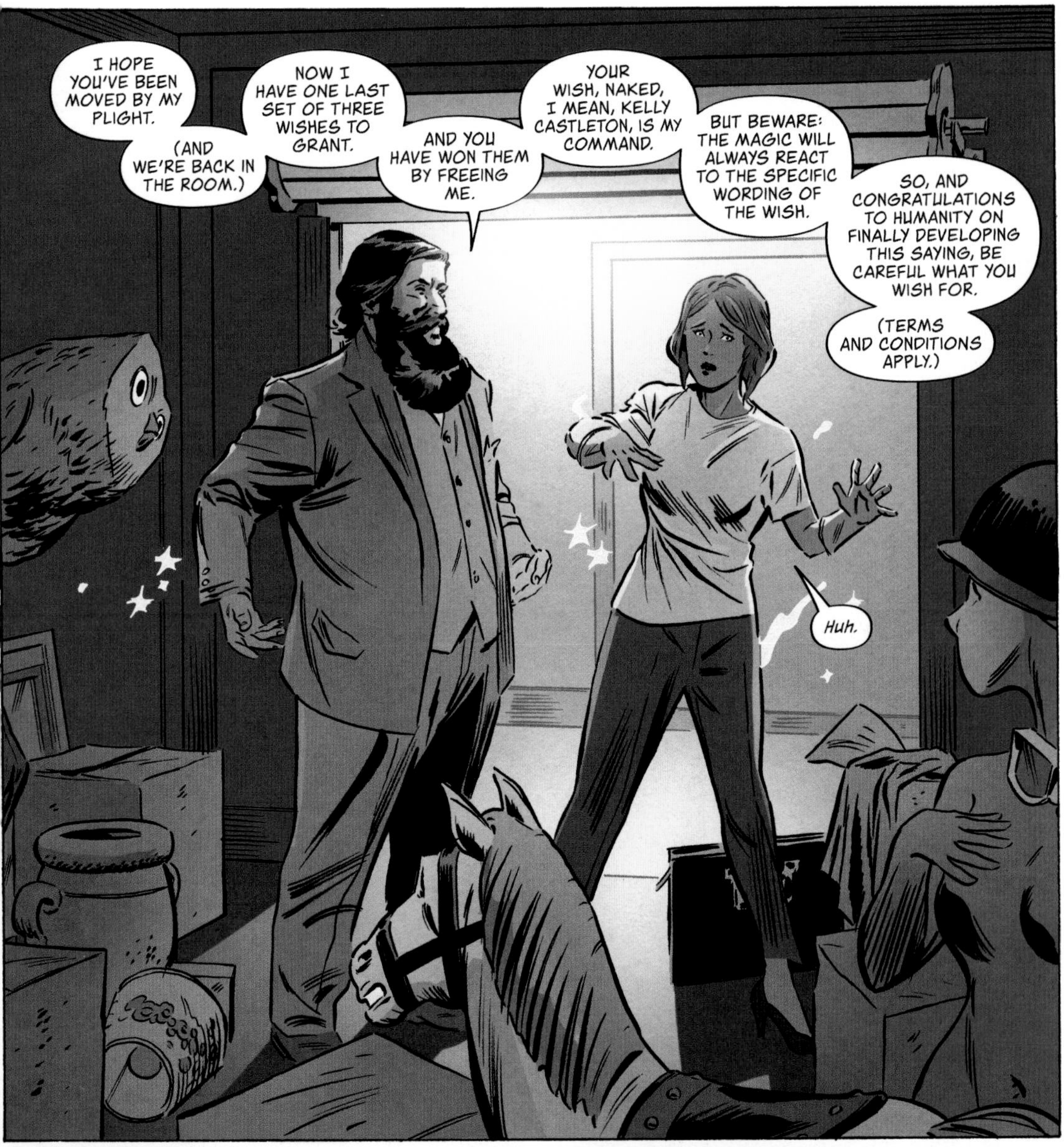
I HOPE YOU'VE BEEN MOVED BY MY PLIGHT.
(AND WE'RE BACK IN THE ROOM.)
NOW I HAVE ONE LAST SET OF THREE WISHES TO GRANT.
AND YOU HAVE WON THEM BY FREEING ME.
YOUR WISH, NAKED, I MEAN, KELLY CASTLETON, IS MY COMMAND.
BUT BEWARE: THE MAGIC WILL ALWAYS REACT TO THE SPECIFIC WORDING OF THE WISH.
SO, AND CONGRATULATIONS TO HUMANITY ON FINALLY DEVELOPING THIS SAYING, BE CAREFUL WHAT YOU WISH FOR.
(TERMS AND CONDITIONS APPLY.)
Huh.

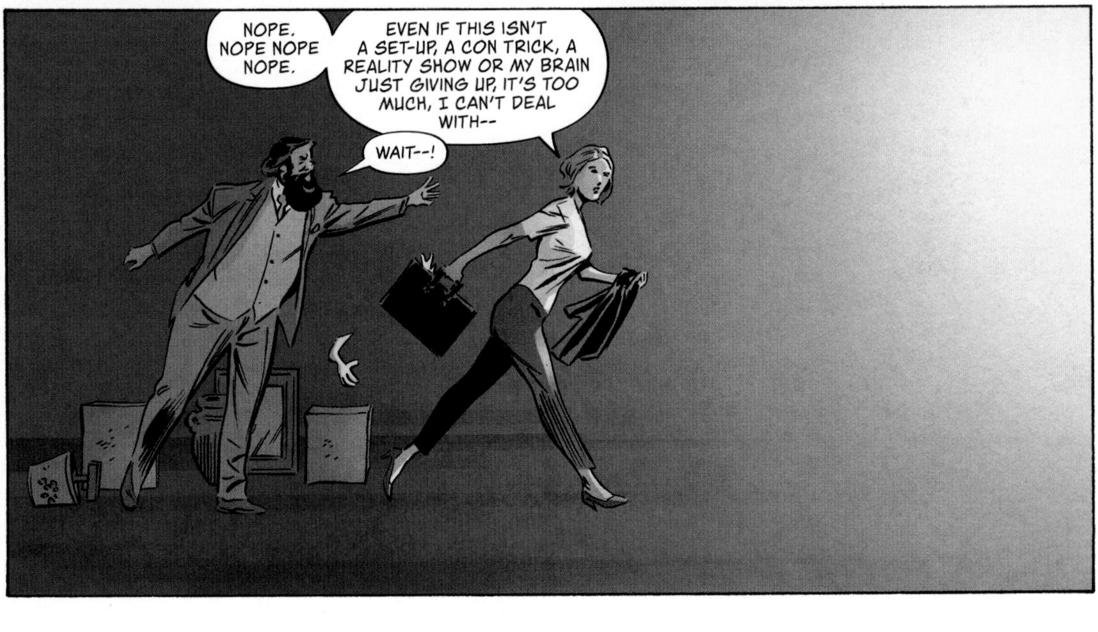
NOPE. NOPE NOPE NOPE.
EVEN IF THIS ISN'T A SET-UP, A CON TRICK, A REALITY SHOW OR MY BRAIN JUST GIVING UP, IT'S TOO MUCH, I CAN'T DEAL WITH--
WAIT--!

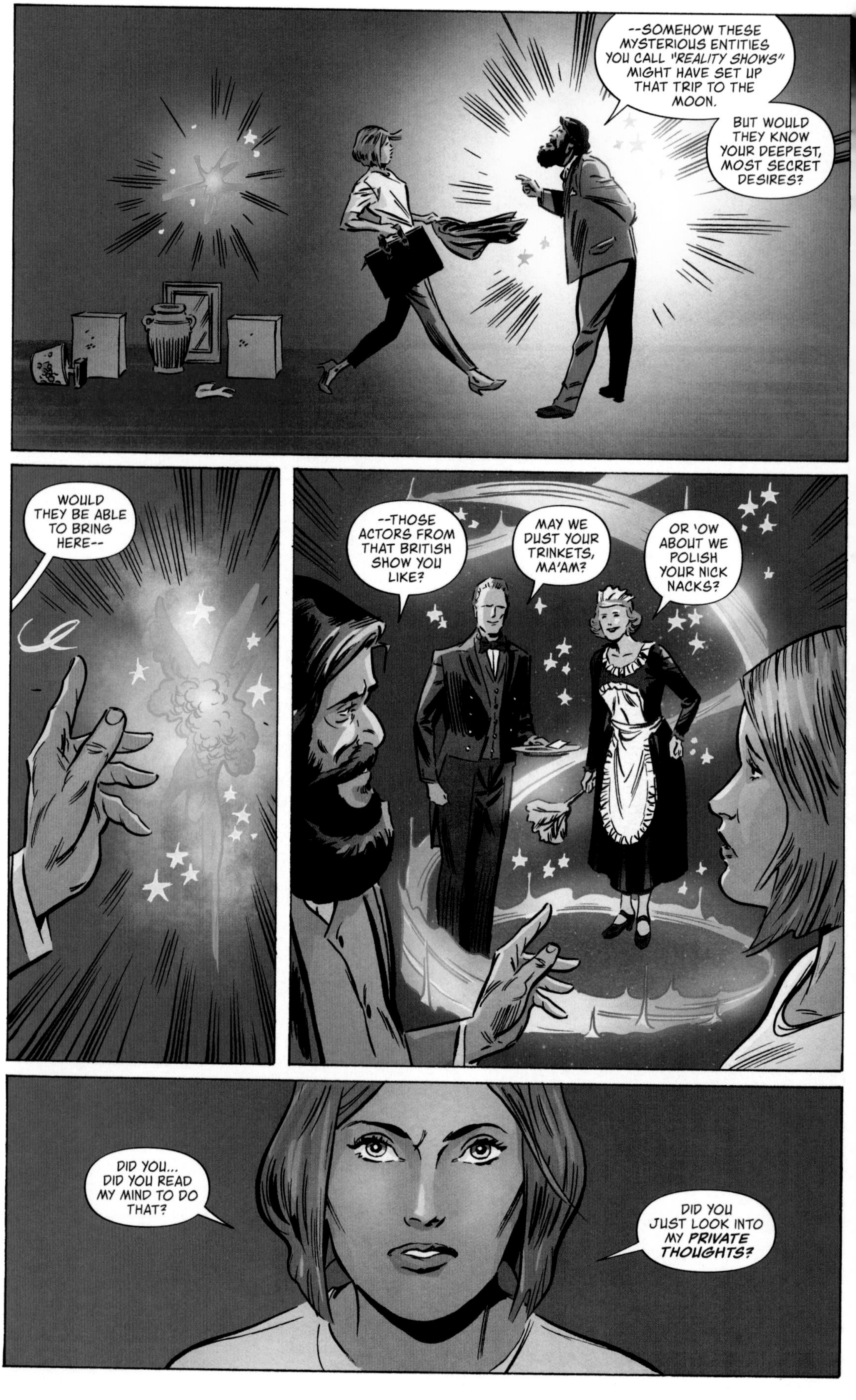
--SOMEHOW THESE MYSTERIOUS ENTITIES YOU CALL "REALITY SHOWS" MIGHT HAVE SET UP THAT TRIP TO THE MOON.
BUT WOULD THEY KNOW YOUR DEEPEST, MOST SECRET DESIRES?
WOULD THEY BE ABLE TO BRING HERE--
--THOSE ACTORS FROM THAT BRITISH SHOW YOU LIKE?
MAY WE DUST YOUR TRINKETS, MA'AM?
OR 'OW ABOUT WE POLISH YOUR NICK NACKS?
DID YOU... DID YOU READ MY MIND TO DO THAT?
DID YOU JUST LOOK INTO MY PRIVATE THOUGHTS?

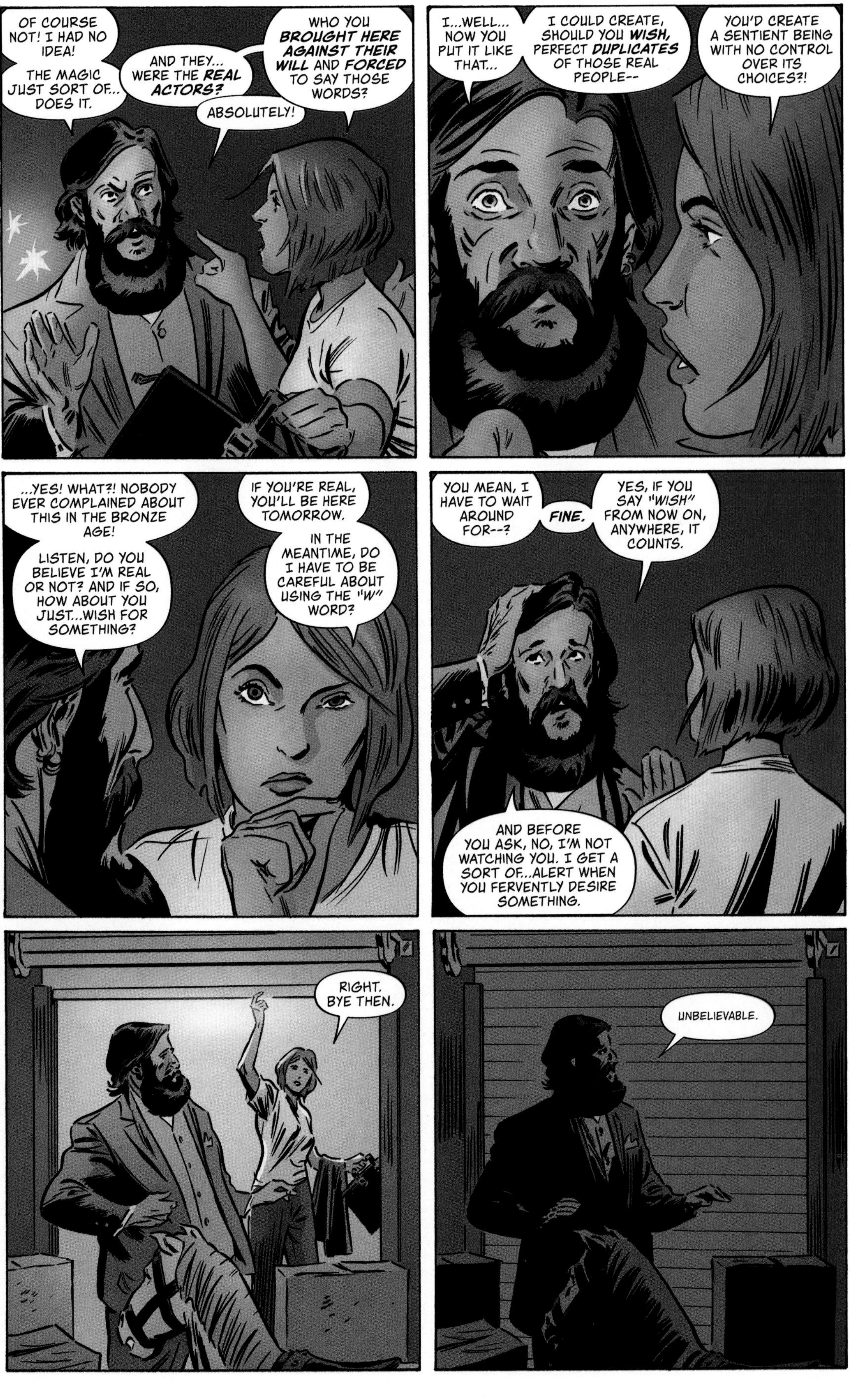

OF COURSE NOT! I HAD NO IDEA!
THE MAGIC JUST SORT OF... DOES IT.
AND THEY... WERE THE REAL ACTORS?
WHO YOU BROUGHT HERE AGAINST THEIR WILL AND FORCED TO SAY THOSE WORDS?
ABSOLUTELY!
I...WELL... NOW YOU PUT IT LIKE THAT...
I COULD CREATE, SHOULD YOU WISH, PERFECT DUPLICATES OF THOSE REAL PEOPLE--
YOU'D CREATE A SENTIENT BEING WITH NO CONTROL OVER ITS CHOICES?!
...YES! WHAT?! NOBODY EVER COMPLAINED ABOUT THIS IN THE BRONZE AGE!
LISTEN, DO YOU BELIEVE I'M REAL OR NOT? AND IF SO, HOW ABOUT YOU JUST...WISH FOR SOMETHING?
IF YOU'RE REAL, YOU'LL BE HERE TOMORROW.
IN THE MEANTIME, DO I HAVE TO BE CAREFUL ABOUT USING THE "W" WORD?
YOU MEAN, I HAVE TO WAIT AROUND FOR--?
FINE.
YES, IF YOU SAY "WISH" FROM NOW ON, ANYWHERE, IT COUNTS.
AND BEFORE YOU ASK, NO, I'M NOT WATCHING YOU. I GET A SORT OF...ALERT WHEN YOU FERVENTLY DESIRE SOMETHING.
RIGHT. BYE THEN.
UNBELIEVABLE.

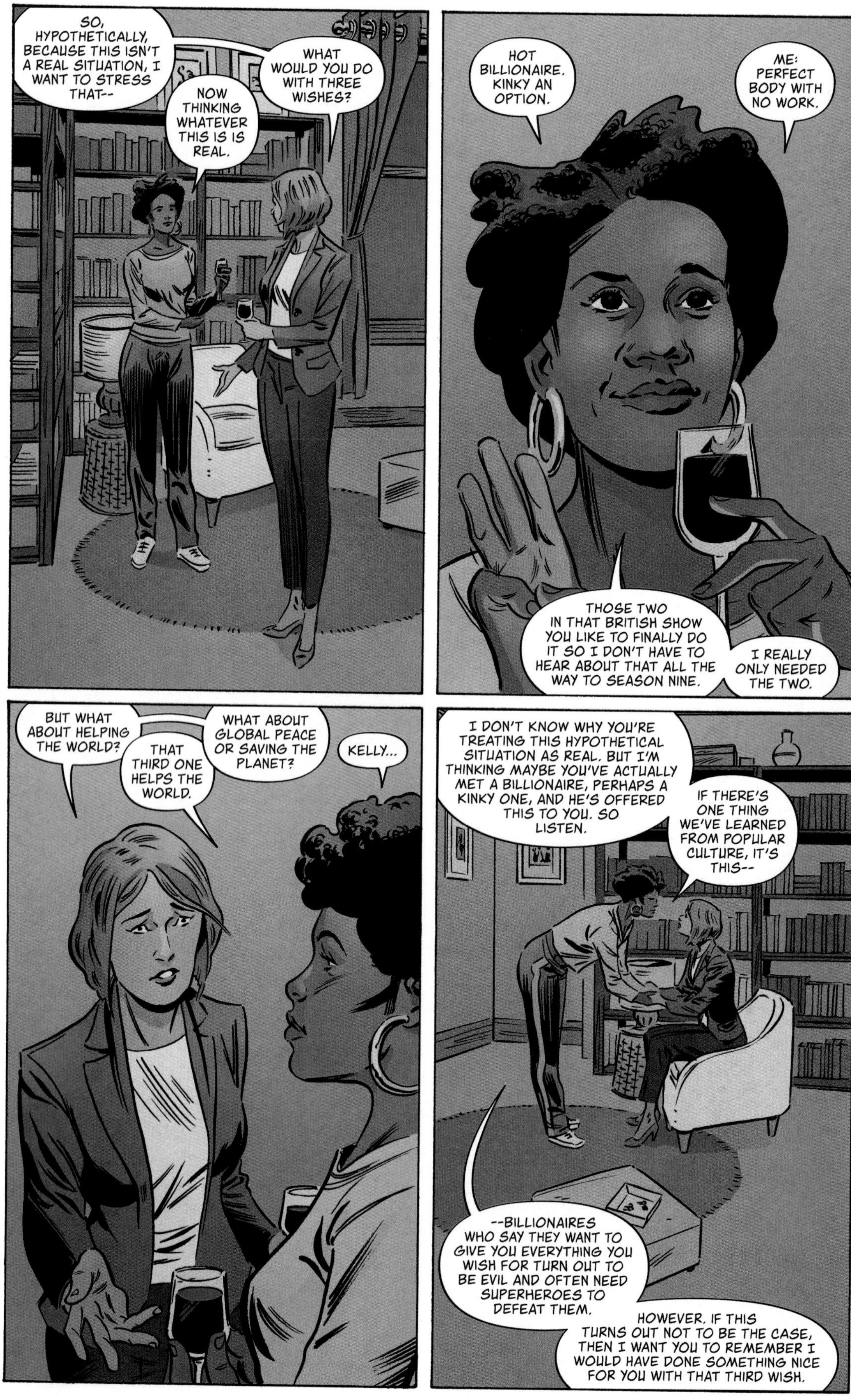
SO, HYPOTHETICALLY, BECAUSE THIS ISN'T A REAL SITUATION, I WANT TO STRESS THAT--
WHAT WOULD YOU DO WITH THREE WISHES?
NOW THINKING WHATEVER THIS IS IS REAL.
HOT BILLIONAIRE. KINKY AN OPTION.
ME: PERFECT BODY WITH NO WORK.
THOSE TWO IN THAT BRITISH SHOW YOU LIKE TO FINALLY DO IT SO I DON'T HAVE TO HEAR ABOUT THAT ALL THE WAY TO SEASON NINE.
I REALLY ONLY NEEDED THE TWO.
BUT WHAT ABOUT HELPING THE WORLD?
WHAT ABOUT GLOBAL PEACE OR SAVING THE PLANET?
THAT THIRD ONE HELPS THE WORLD.
KELLY...
I DON'T KNOW WHY YOU'RE TREATING THIS HYPOTHETICAL SITUATION AS REAL. BUT I'M THINKING MAYBE YOU'VE ACTUALLY MET A BILLIONAIRE, PERHAPS A KINKY ONE, AND HE'S OFFERED THIS TO YOU. SO LISTEN.
IF THERE'S ONE THING WE'VE LEARNED FROM POPULAR CULTURE, IT'S THIS--
--BILLIONAIRES WHO SAY THEY WANT TO GIVE YOU EVERYTHING YOU WISH FOR TURN OUT TO BE EVIL AND OFTEN NEED SUPERHEROES TO DEFEAT THEM.
HOWEVER, IF THIS TURNS OUT NOT TO BE THE CASE, THEN I WANT YOU TO REMEMBER I WOULD HAVE DONE SOMETHING NICE FOR YOU WITH THAT THIRD WISH.

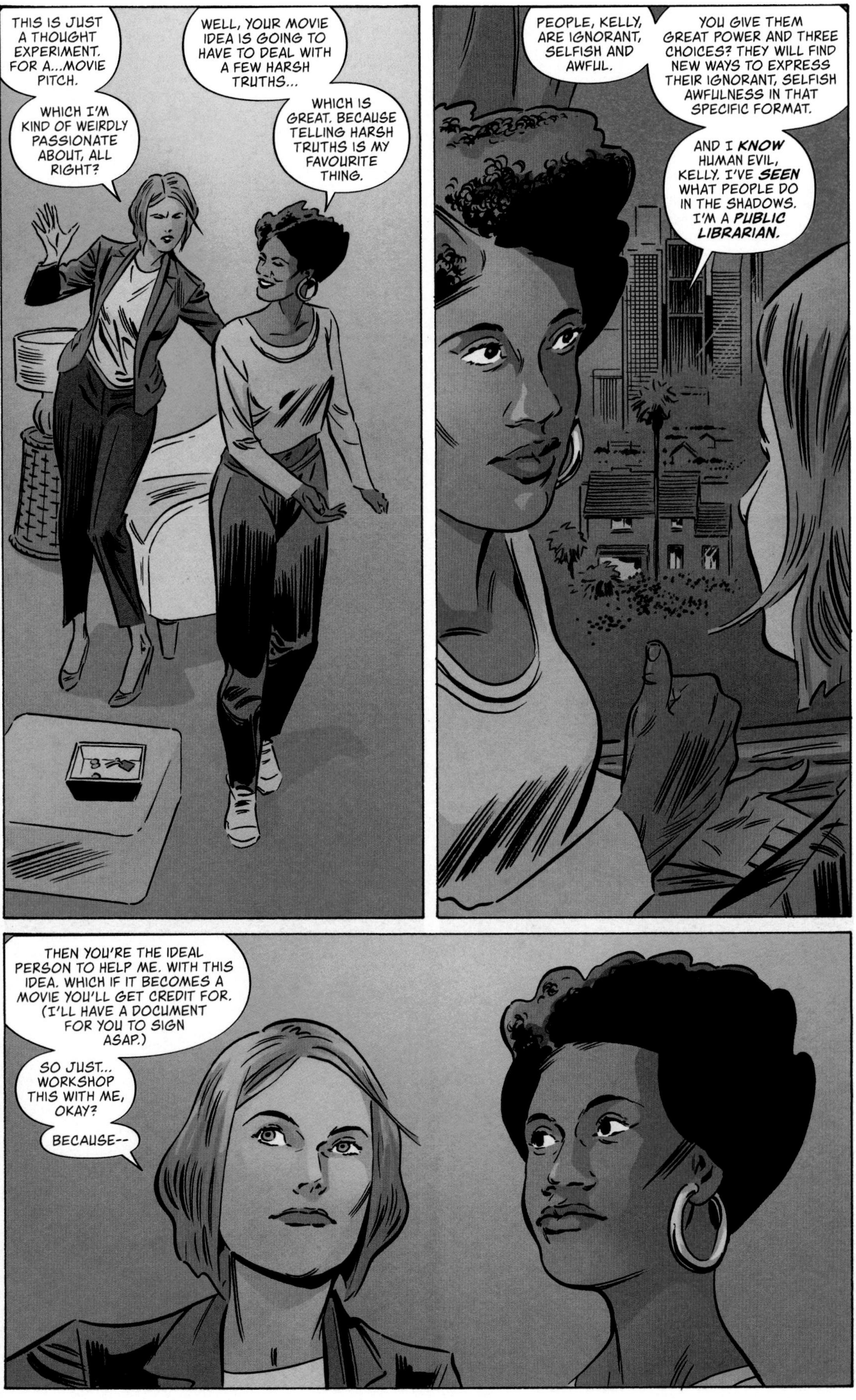
THIS IS JUST A THOUGHT EXPERIMENT. FOR A...MOVIE PITCH.
WHICH I'M KIND OF WEIRDLY PASSIONATE ABOUT, ALL RIGHT?
WELL, YOUR MOVIE IDEA IS GOING TO HAVE TO DEAL WITH A FEW HARSH TRUTHS...
WHICH IS GREAT. BECAUSE TELLING HARSH TRUTHS IS MY FAVOURITE THING.
PEOPLE, KELLY, ARE IGNORANT, SELFISH AND AWFUL.
YOU GIVE THEM GREAT POWER AND THREE CHOICES? THEY WILL FIND NEW WAYS TO EXPRESS THEIR IGNORANT, SELFISH AWFULNESS IN THAT SPECIFIC FORMAT.
AND I *KNOW* HUMAN EVIL, KELLY. I'VE *SEEN* WHAT PEOPLE DO IN THE SHADOWS. I'M A *PUBLIC LIBRARIAN.*
THEN YOU'RE THE IDEAL PERSON TO HELP ME. WITH THIS IDEA. WHICH IF IT BECOMES A MOVIE YOU'LL GET CREDIT FOR. (I'LL HAVE A DOCUMENT FOR YOU TO SIGN ASAP.)
SO JUST... WORKSHOP THIS WITH ME, OKAY?
BECAUSE--

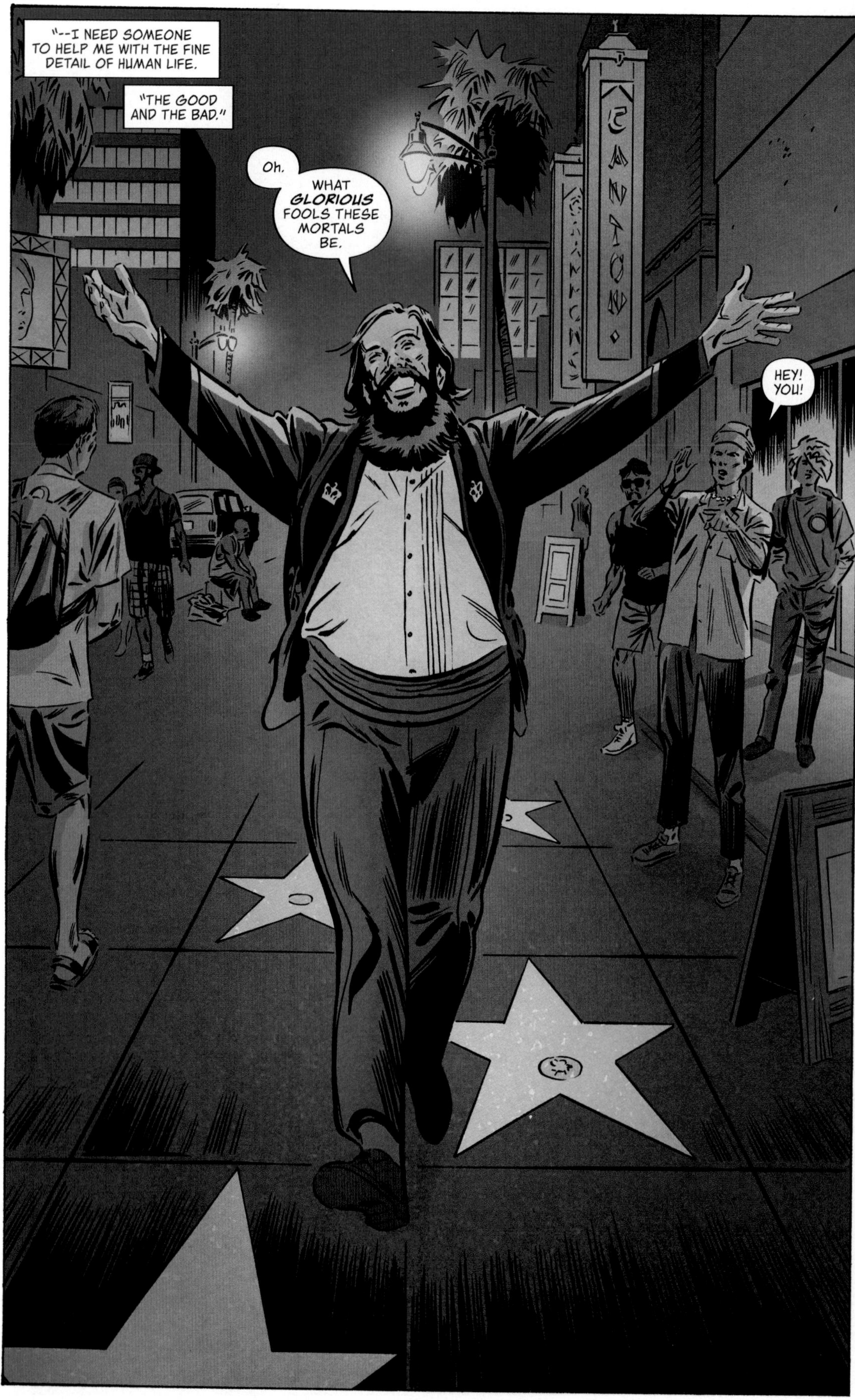
"--I NEED SOMEONE TO HELP ME WITH THE FINE DETAIL OF HUMAN LIFE.
"THE GOOD AND THE BAD."
Oh.
WHAT GLORIOUS FOOLS THESE MORTALS BE.
HEY! YOU!

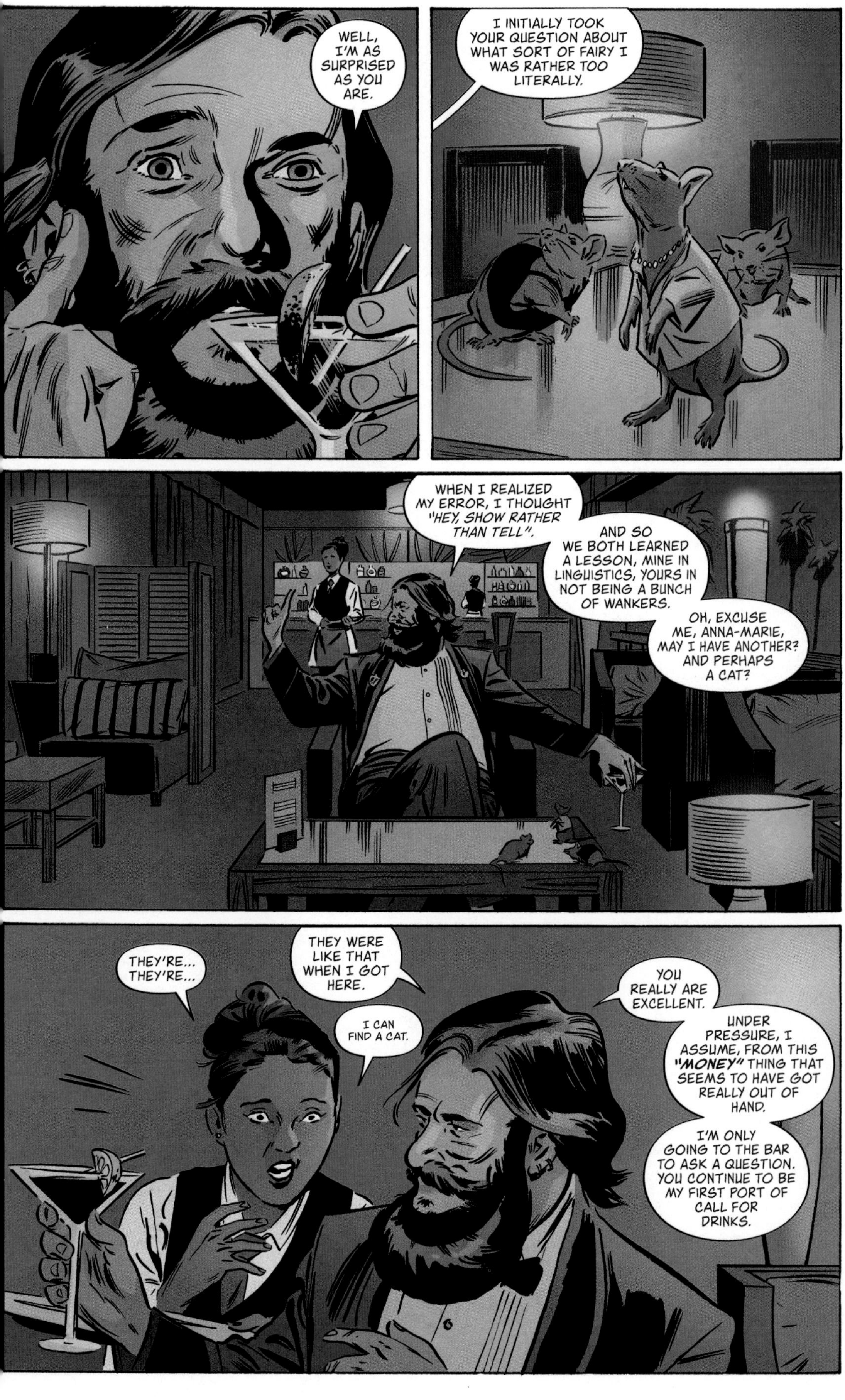
WELL, I'M AS SURPRISED AS YOU ARE.
I INITIALLY TOOK YOUR QUESTION ABOUT WHAT SORT OF FAIRY I WAS RATHER TOO LITERALLY.
WHEN I REALIZED MY ERROR, I THOUGHT *"HEY, SHOW RATHER THAN TELL".*
AND SO WE BOTH LEARNED A LESSON, MINE IN LINGUISTICS, YOURS IN NOT BEING A BUNCH OF WANKERS.
OH, EXCUSE ME, ANNA-MARIE, MAY I HAVE ANOTHER? AND PERHAPS A CAT?
THEY'RE... THEY'RE...
THEY WERE LIKE THAT WHEN I GOT HERE.
I CAN FIND A CAT.
YOU REALLY ARE EXCELLENT.
UNDER PRESSURE, I ASSUME, FROM THIS ***"MONEY"*** THING THAT SEEMS TO HAVE GOT REALLY OUT OF HAND.
I'M ONLY GOING TO THE BAR TO ASK A QUESTION. YOU CONTINUE TO BE MY FIRST PORT OF CALL FOR DRINKS.

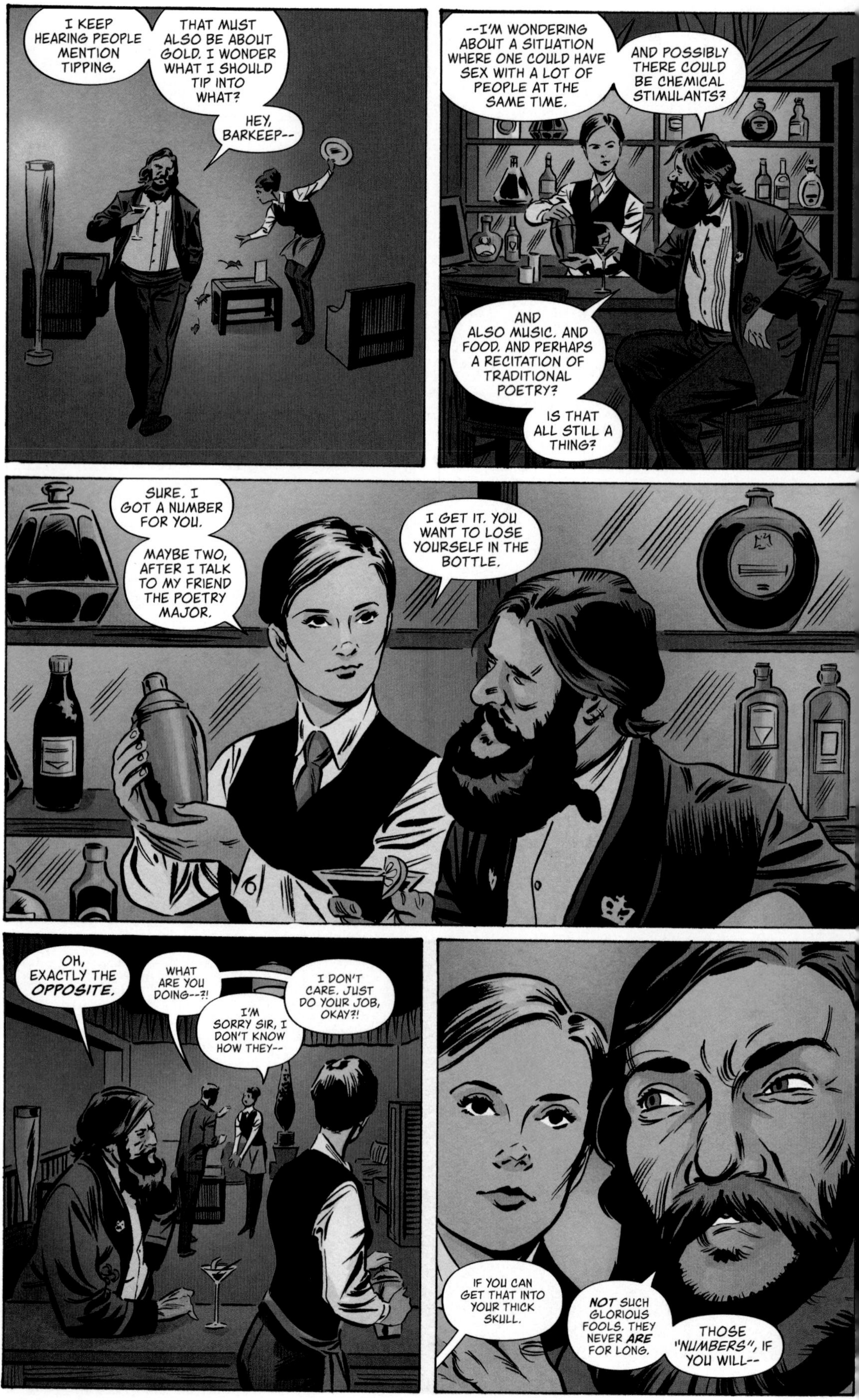
I KEEP HEARING PEOPLE MENTION TIPPING.
THAT MUST ALSO BE ABOUT GOLD. I WONDER WHAT I SHOULD TIP INTO WHAT?
HEY, BARKEEP--
--I'M WONDERING ABOUT A SITUATION WHERE ONE COULD HAVE SEX WITH A LOT OF PEOPLE AT THE SAME TIME.
AND POSSIBLY THERE COULD BE CHEMICAL STIMULANTS?
AND ALSO MUSIC. AND FOOD. AND PERHAPS A RECITATION OF TRADITIONAL POETRY?
IS THAT ALL STILL A THING?
SURE. I GOT A NUMBER FOR YOU.
MAYBE TWO, AFTER I TALK TO MY FRIEND THE POETRY MAJOR.
I GET IT. YOU WANT TO LOSE YOURSELF IN THE BOTTLE.
OH, EXACTLY THE ***OPPOSITE.***
WHAT ARE YOU DOING--?!
I'M SORRY SIR, I DON'T KNOW HOW THEY--
I DON'T CARE. JUST DO YOUR JOB, OKAY?!
IF YOU CAN GET THAT INTO YOUR THICK SKULL.
NOT SUCH GLORIOUS FOOLS. THEY NEVER ***ARE*** FOR LONG.
THOSE *"NUMBERS"*, IF YOU WILL--

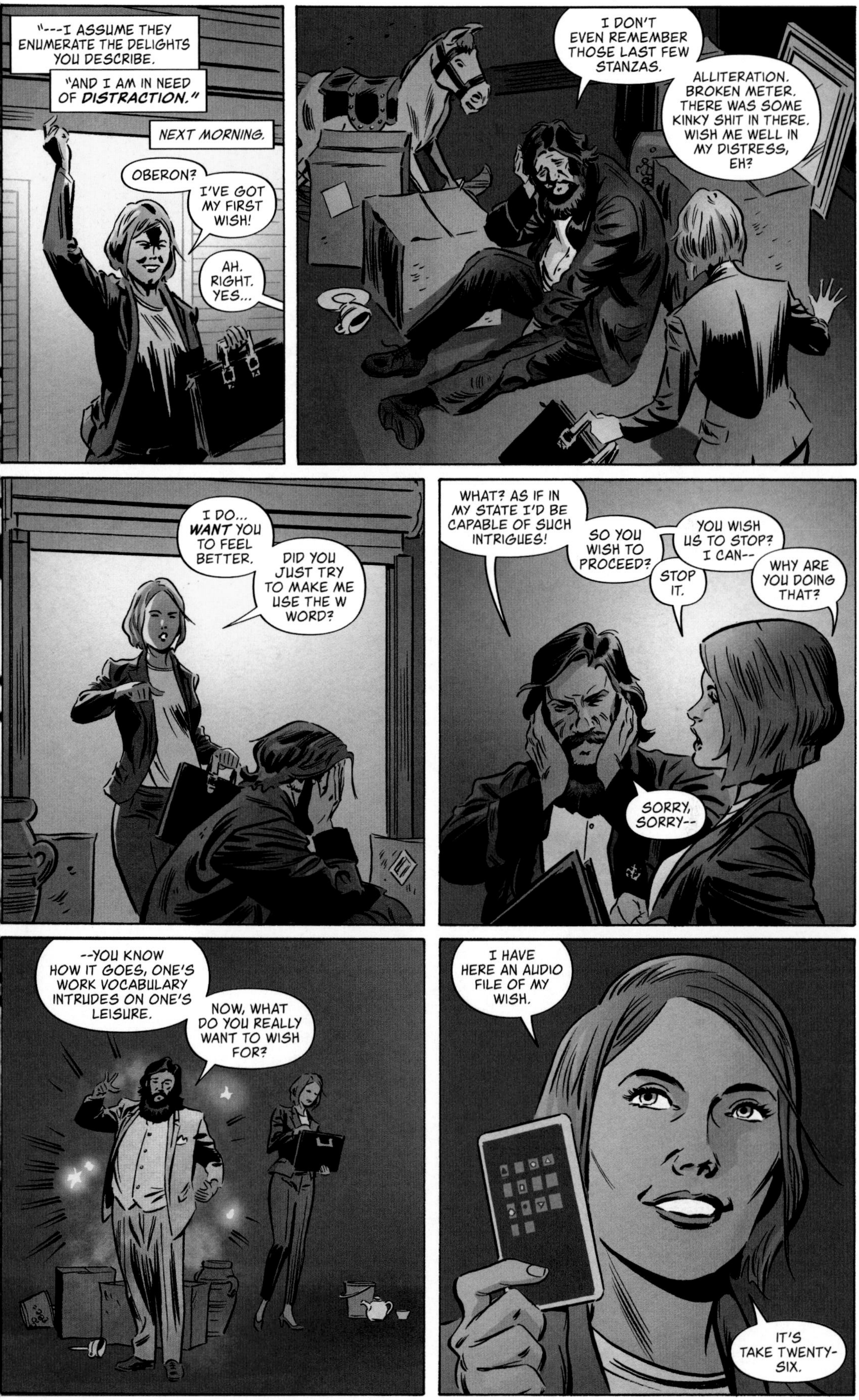

"---I ASSUME THEY ENUMERATE THE DELIGHTS YOU DESCRIBE.
"AND I AM IN NEED OF ***DISTRACTION.***"
NEXT MORNING.
OBERON?
I'VE GOT MY FIRST WISH!
AH. RIGHT. YES...
I DON'T EVEN REMEMBER THOSE LAST FEW STANZAS.
ALLITERATION. BROKEN METER. THERE WAS SOME KINKY SHIT IN THERE. WISH ME WELL IN MY DISTRESS, EH?
I DO... ***WANT*** YOU TO FEEL BETTER.
DID YOU JUST TRY TO MAKE ME USE THE W WORD?
WHAT? AS IF IN MY STATE I'D BE CAPABLE OF SUCH INTRIGUES!
SO YOU WISH TO PROCEED?
YOU WISH US TO STOP? I CAN--
STOP IT.
WHY ARE YOU DOING THAT?
SORRY, SORRY--
--YOU KNOW HOW IT GOES, ONE'S WORK VOCABULARY INTRUDES ON ONE'S LEISURE.
NOW, WHAT DO YOU REALLY WANT TO WISH FOR?
I HAVE HERE AN AUDIO FILE OF MY WISH.
IT'S TAKE TWENTY-SIX.

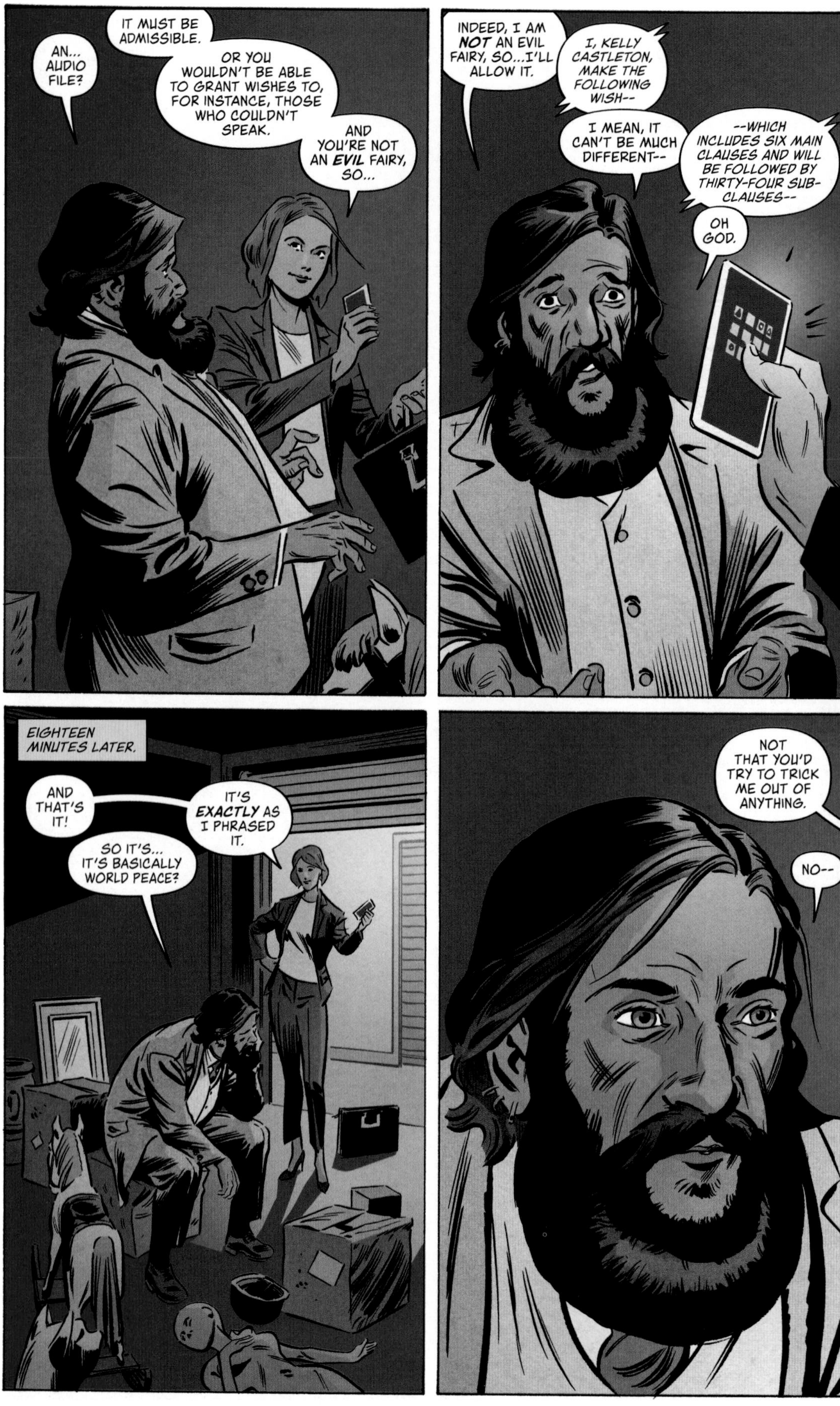
AN... AUDIO FILE?
IT MUST BE ADMISSIBLE.
OR YOU WOULDN'T BE ABLE TO GRANT WISHES TO, FOR INSTANCE, THOSE WHO COULDN'T SPEAK.
AND YOU'RE NOT AN EVIL FAIRY, SO...
INDEED, I AM NOT AN EVIL FAIRY, SO...I'LL ALLOW IT.
I, KELLY CASTLETON, MAKE THE FOLLOWING WISH--
I MEAN, IT CAN'T BE MUCH DIFFERENT--
--WHICH INCLUDES SIX MAIN CLAUSES AND WILL BE FOLLOWED BY THIRTY-FOUR SUB-CLAUSES--
OH GOD.
EIGHTEEN MINUTES LATER.
AND THAT'S IT!
IT'S EXACTLY AS I PHRASED IT.
SO IT'S... IT'S BASICALLY WORLD PEACE?
NOT THAT YOU'D TRY TO TRICK ME OUT OF ANYTHING.
NO--

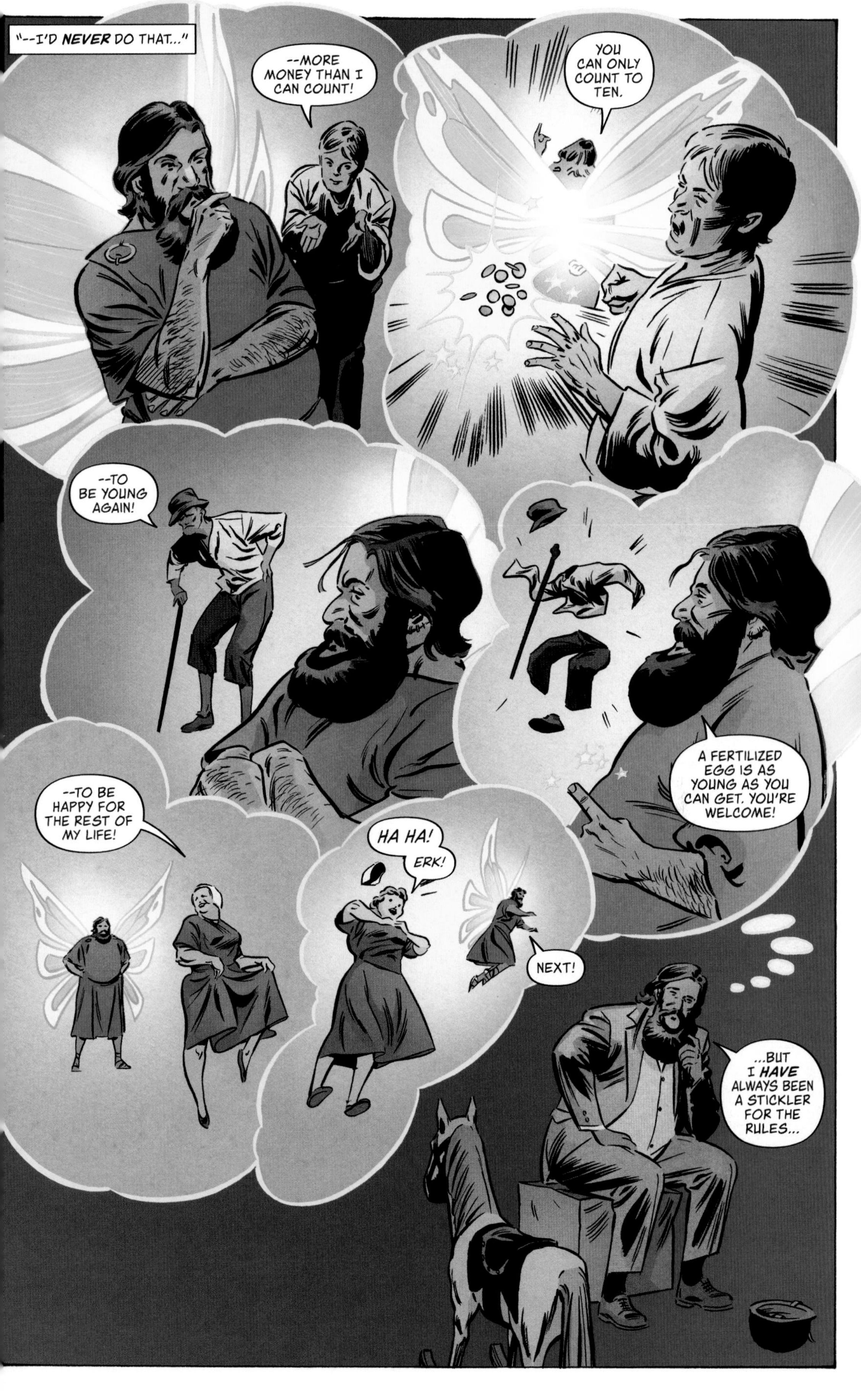
"--I'D NEVER DO THAT..."
--MORE MONEY THAN I CAN COUNT!
YOU CAN ONLY COUNT TO TEN.
--TO BE YOUNG AGAIN!
A FERTILIZED EGG IS AS YOUNG AS YOU CAN GET. YOU'RE WELCOME!
--TO BE HAPPY FOR THE REST OF MY LIFE!
HA HA!
ERK!
NEXT!
...BUT I HAVE ALWAYS BEEN A STICKLER FOR THE RULES...

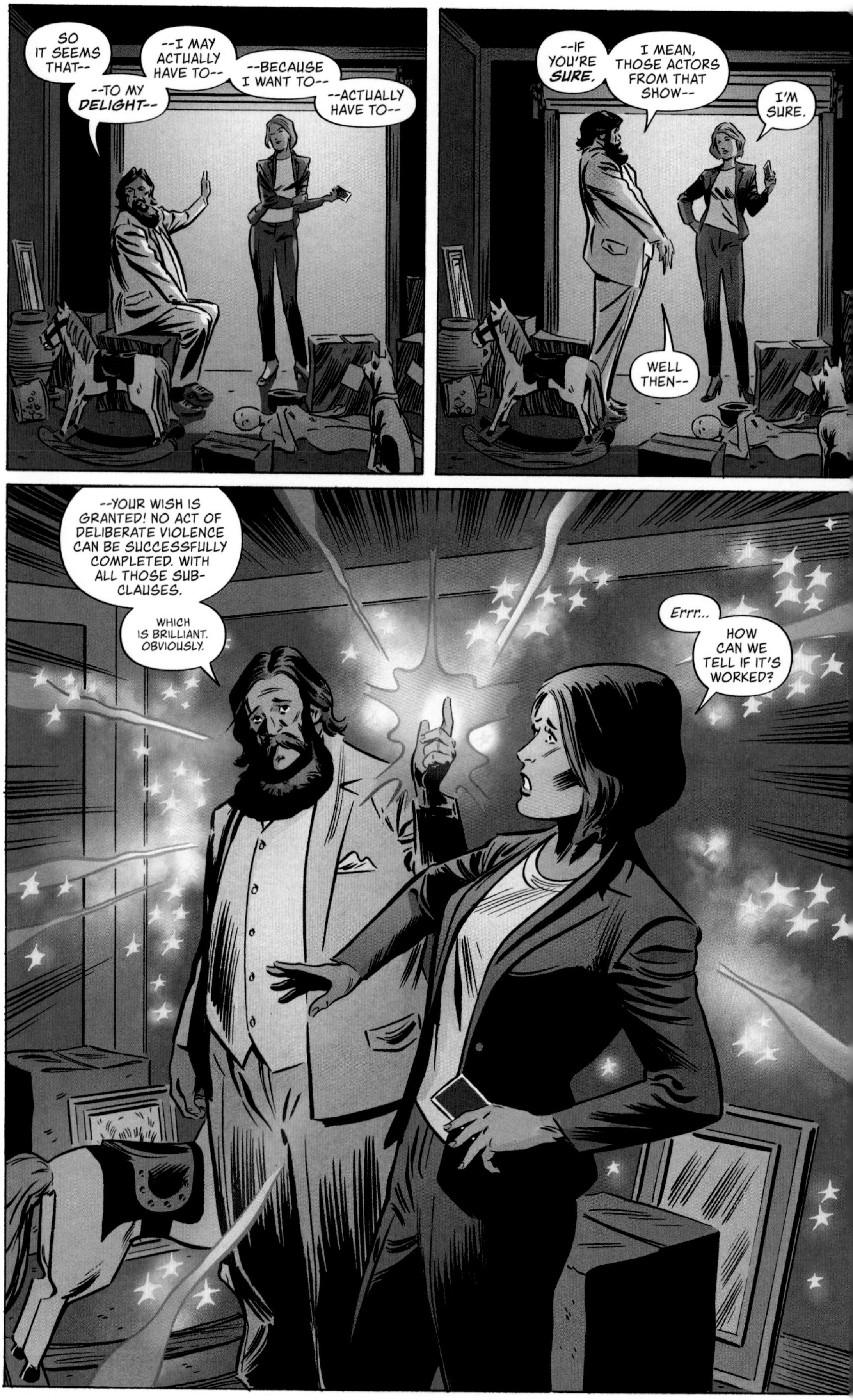
SO IT SEEMS THAT--
--TO MY DELIGHT--
--I MAY ACTUALLY HAVE TO--
--BECAUSE I WANT TO--
--ACTUALLY HAVE TO--
--IF YOU'RE SURE.
I MEAN, THOSE ACTORS FROM THAT SHOW--
I'M SURE.
WELL THEN--
--YOUR WISH IS GRANTED! NO ACT OF DELIBERATE VIOLENCE CAN BE SUCCESSFULLY COMPLETED. WITH ALL THOSE SUB-CLAUSES.
WHICH IS BRILLIANT. OBVIOUSLY.
Errr...
HOW CAN WE TELL IF IT'S WORKED?

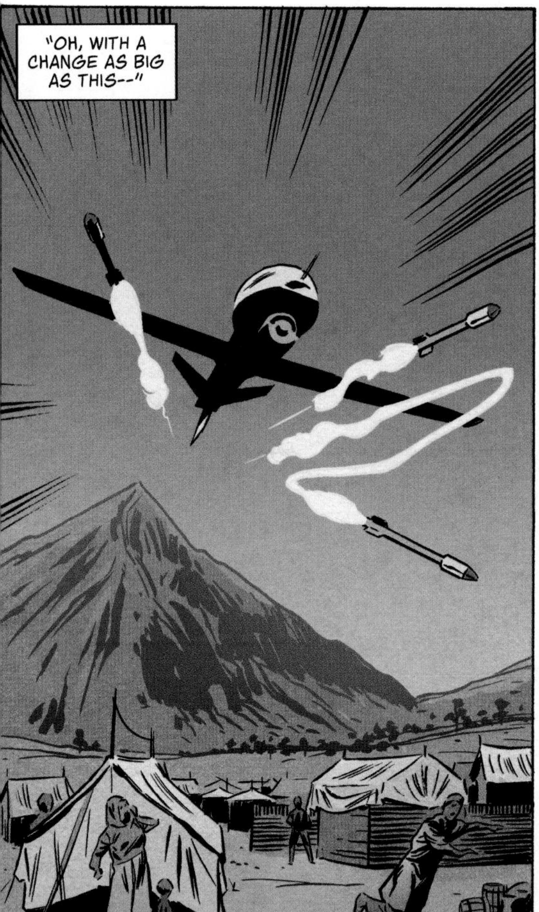
"OH, WITH A CHANGE AS BIG AS THIS--"
<WRONG TARGET! WE ARE NOT MILITARY!>

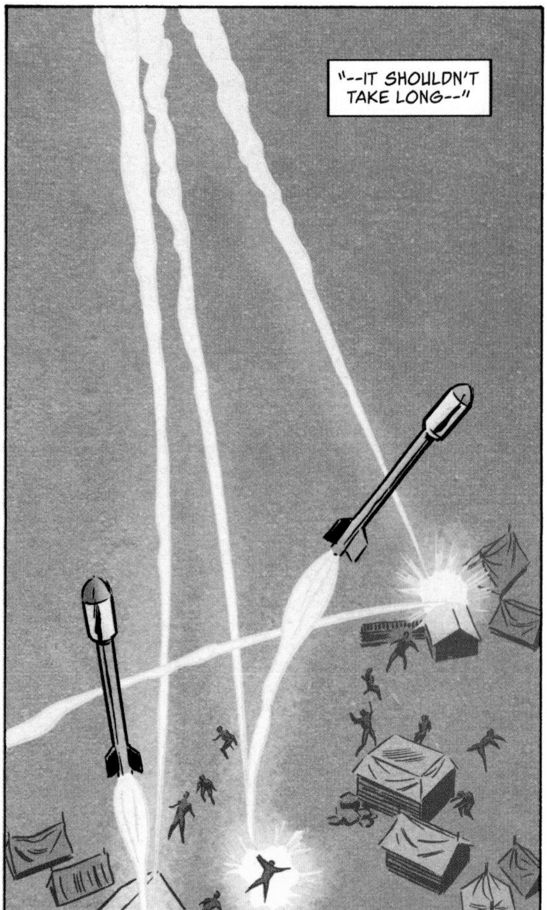
"--IT SHOULDN'T TAKE LONG--"

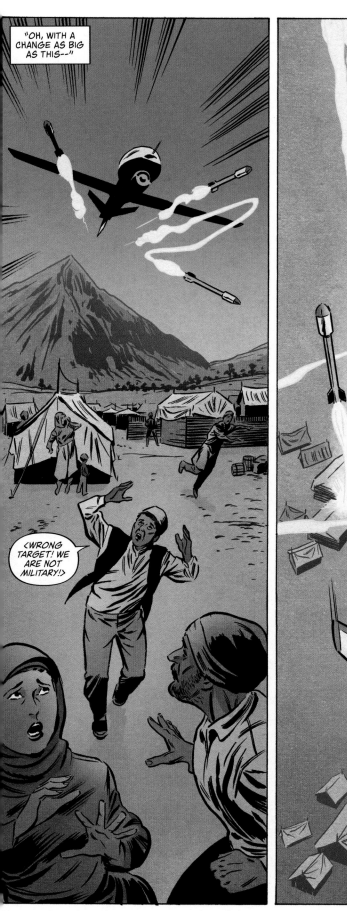

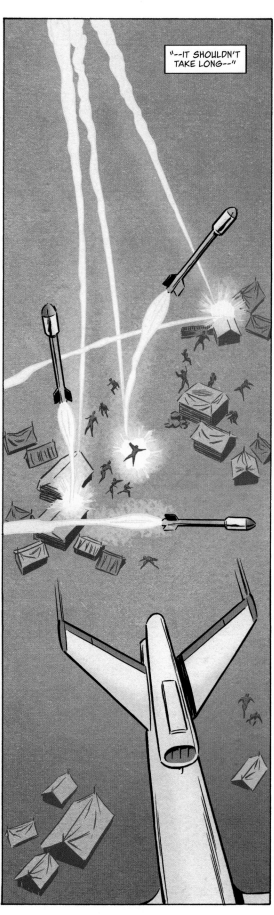

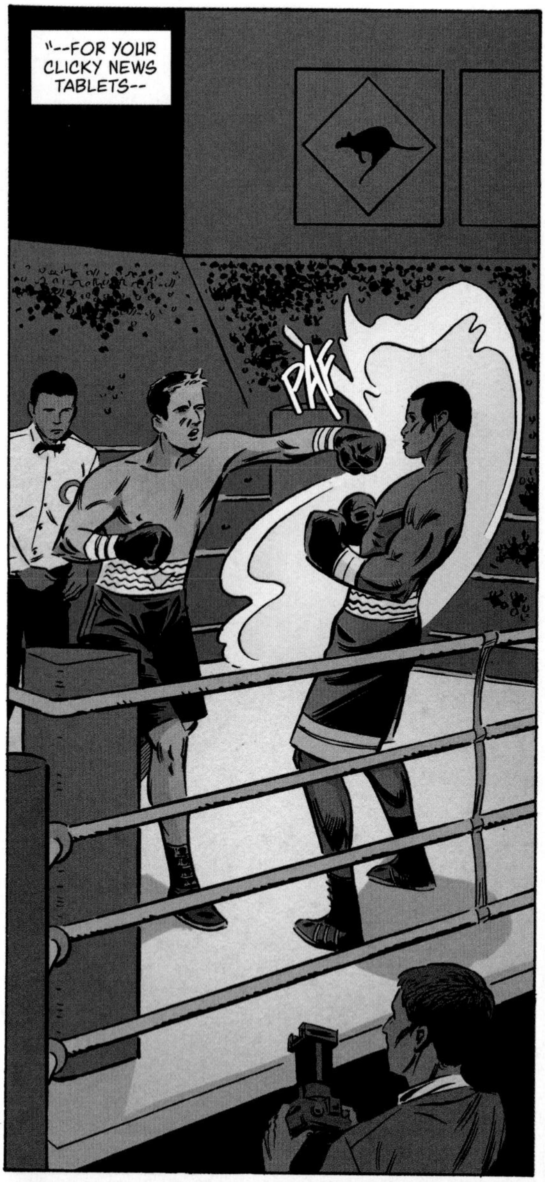
"--FOR YOUR CLICKY NEWS TABLETS--
PAF

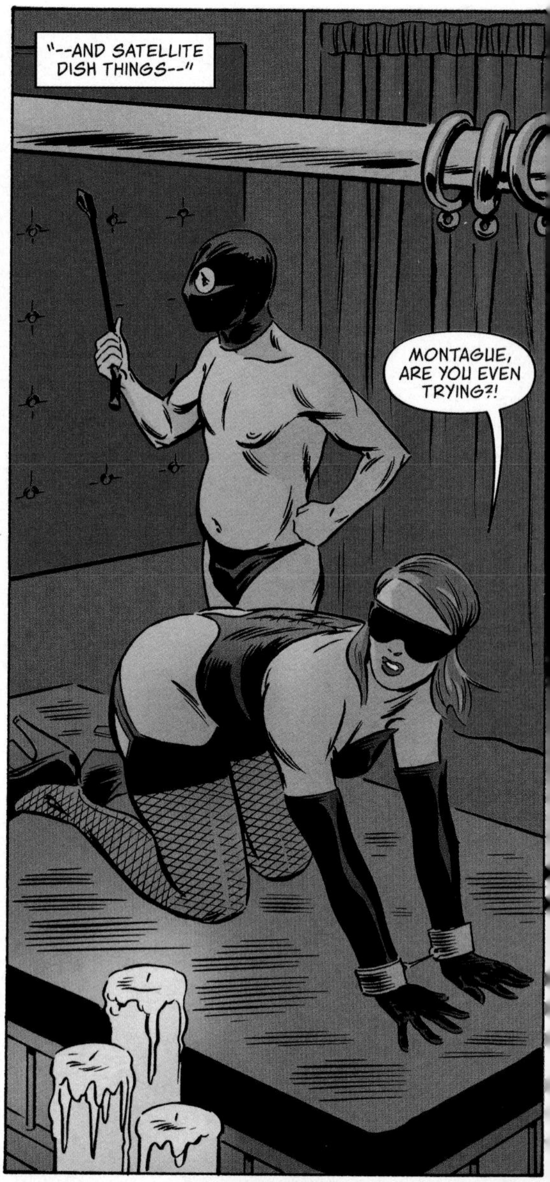
"--AND SATELLITE DISH THINGS--"
MONTAGUE, ARE YOU EVEN TRYING?!

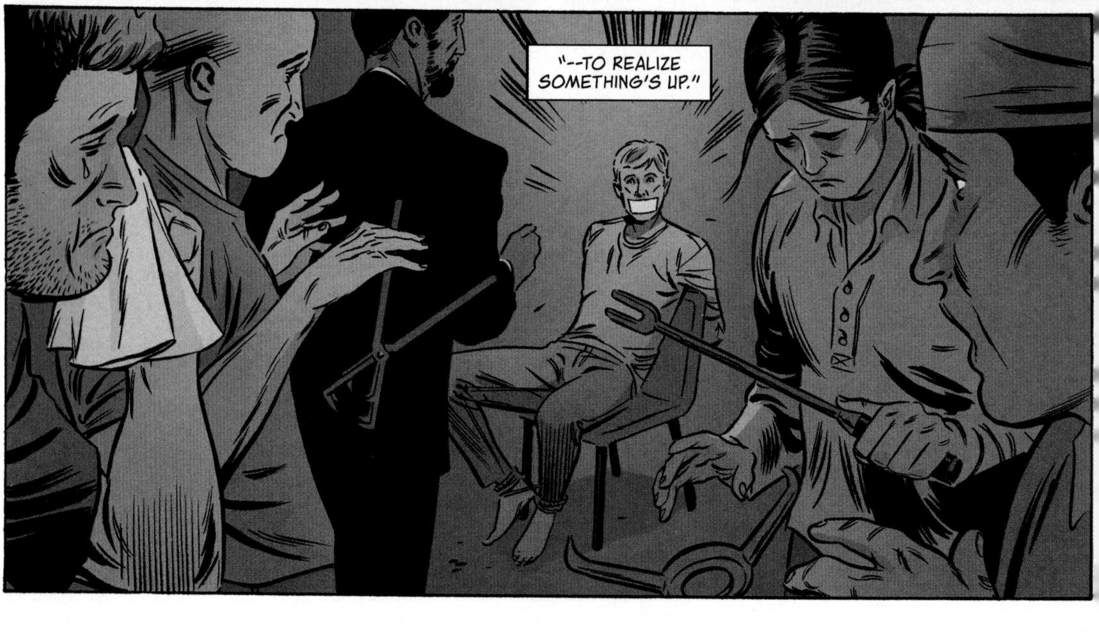
"--TO REALIZE SOMETHING'S UP."

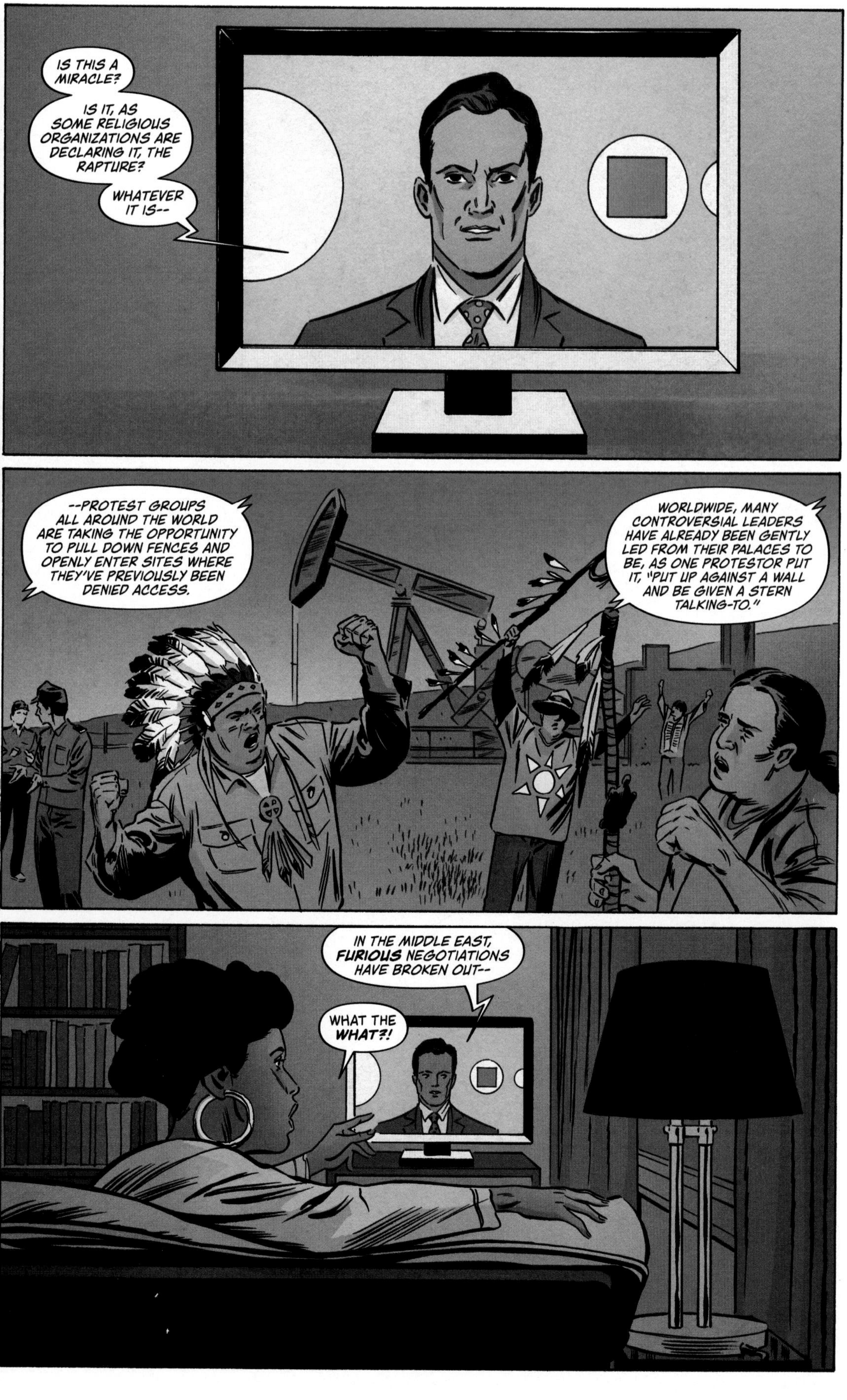
IS THIS A MIRACLE?
IS IT, AS SOME RELIGIOUS ORGANIZATIONS ARE DECLARING IT, THE RAPTURE?
WHATEVER IT IS--
--PROTEST GROUPS ALL AROUND THE WORLD ARE TAKING THE OPPORTUNITY TO PULL DOWN FENCES AND OPENLY ENTER SITES WHERE THEY'VE PREVIOUSLY BEEN DENIED ACCESS.
WORLDWIDE, MANY CONTROVERSIAL LEADERS HAVE ALREADY BEEN GENTLY LED FROM THEIR PALACES TO BE, AS ONE PROTESTOR PUT IT, "PUT UP AGAINST A WALL AND BE GIVEN A STERN TALKING-TO."
IN THE MIDDLE EAST, FURIOUS NEGOTIATIONS HAVE BROKEN OUT--
WHAT THE WHAT?!

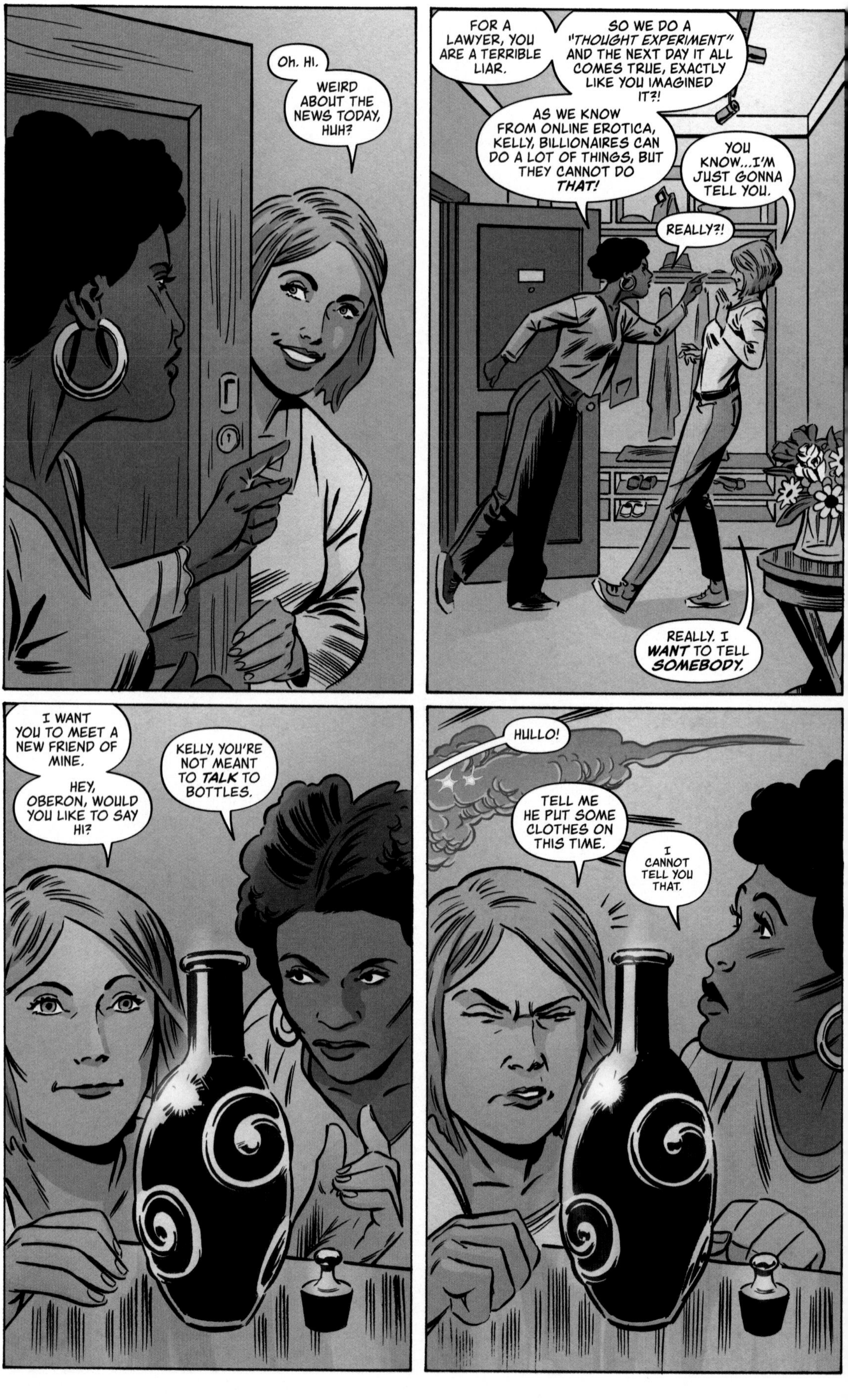
Oh. HI.
WEIRD ABOUT THE NEWS TODAY, HUH?
FOR A LAWYER, YOU ARE A TERRIBLE LIAR.
SO WE DO A "THOUGHT EXPERIMENT" AND THE NEXT DAY IT ALL COMES TRUE, EXACTLY LIKE YOU IMAGINED IT?!
AS WE KNOW FROM ONLINE EROTICA, KELLY, BILLIONAIRES CAN DO A LOT OF THINGS, BUT THEY CANNOT DO THAT!
YOU KNOW...I'M JUST GONNA TELL YOU.
REALLY?!
REALLY. I WANT TO TELL SOMEBODY.
I WANT YOU TO MEET A NEW FRIEND OF MINE.
HEY, OBERON, WOULD YOU LIKE TO SAY HI?
KELLY, YOU'RE NOT MEANT TO TALK TO BOTTLES.
HULLO!
TELL ME HE PUT SOME CLOTHES ON THIS TIME.
I CANNOT TELL YOU THAT.

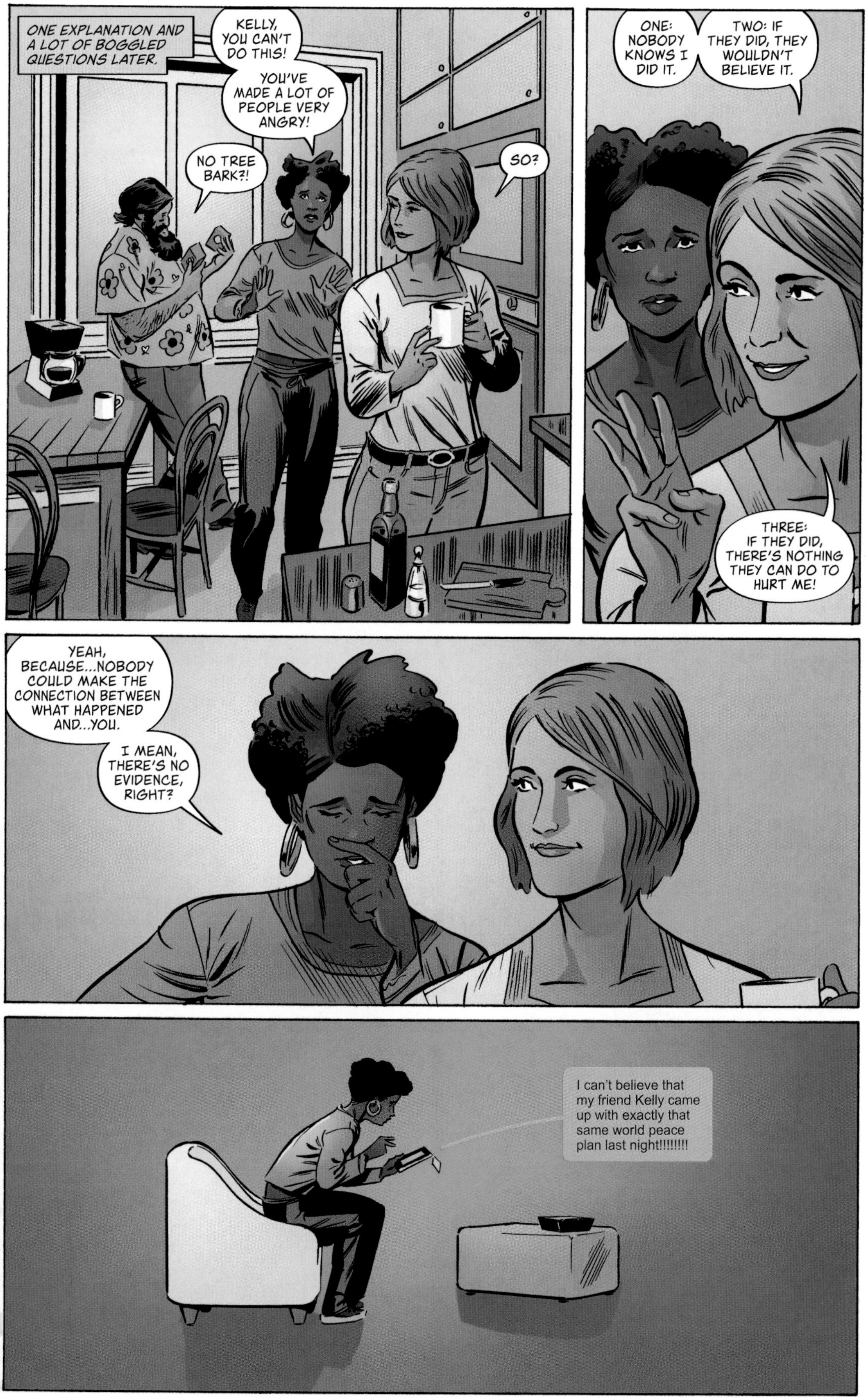
ONE EXPLANATION AND A LOT OF BOGGLED QUESTIONS LATER.
KELLY, YOU CAN'T DO THIS!
YOU'VE MADE A LOT OF PEOPLE VERY ANGRY!
NO TREE BARK?!
SO?
ONE: NOBODY KNOWS I DID IT.
TWO: IF THEY DID, THEY WOULDN'T BELIEVE IT.
THREE: IF THEY DID, THERE'S NOTHING THEY CAN DO TO HURT ME!
YEAH, BECAUSE...NOBODY COULD MAKE THE CONNECTION BETWEEN WHAT HAPPENED AND...YOU.
I MEAN, THERE'S NO EVIDENCE, RIGHT?
I can't believe that my friend Kelly came up with exactly that same world peace plan last night!!!!!!!!

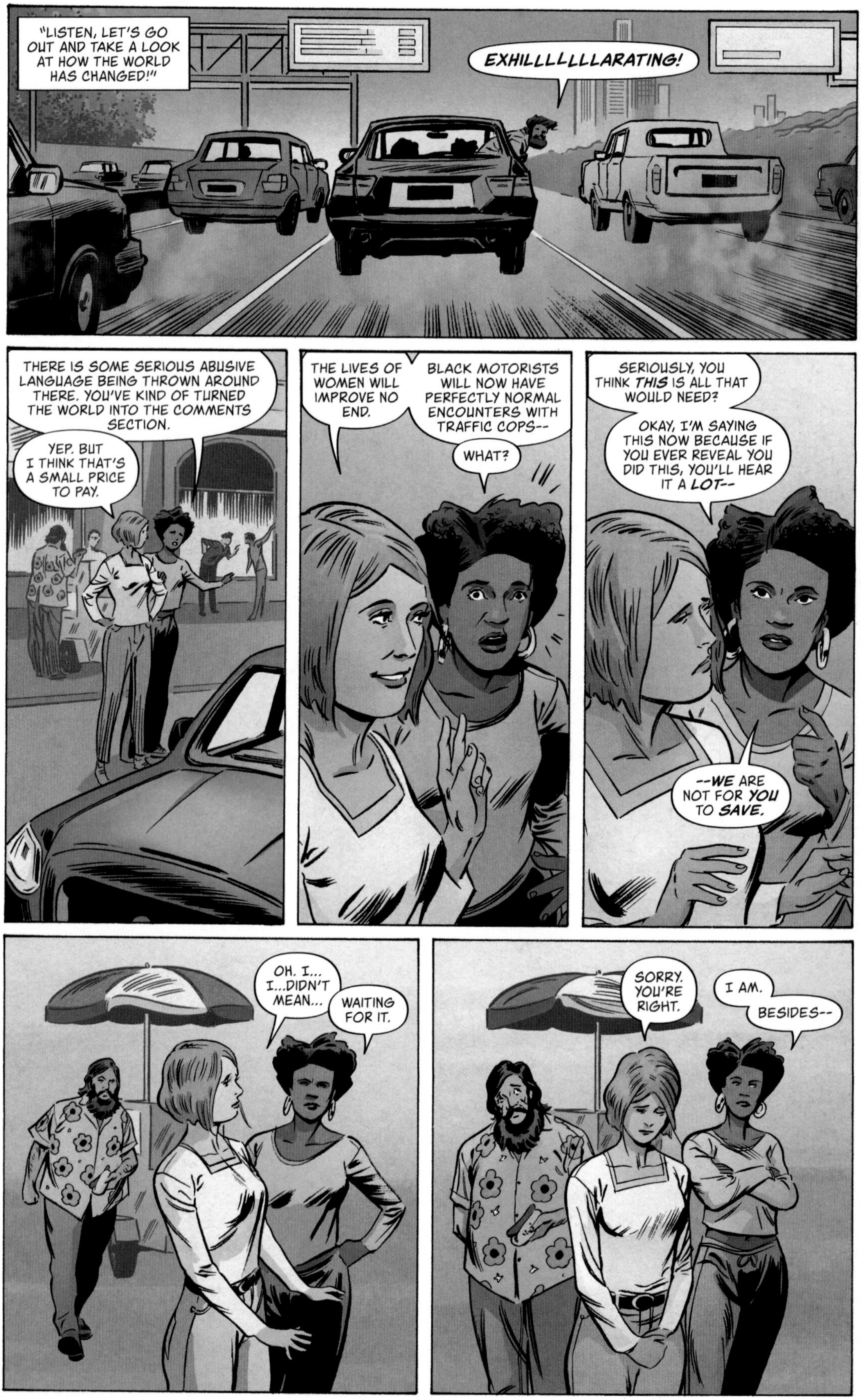
"LISTEN, LET'S GO OUT AND TAKE A LOOK AT HOW THE WORLD HAS CHANGED!"
EXHILLLLLLLARATING!
THERE IS SOME SERIOUS ABUSIVE LANGUAGE BEING THROWN AROUND THERE. YOU'VE KIND OF TURNED THE WORLD INTO THE COMMENTS SECTION.
YEP. BUT I THINK THAT'S A SMALL PRICE TO PAY.
THE LIVES OF WOMEN WILL IMPROVE NO END.
BLACK MOTORISTS WILL NOW HAVE PERFECTLY NORMAL ENCOUNTERS WITH TRAFFIC COPS--
WHAT?
SERIOUSLY, YOU THINK *THIS* IS ALL THAT WOULD NEED?
OKAY, I'M SAYING THIS NOW BECAUSE IF YOU EVER REVEAL YOU DID THIS, YOU'LL HEAR IT A *LOT*--
--*WE* ARE NOT FOR *YOU* TO *SAVE.*
OH. I... I...DIDN'T MEAN...
WAITING FOR IT.
SORRY. YOU'RE RIGHT.
I AM.
BESIDES--

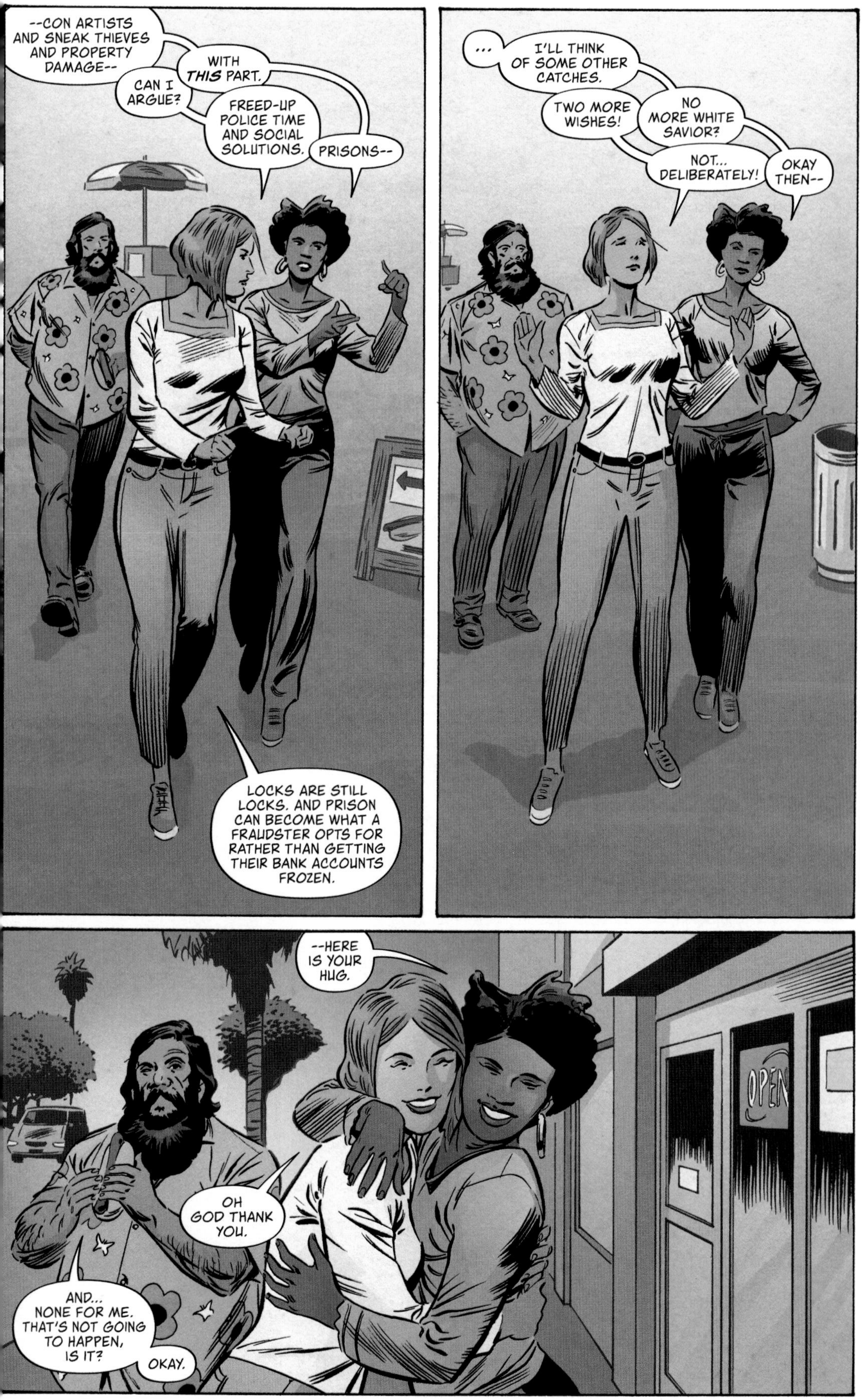
--CON ARTISTS AND SNEAK THIEVES AND PROPERTY DAMAGE--
CAN I ARGUE?
WITH *THIS* PART.
FREED-UP POLICE TIME AND SOCIAL SOLUTIONS.
PRISONS--
LOCKS ARE STILL LOCKS. AND PRISON CAN BECOME WHAT A FRAUDSTER OPTS FOR RATHER THAN GETTING THEIR BANK ACCOUNTS FROZEN.
...
I'LL THINK OF SOME OTHER CATCHES.
TWO MORE WISHES!
NO MORE WHITE SAVIOR?
NOT... DELIBERATELY!
OKAY THEN--
--HERE IS YOUR HUG.
OH GOD THANK YOU.
AND... NONE FOR ME. THAT'S NOT GOING TO HAPPEN, IS IT?
OKAY.
OPEN

SO, MAYBE YOU COULD USE A WISH FOR SOMETHING...LESS SELFLESS?

SOMETHING IMPULSIVE!

AH, YOUR FRIEND IS WISE!

ANNIE...I HAVE TWO MORE CHANCES TO MAKE THE WORLD BETTER.

I AM GOING TO USE THEM *WISELY*.

THERE STILL EXISTS CHEESE!

I REMEMBER WHEN THEY INVENTED CHEESE.

IT WAS LIKE: "WHAAAT, THE MILK WENT OFF AND IT TURNED INTO *THAT*?"

SO THEN THEY TRIED LETTING EVERYTHING ELSE GO OFF. AND THAT WASN'T SO GREAT.

...A SPOKESWOMAN FOR THE GUN LOBBY--

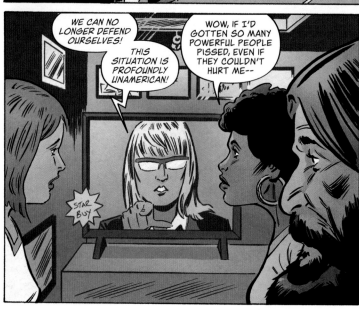

WE CAN NO LONGER DEFEND OURSELVES!

THIS SITUATION IS PROFOUNDLY UNAMERICAN!

WOW, IF I'D GOTTEN SO MANY POWERFUL PEOPLE PISSED, EVEN IF THEY COULDN'T HURT ME--

STAR BUY

--I MIGHT, I DON'T KNOW, GO INTO HIDING OR SOMETHING?

YOU KNOW--

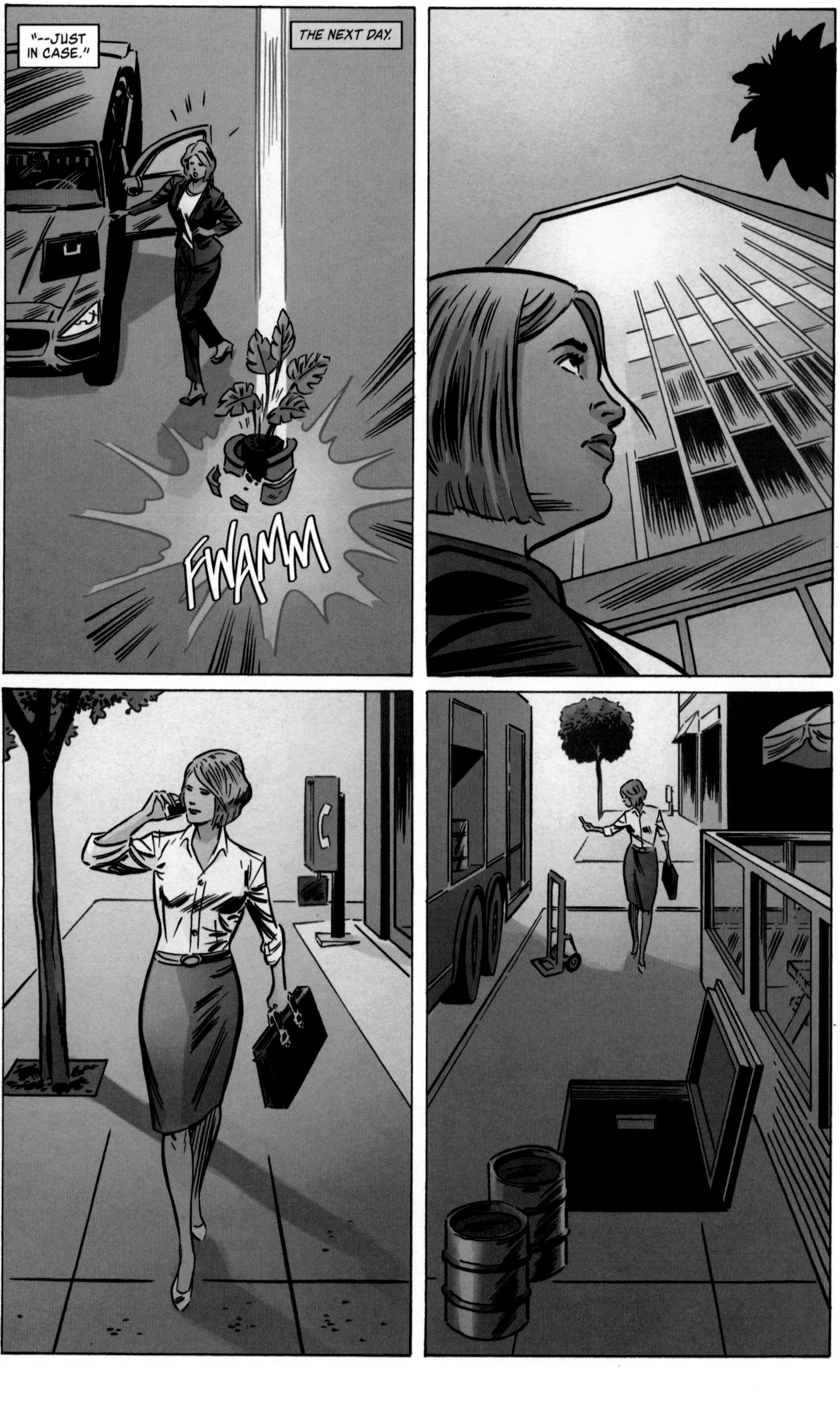
"--JUST IN CASE."
THE NEXT DAY.
FWAMM

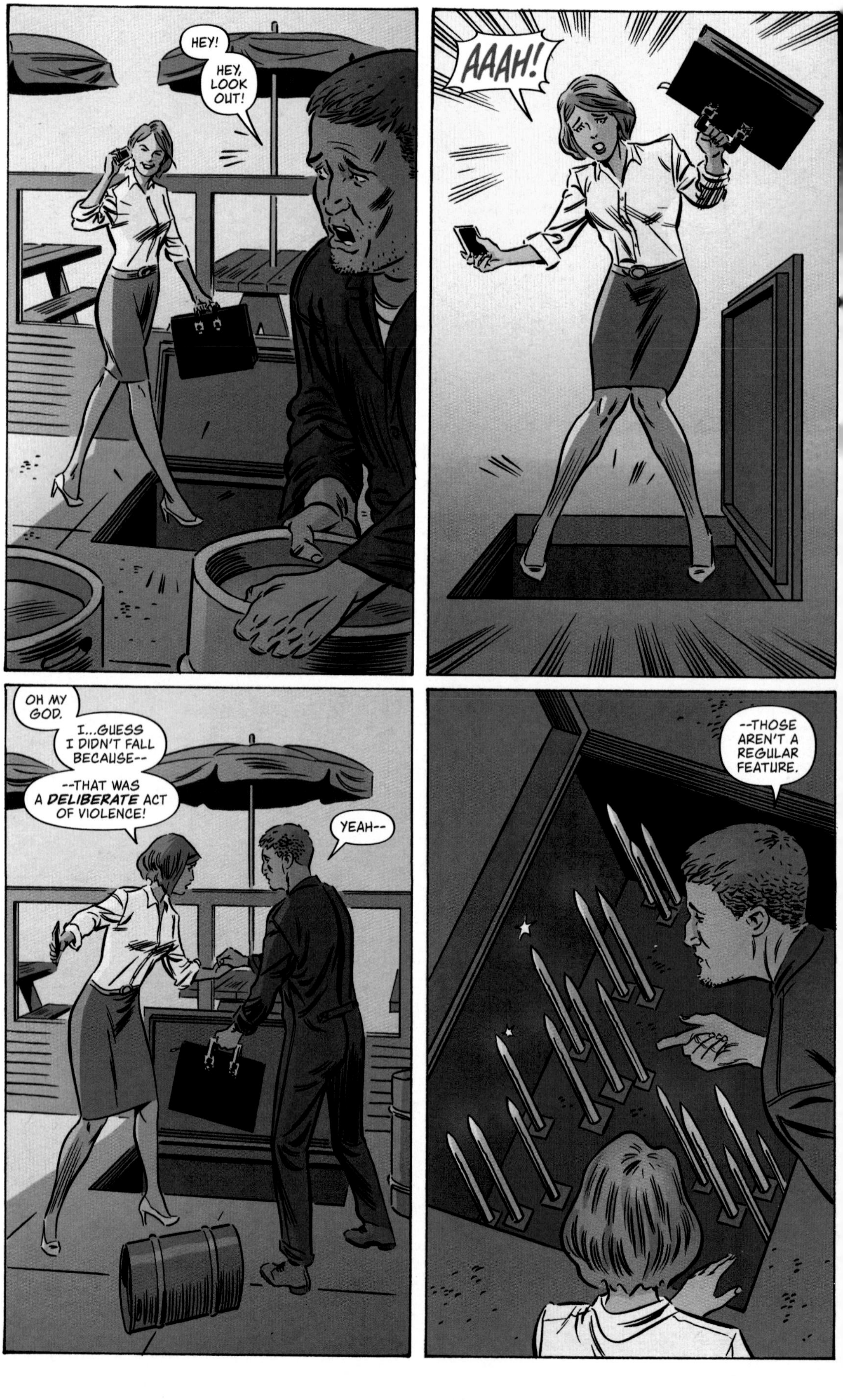
HEY!
HEY, LOOK OUT!
AAAH!
OH MY GOD.
I...GUESS I DIDN'T FALL BECAUSE--
--THAT WAS A DELIBERATE ACT OF VIOLENCE!
YEAH--
--THOSE AREN'T A REGULAR FEATURE.

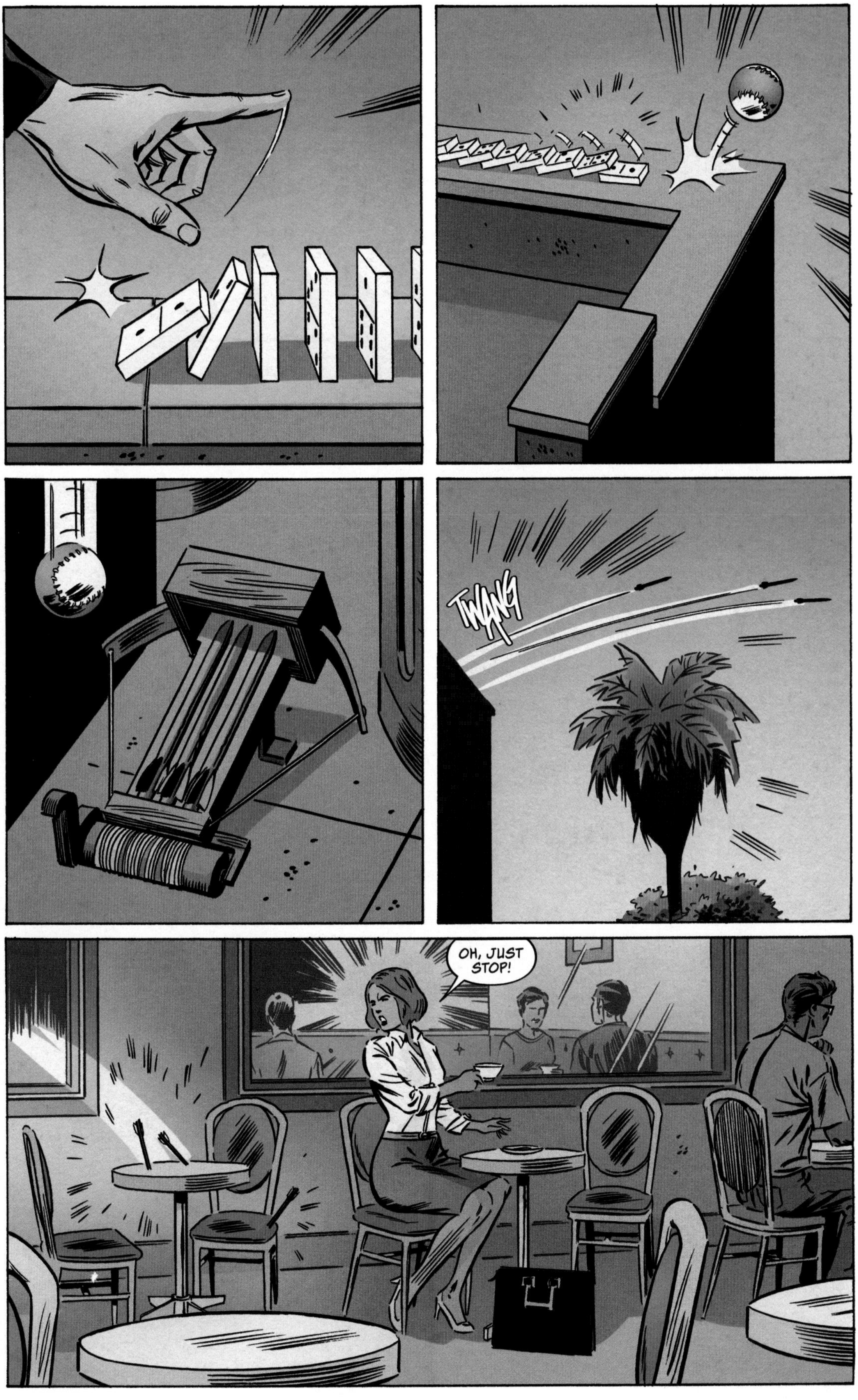
TWANG
OH, JUST STOP!

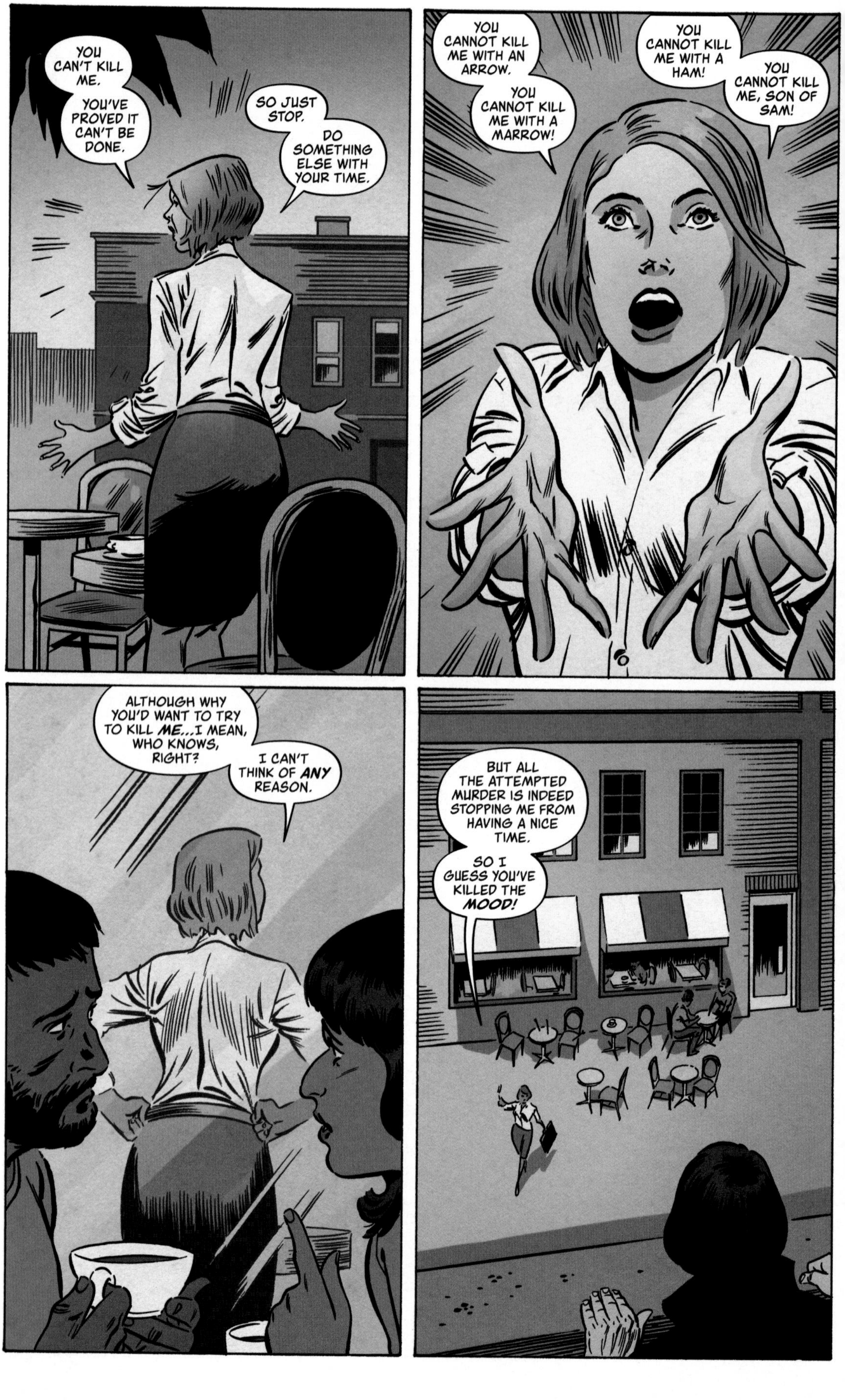
YOU CAN'T KILL ME.
YOU'VE PROVED IT CAN'T BE DONE.
SO JUST STOP.
DO SOMETHING ELSE WITH YOUR TIME.
YOU CANNOT KILL ME WITH AN ARROW.
YOU CANNOT KILL ME WITH A MARROW!
YOU CANNOT KILL ME WITH A HAM!
YOU CANNOT KILL ME, SON OF SAM!
ALTHOUGH WHY YOU'D WANT TO TRY TO KILL ME...I MEAN, WHO KNOWS, RIGHT?
I CAN'T THINK OF ANY REASON.
BUT ALL THE ATTEMPTED MURDER IS INDEED STOPPING ME FROM HAVING A NICE TIME.
SO I GUESS YOU'VE KILLED THE MOOD!

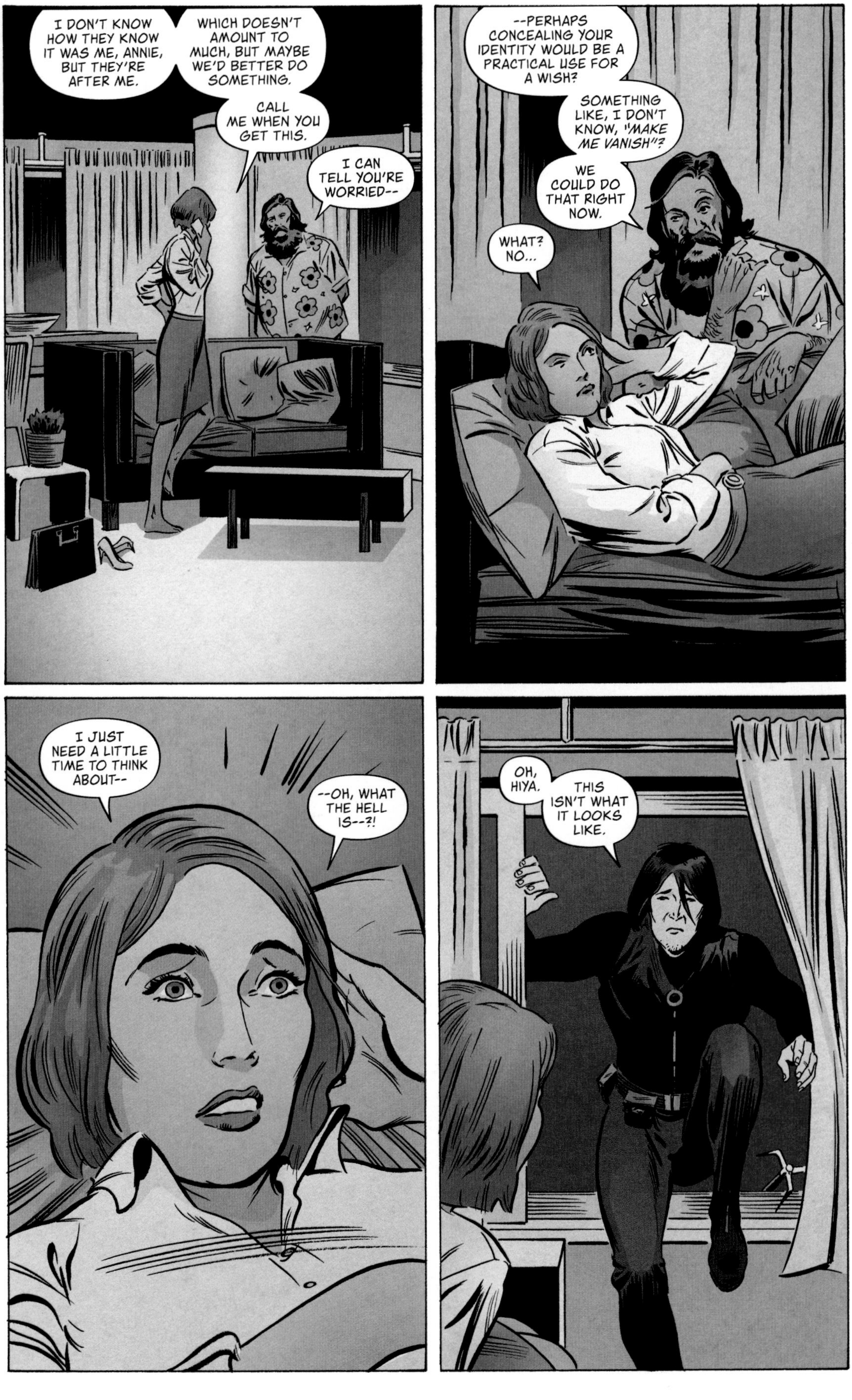
I DON'T KNOW HOW THEY KNOW IT WAS ME, ANNIE, BUT THEY'RE AFTER ME.
WHICH DOESN'T AMOUNT TO MUCH, BUT MAYBE WE'D BETTER DO SOMETHING.
CALL ME WHEN YOU GET THIS.
I CAN TELL YOU'RE WORRIED--
--PERHAPS CONCEALING YOUR IDENTITY WOULD BE A PRACTICAL USE FOR A WISH?
SOMETHING LIKE, I DON'T KNOW, "MAKE ME VANISH"?
WE COULD DO THAT RIGHT NOW.
WHAT? NO...
I JUST NEED A LITTLE TIME TO THINK ABOUT--
--OH, WHAT THE HELL IS--?!
OH, HIYA.
THIS ISN'T WHAT IT LOOKS LIKE.

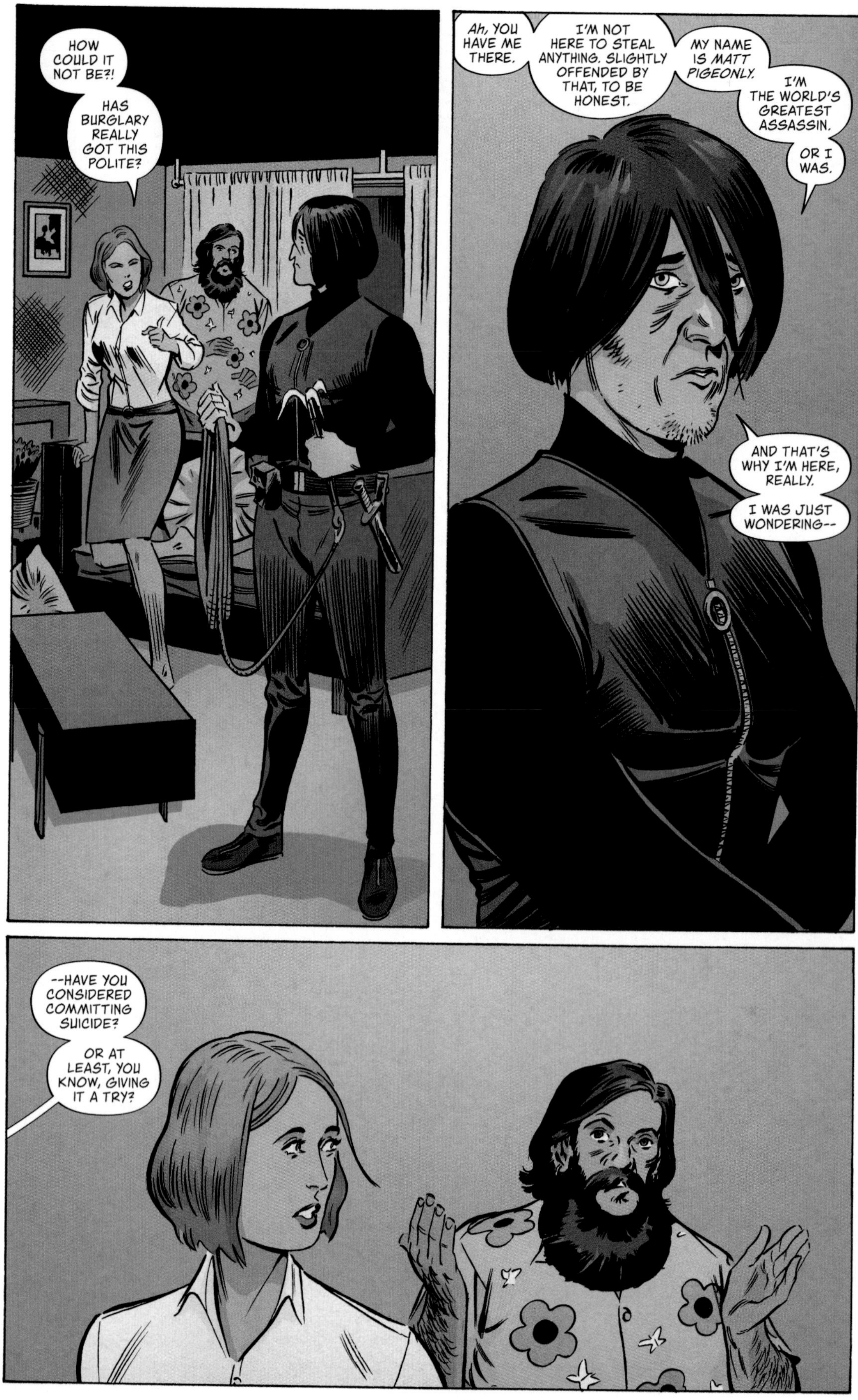
HOW COULD IT NOT BE?!
HAS BURGLARY REALLY GOT THIS POLITE?
Ah, YOU HAVE ME THERE.
I'M NOT HERE TO STEAL ANYTHING. SLIGHTLY OFFENDED BY THAT, TO BE HONEST.
MY NAME IS MATT PIGEONLY.
I'M THE WORLD'S GREATEST ASSASSIN.
OR I WAS.
AND THAT'S WHY I'M HERE, REALLY.
I WAS JUST WONDERING--
--HAVE YOU CONSIDERED COMMITTING SUICIDE?
OR AT LEAST, YOU KNOW, GIVING IT A TRY?

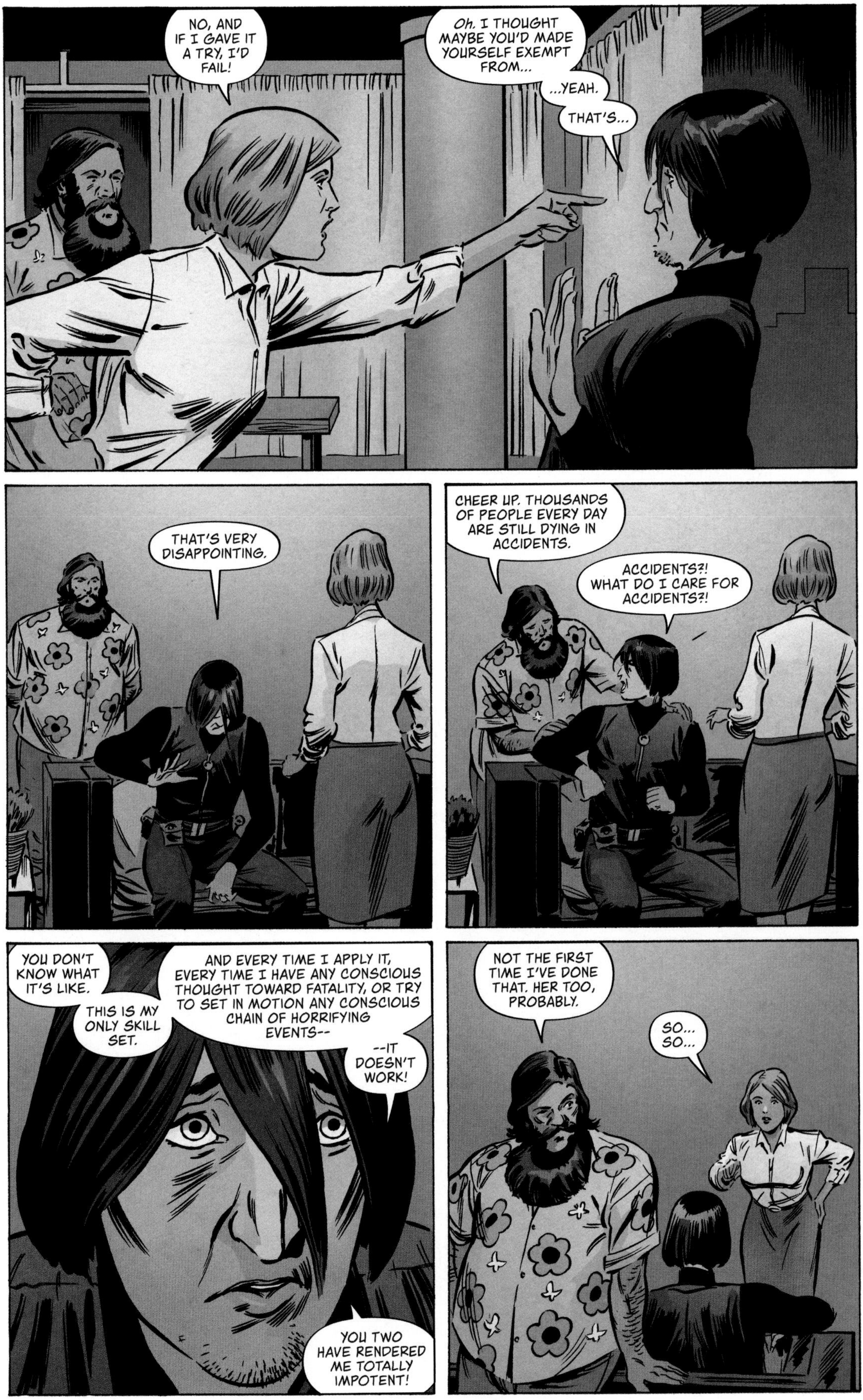
NO, AND IF I GAVE IT A TRY, I'D FAIL!
Oh. I THOUGHT MAYBE YOU'D MADE YOURSELF EXEMPT FROM...
...YEAH.
THAT'S...
THAT'S VERY DISAPPOINTING.
CHEER UP. THOUSANDS OF PEOPLE EVERY DAY ARE STILL DYING IN ACCIDENTS.
ACCIDENTS?! WHAT DO I CARE FOR ACCIDENTS?!
YOU DON'T KNOW WHAT IT'S LIKE.
THIS IS MY ONLY SKILL SET.
AND EVERY TIME I APPLY IT, EVERY TIME I HAVE ANY CONSCIOUS THOUGHT TOWARD FATALITY, OR TRY TO SET IN MOTION ANY CONSCIOUS CHAIN OF HORRIFYING EVENTS--
--IT DOESN'T WORK!
YOU TWO HAVE RENDERED ME TOTALLY IMPOTENT!
NOT THE FIRST TIME I'VE DONE THAT. HER TOO, PROBABLY.
SO... SO...

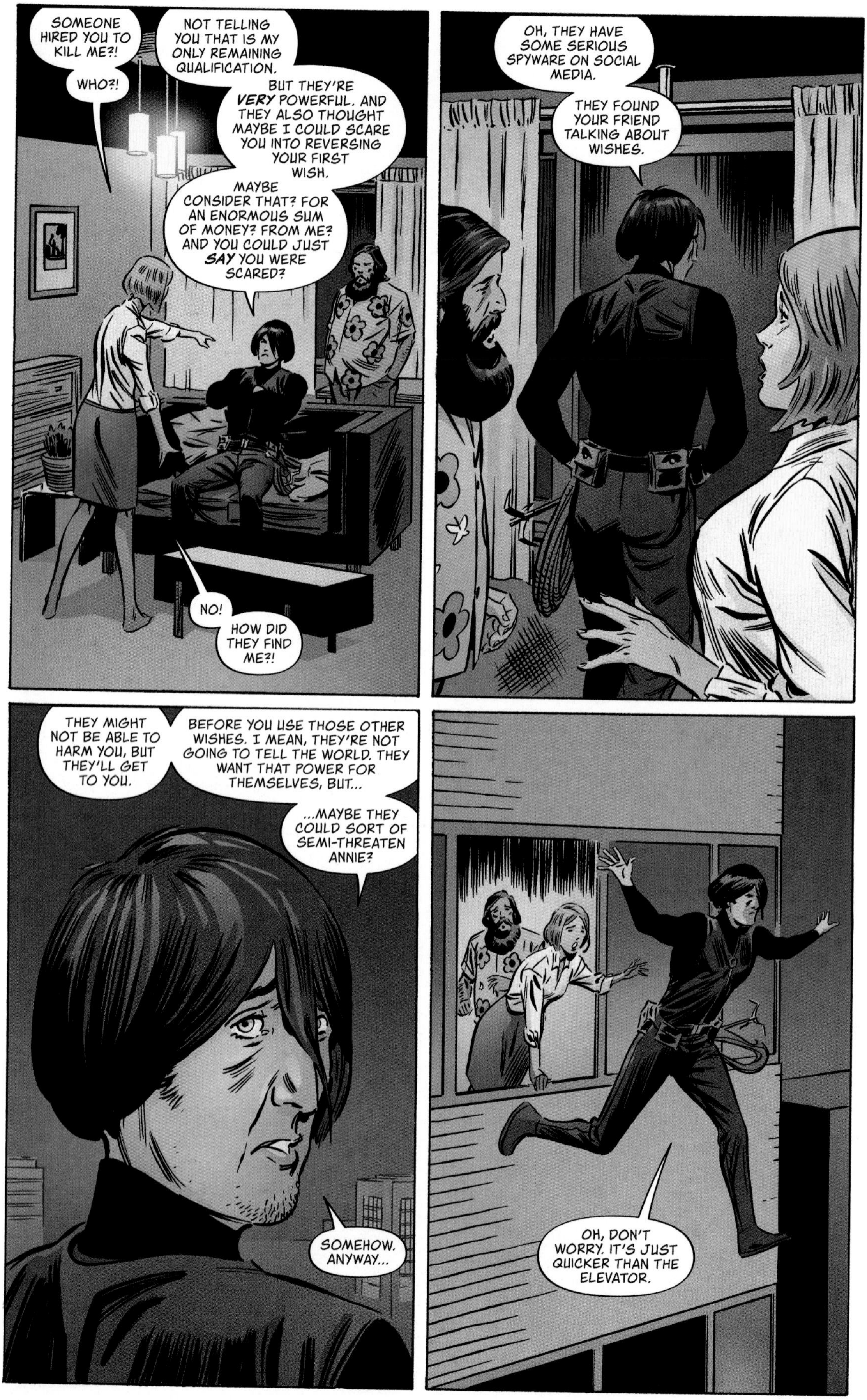
SOMEONE HIRED YOU TO KILL ME?!
WHO?!
NOT TELLING YOU THAT IS MY ONLY REMAINING QUALIFICATION.
BUT THEY'RE *VERY* POWERFUL. AND THEY ALSO THOUGHT MAYBE I COULD SCARE YOU INTO REVERSING YOUR FIRST WISH.
MAYBE CONSIDER THAT? FOR AN ENORMOUS SUM OF MONEY? FROM ME? AND YOU COULD JUST *SAY* YOU WERE SCARED?
NO!
HOW DID THEY FIND ME?!
OH, THEY HAVE SOME SERIOUS SPYWARE ON SOCIAL MEDIA.
THEY FOUND YOUR FRIEND TALKING ABOUT WISHES.
THEY MIGHT NOT BE ABLE TO HARM YOU, BUT THEY'LL GET TO YOU.
BEFORE YOU USE THOSE OTHER WISHES. I MEAN, THEY'RE NOT GOING TO TELL THE WORLD. THEY WANT THAT POWER FOR THEMSELVES, BUT...
...MAYBE THEY COULD SORT OF SEMI-THREATEN ANNIE?
SOMEHOW. ANYWAY...
OH, DON'T WORRY. IT'S JUST QUICKER THAN THE ELEVATOR.

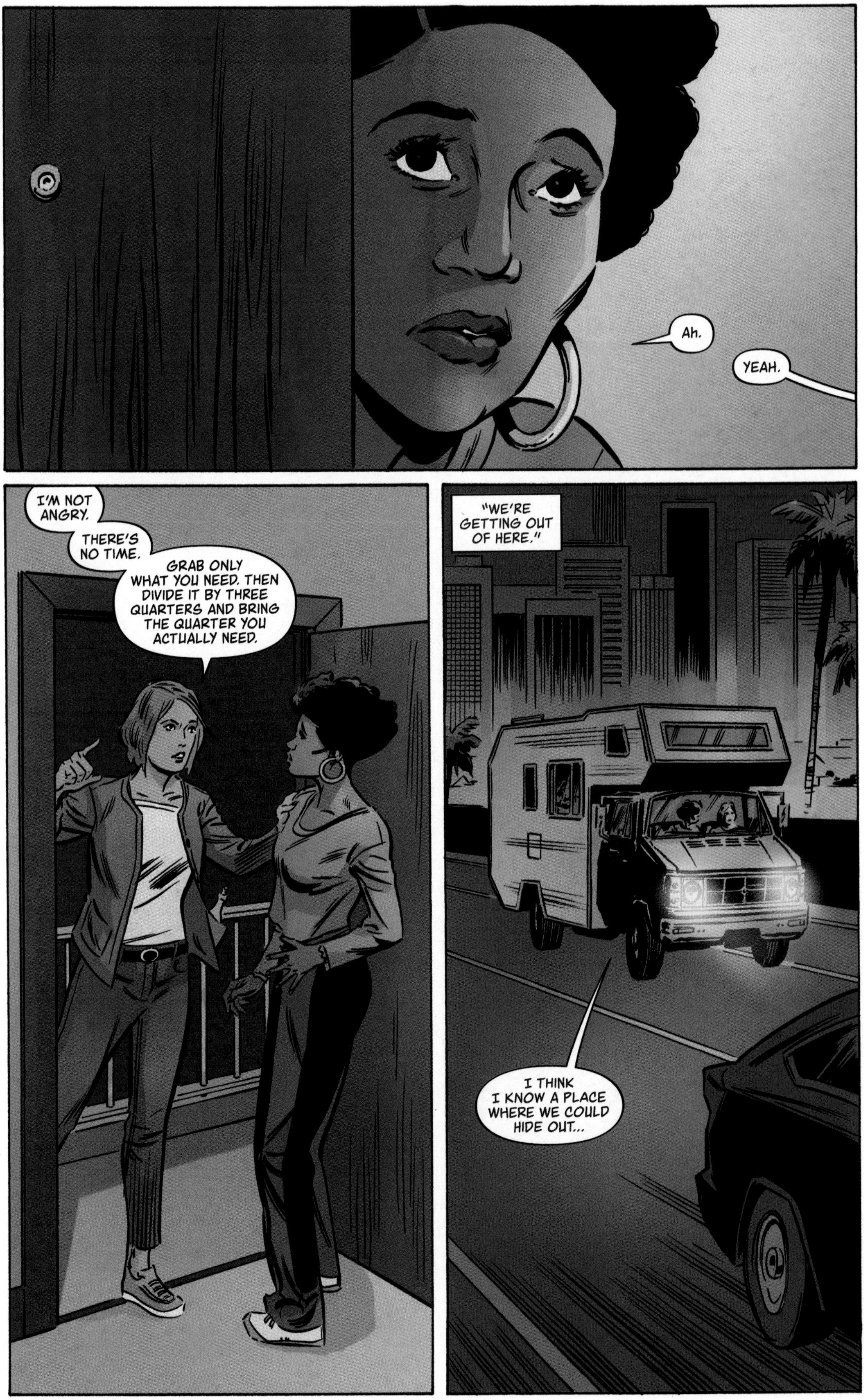

Ah.
YEAH.
I'M NOT ANGRY.
THERE'S NO TIME.
GRAB ONLY WHAT YOU NEED. THEN DIVIDE IT BY THREE QUARTERS AND BRING THE QUARTER YOU ACTUALLY NEED.
"WE'RE GETTING OUT OF HERE."
I THINK I KNOW A PLACE WHERE WE COULD HIDE OUT...

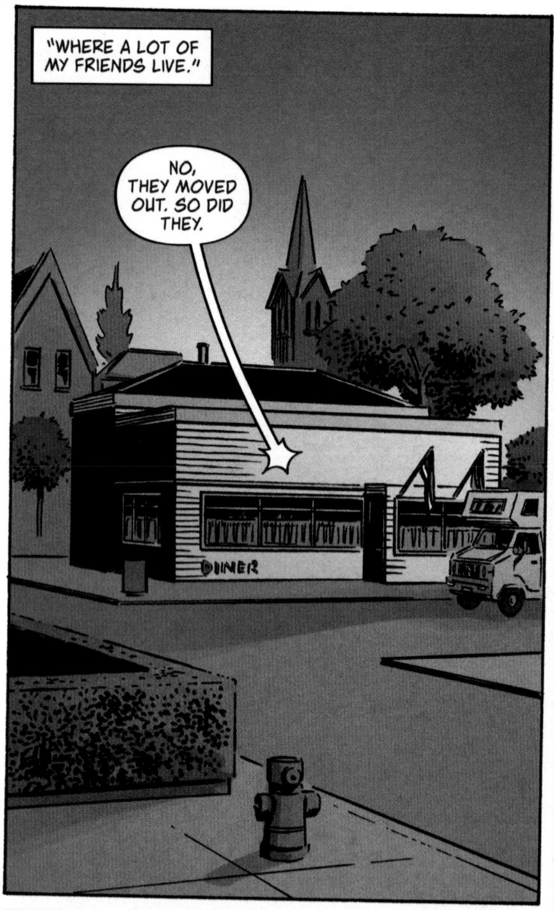
"WHERE A LOT OF MY FRIENDS LIVE."
NO, THEY MOVED OUT. SO DID THEY.
DINER

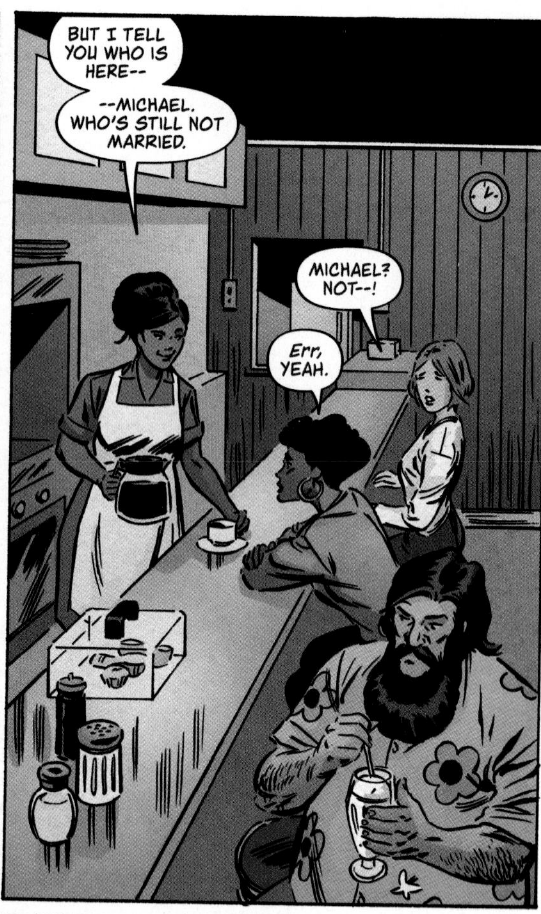
BUT I TELL YOU WHO IS HERE--
--MICHAEL. WHO'S STILL NOT MARRIED.
MICHAEL? NOT--!
Err, YEAH.

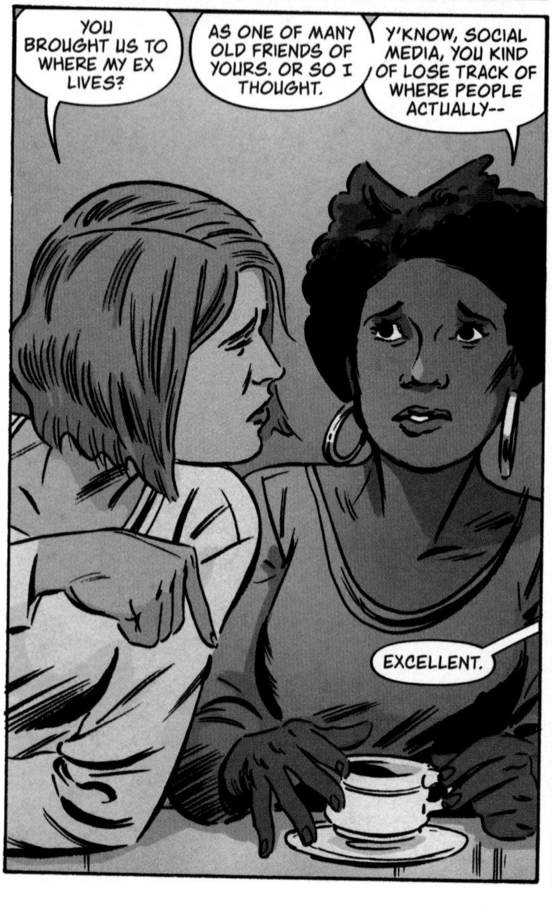
YOU BROUGHT US TO WHERE MY EX LIVES?
AS ONE OF MANY OLD FRIENDS OF YOURS. OR SO I THOUGHT.
Y'KNOW, SOCIAL MEDIA, YOU KIND OF LOSE TRACK OF WHERE PEOPLE ACTUALLY--
EXCELLENT.

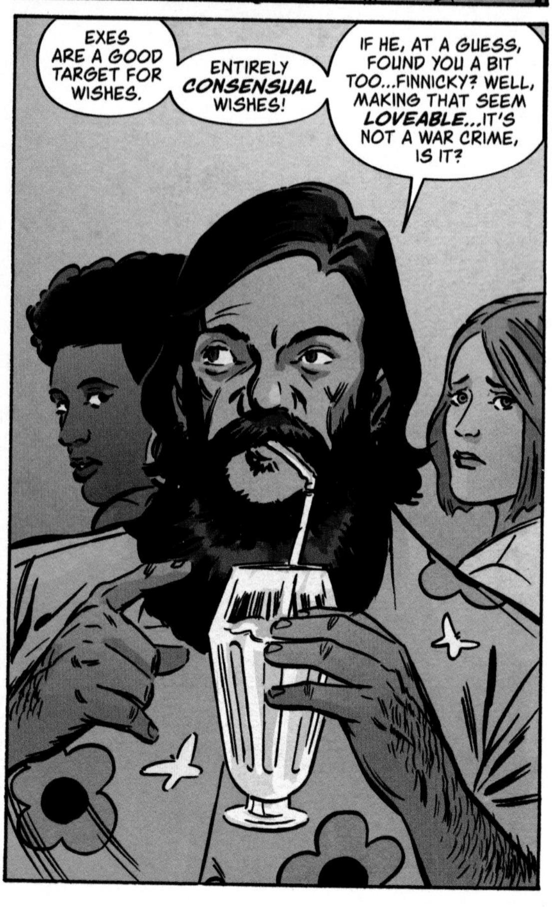
EXES ARE A GOOD TARGET FOR WISHES.
ENTIRELY CONSENSUAL WISHES!
IF HE, AT A GUESS, FOUND YOU A BIT TOO...FINNICKY? WELL, MAKING THAT SEEM LOVEABLE...IT'S NOT A WAR CRIME, IS IT?

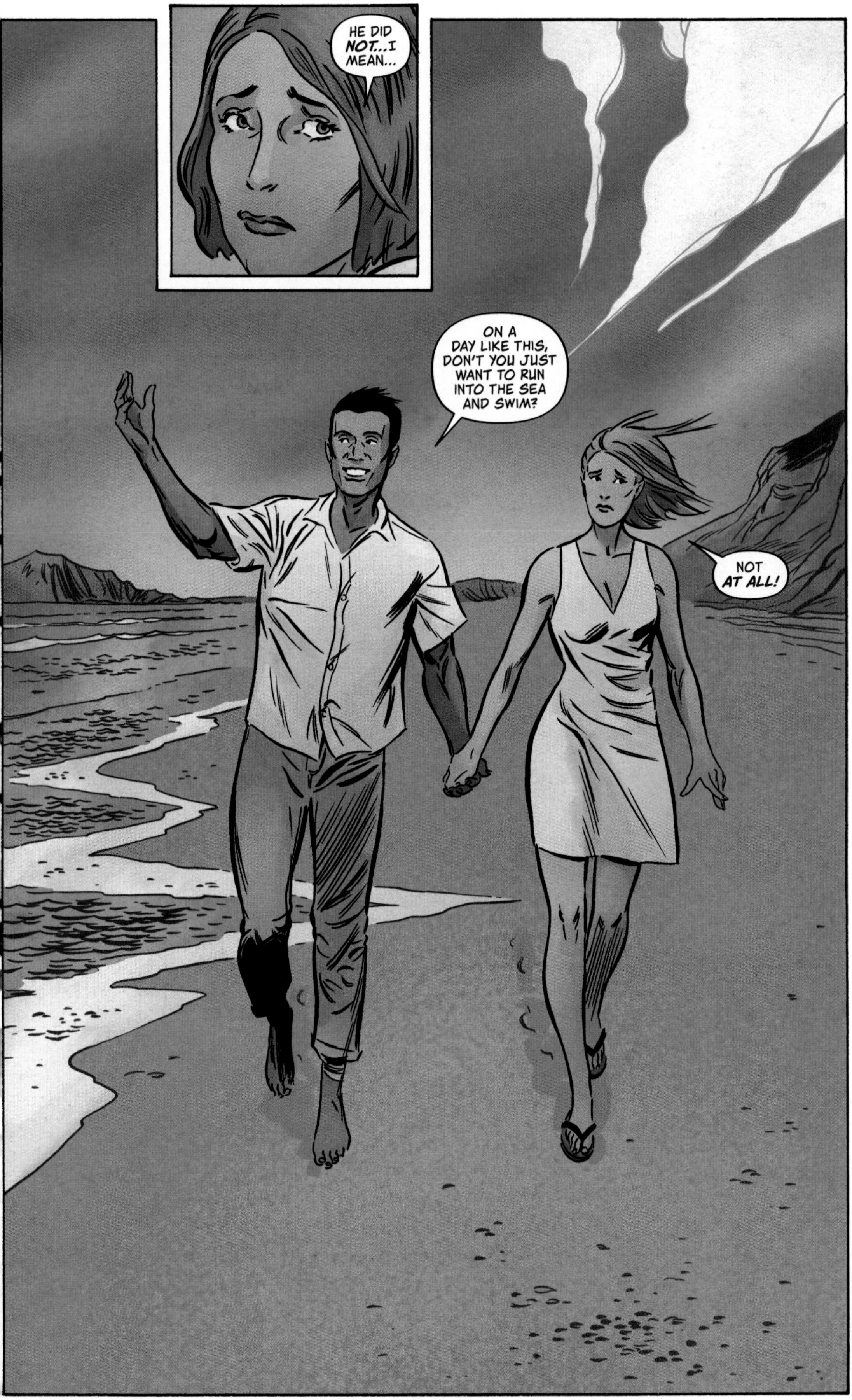
HE DID NOT...I MEAN...
ON A DAY LIKE THIS, DON'T YOU JUST WANT TO RUN INTO THE SEA AND SWIM?
NOT AT ALL!

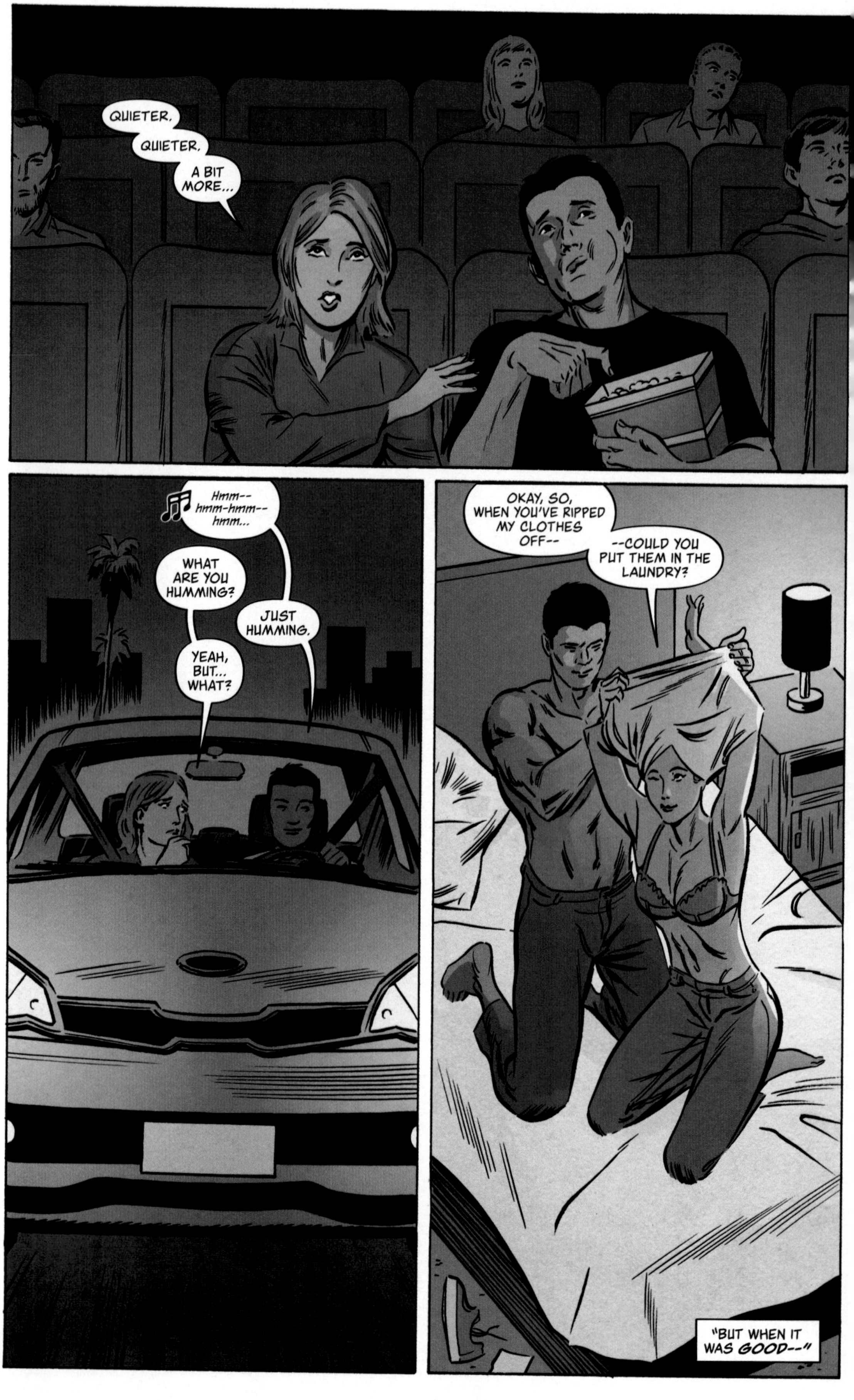
QUIETER.
QUIETER.
A BIT MORE...
Hmm--hmm-hmm--hmm...
WHAT ARE YOU HUMMING?
JUST HUMMING.
YEAH, BUT... WHAT?
OKAY, SO, WHEN YOU'VE RIPPED MY CLOTHES OFF--
--COULD YOU PUT THEM IN THE LAUNDRY?
"BUT WHEN IT WAS GOOD--"

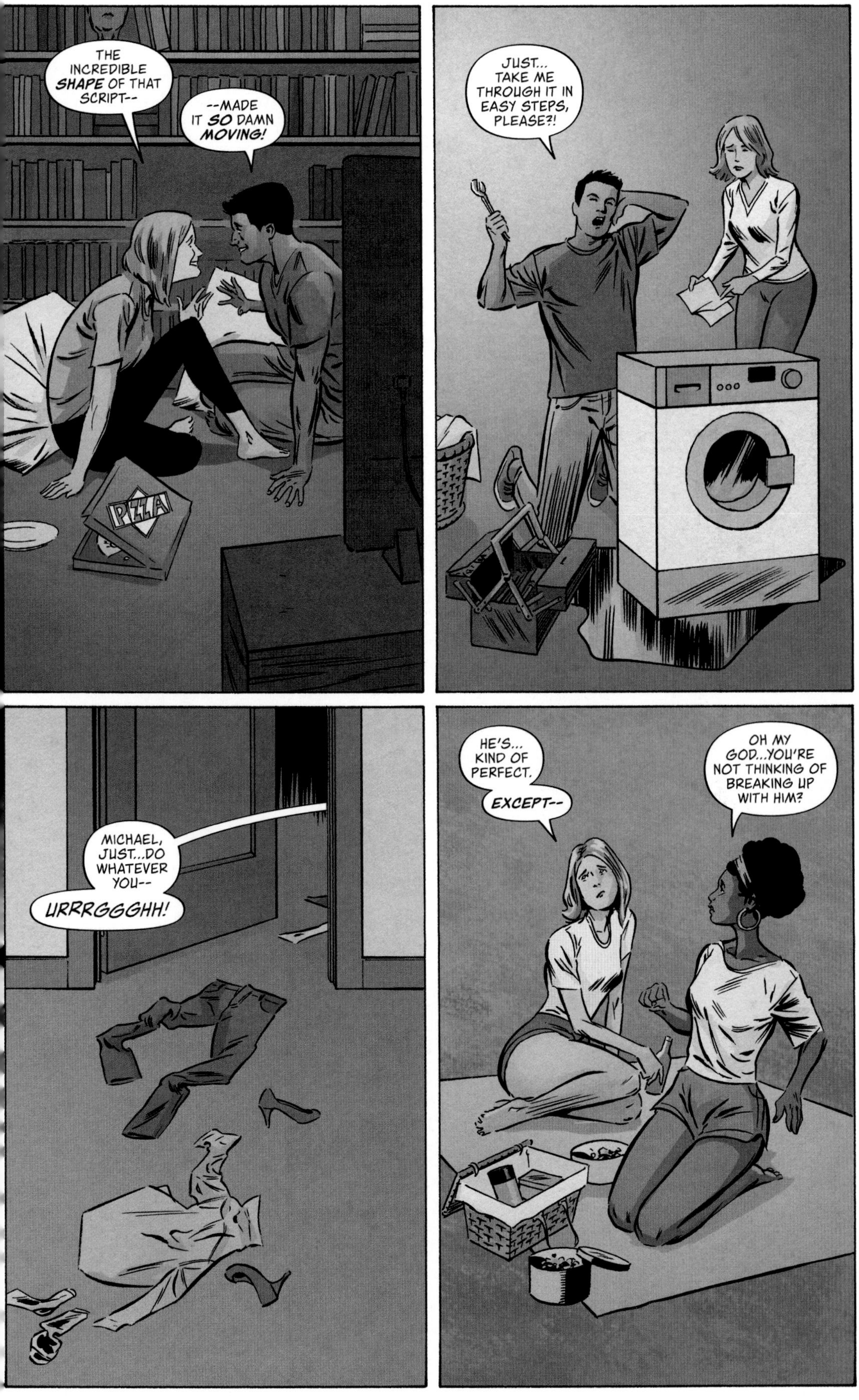
THE INCREDIBLE SHAPE OF THAT SCRIPT--
--MADE IT SO DAMN MOVING!
JUST... TAKE ME THROUGH IT IN EASY STEPS, PLEASE?!
PIZZA
MICHAEL, JUST...DO WHATEVER YOU--
URRRGGGHH!
HE'S... KIND OF PERFECT.
EXCEPT--
OH MY GOD...YOU'RE NOT THINKING OF BREAKING UP WITH HIM?

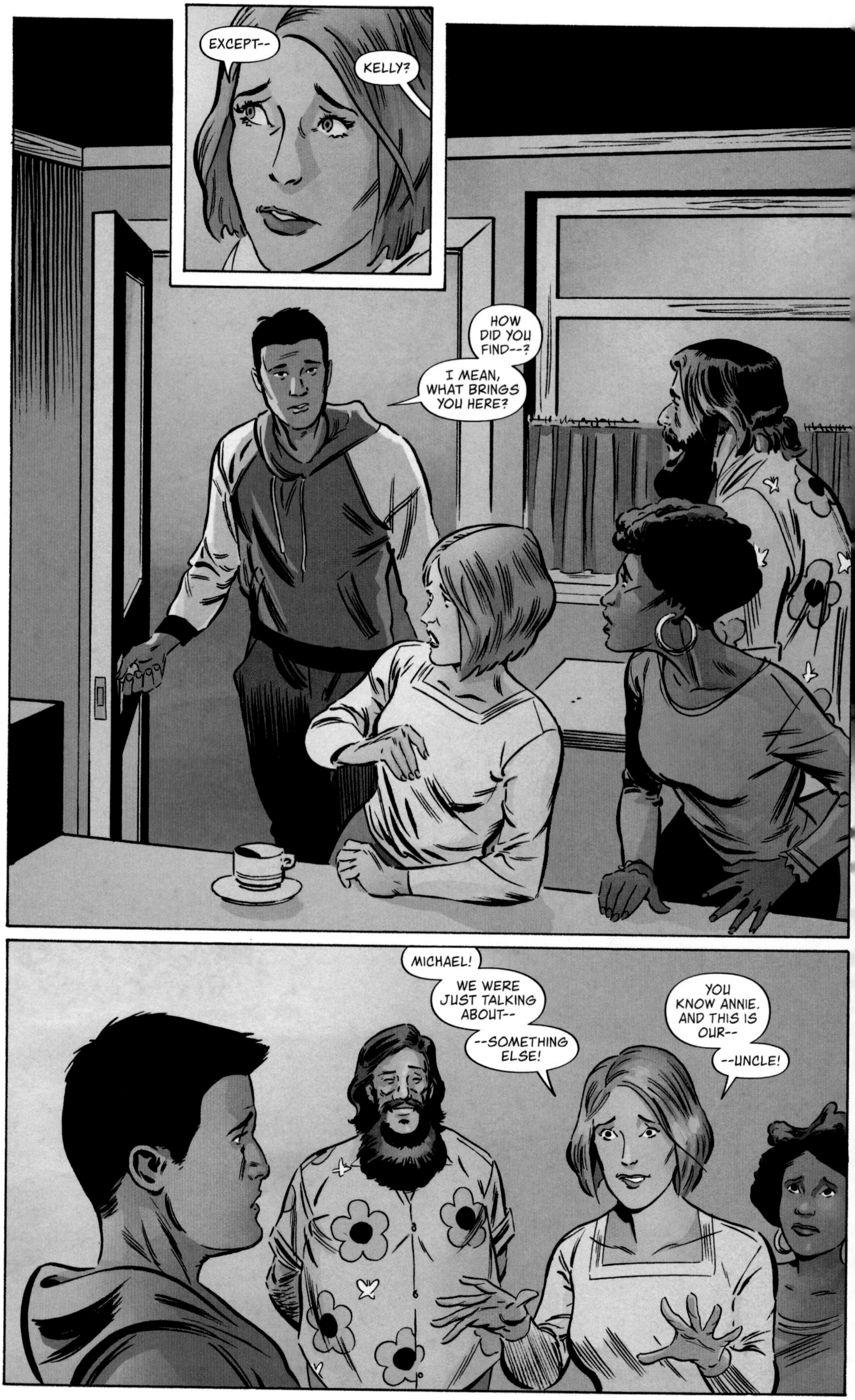
EXCEPT--
KELLY?
HOW DID YOU FIND--?
I MEAN, WHAT BRINGS YOU HERE?
MICHAEL!
WE WERE JUST TALKING ABOUT--
--SOMETHING ELSE!
YOU KNOW ANNIE. AND THIS IS OUR--
--UNCLE!

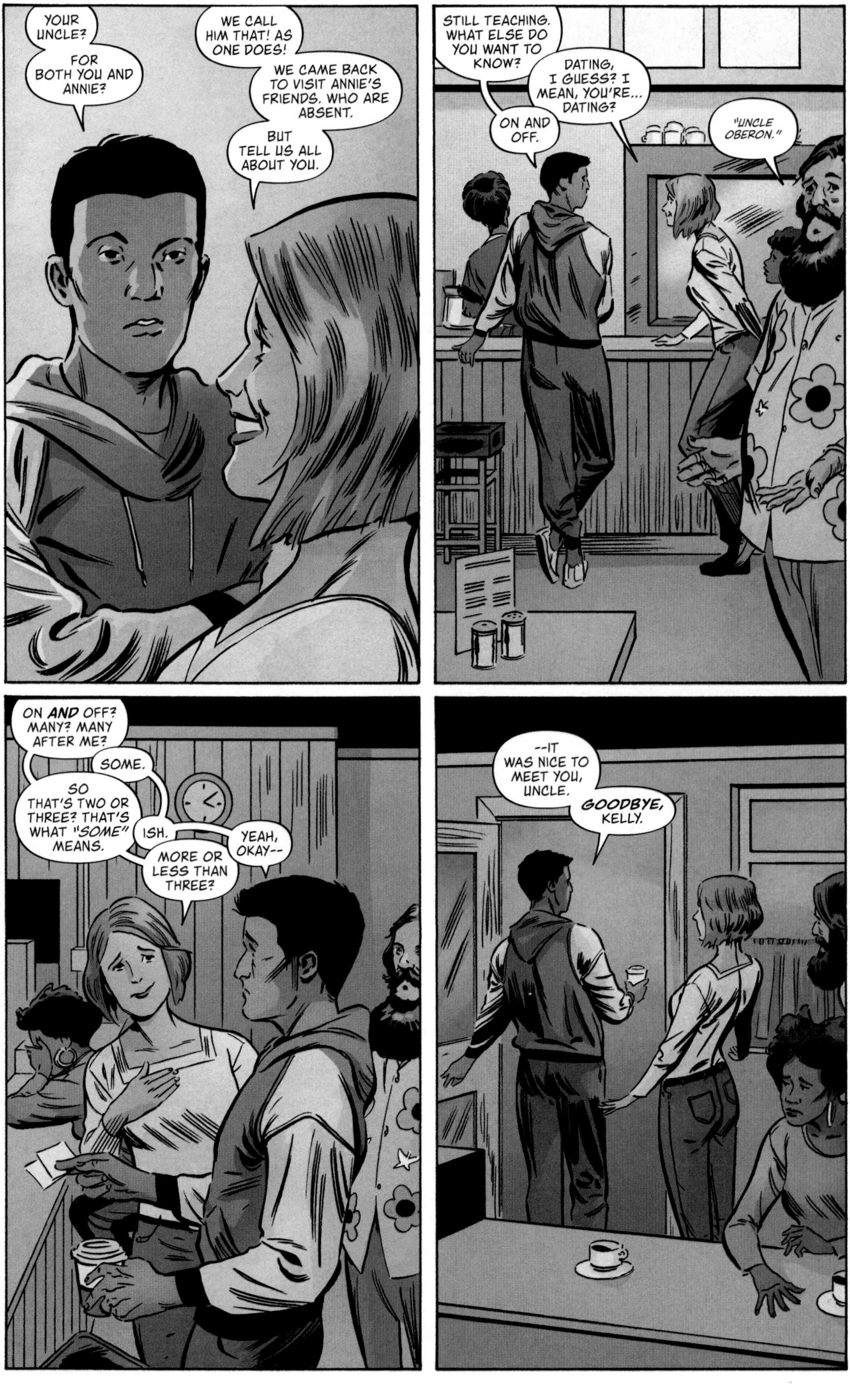
YOUR UNCLE?
FOR BOTH YOU AND ANNIE?
WE CALL HIM THAT! AS ONE DOES!
WE CAME BACK TO VISIT ANNIE'S FRIENDS. WHO ARE ABSENT.
BUT TELL US ALL ABOUT YOU.
STILL TEACHING. WHAT ELSE DO YOU WANT TO KNOW?
DATING, I GUESS? I MEAN, YOU'RE... DATING?
ON AND OFF.
"UNCLE OBERON."
ON AND OFF? MANY? MANY AFTER ME?
SOME.
SO THAT'S TWO OR THREE? THAT'S WHAT "SOME" MEANS.
ISH.
YEAH, OKAY--
MORE OR LESS THAN THREE?
--IT WAS NICE TO MEET YOU, UNCLE.
GOODBYE, KELLY.

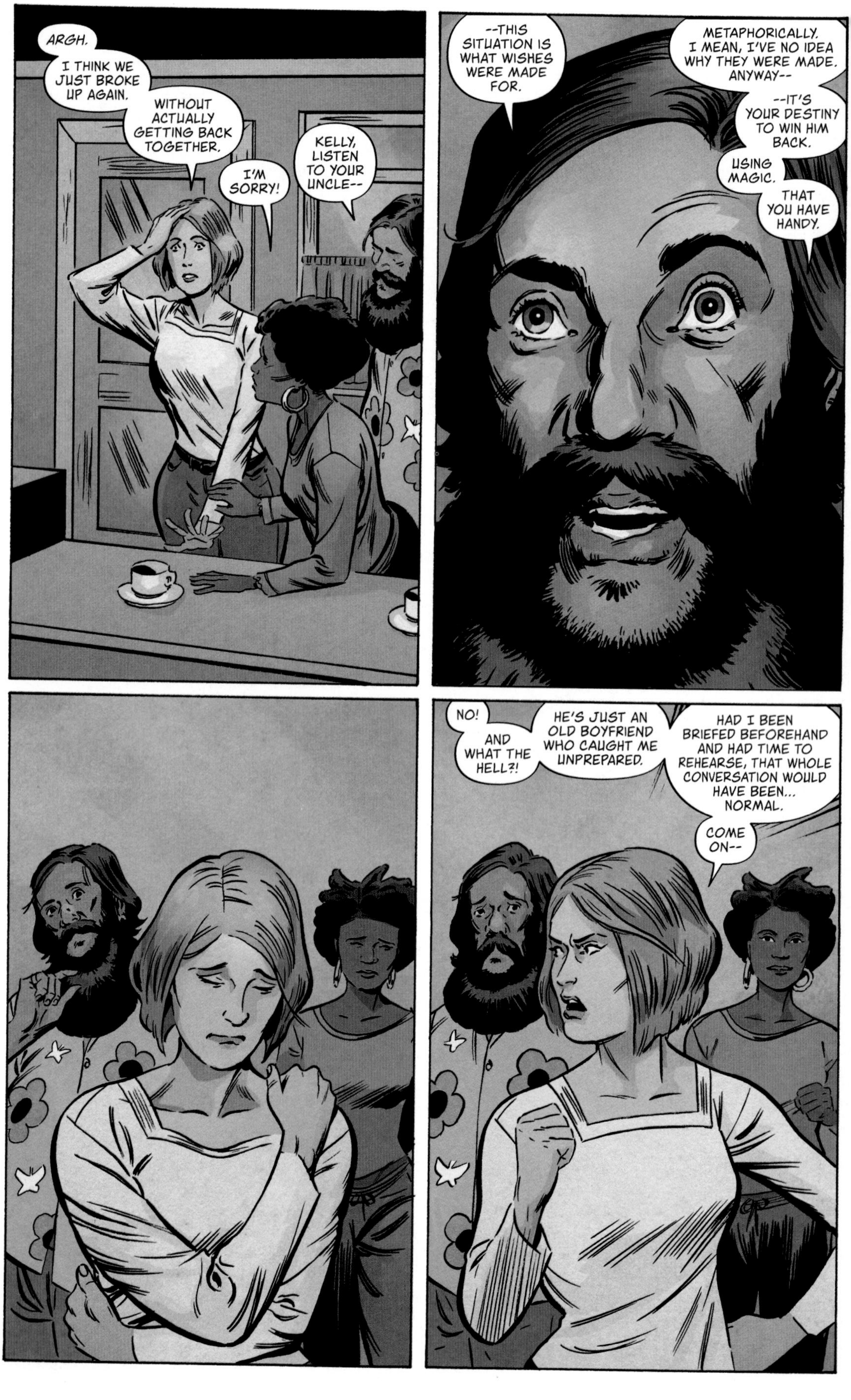
ARGH.
I THINK WE JUST BROKE UP AGAIN.
WITHOUT ACTUALLY GETTING BACK TOGETHER.
I'M SORRY!
KELLY, LISTEN TO YOUR UNCLE--
--THIS SITUATION IS WHAT WISHES WERE MADE FOR.
METAPHORICALLY. I MEAN, I'VE NO IDEA WHY THEY WERE MADE. ANYWAY--
--IT'S YOUR DESTINY TO WIN HIM BACK.
USING MAGIC.
THAT YOU HAVE HANDY.
NO!
AND WHAT THE HELL?!
HE'S JUST AN OLD BOYFRIEND WHO CAUGHT ME UNPREPARED.
HAD I BEEN BRIEFED BEFOREHAND AND HAD TIME TO REHEARSE, THAT WHOLE CONVERSATION WOULD HAVE BEEN... NORMAL.
COME ON--

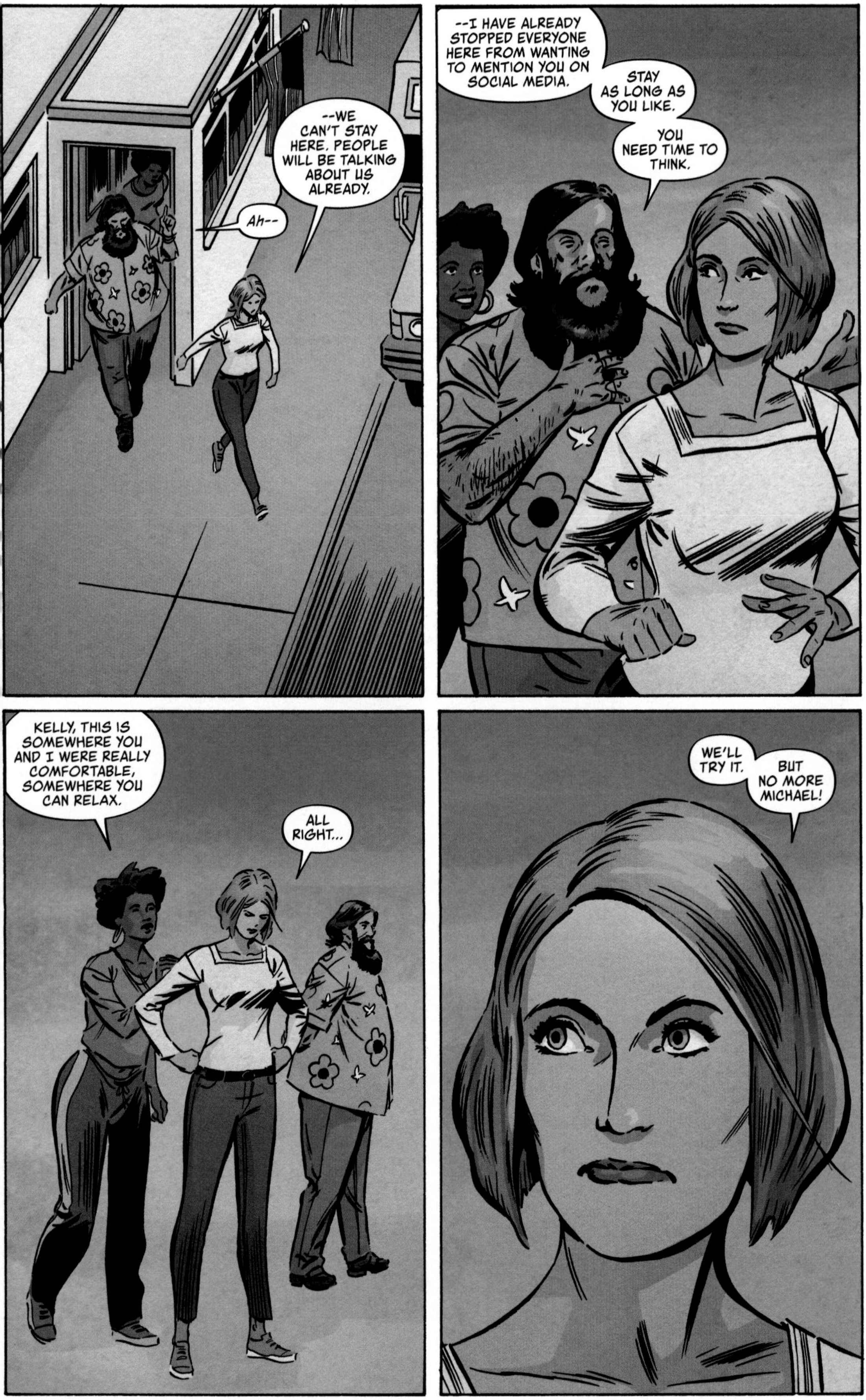
--WE CAN'T STAY HERE. PEOPLE WILL BE TALKING ABOUT US ALREADY.
Ah--
--I HAVE ALREADY STOPPED EVERYONE HERE FROM WANTING TO MENTION YOU ON SOCIAL MEDIA.
STAY AS LONG AS YOU LIKE.
YOU NEED TIME TO THINK.
KELLY, THIS IS SOMEWHERE YOU AND I WERE REALLY COMFORTABLE, SOMEWHERE YOU CAN RELAX.
ALL RIGHT...
WE'LL TRY IT.
BUT NO MORE MICHAEL!

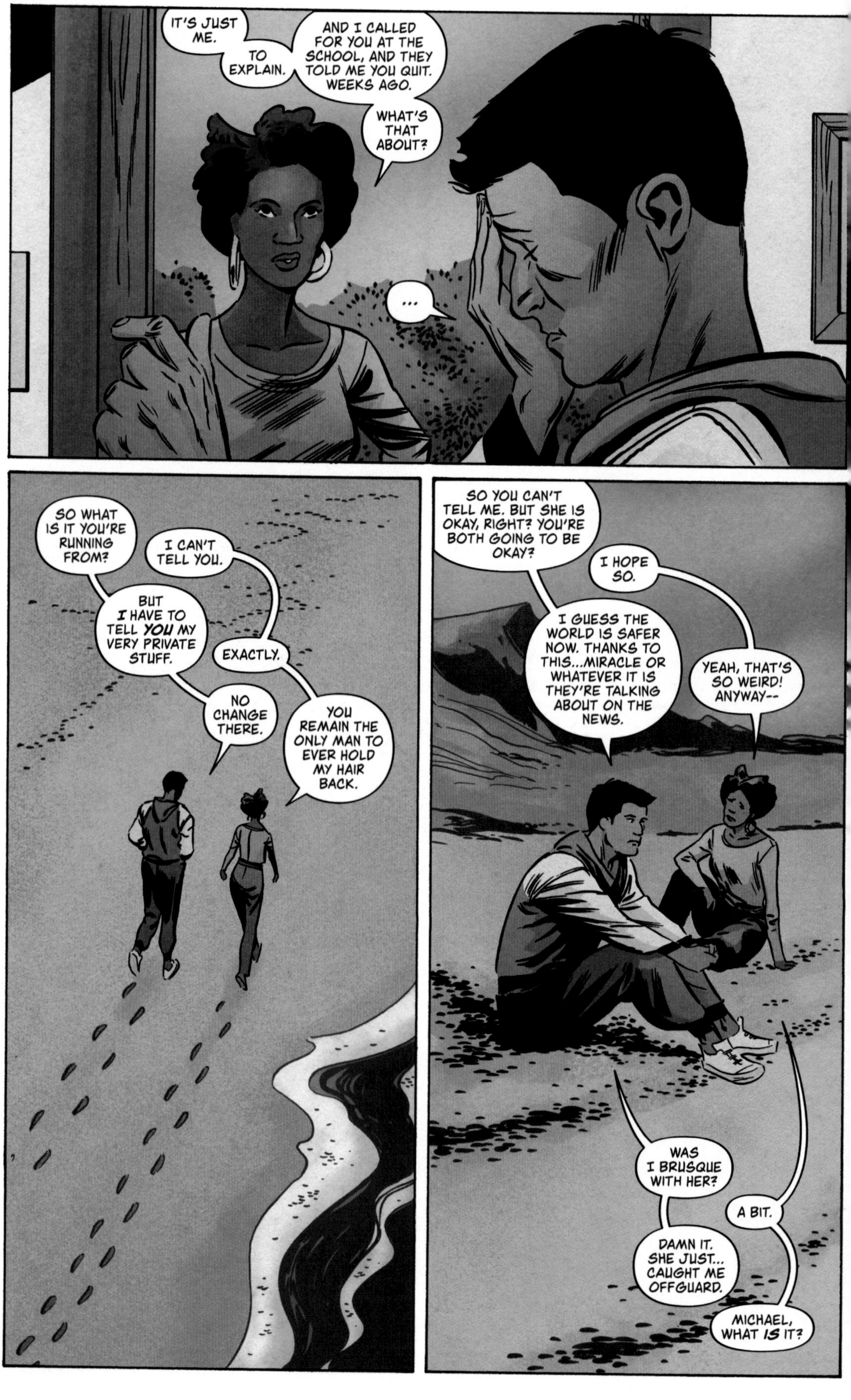
IT'S JUST ME.
TO EXPLAIN.
AND I CALLED FOR YOU AT THE SCHOOL, AND THEY TOLD ME YOU QUIT. WEEKS AGO.
WHAT'S THAT ABOUT?
...
SO WHAT IS IT YOU'RE RUNNING FROM?
I CAN'T TELL YOU.
BUT I HAVE TO TELL YOU MY VERY PRIVATE STUFF.
EXACTLY.
NO CHANGE THERE.
YOU REMAIN THE ONLY MAN TO EVER HOLD MY HAIR BACK.
SO YOU CAN'T TELL ME. BUT SHE IS OKAY, RIGHT? YOU'RE BOTH GOING TO BE OKAY?
I HOPE SO.
I GUESS THE WORLD IS SAFER NOW. THANKS TO THIS...MIRACLE OR WHATEVER IT IS THEY'RE TALKING ABOUT ON THE NEWS.
YEAH, THAT'S SO WEIRD! ANYWAY--
WAS I BRUSQUE WITH HER?
A BIT.
DAMN IT. SHE JUST... CAUGHT ME OFFGUARD.
MICHAEL, WHAT IS IT?

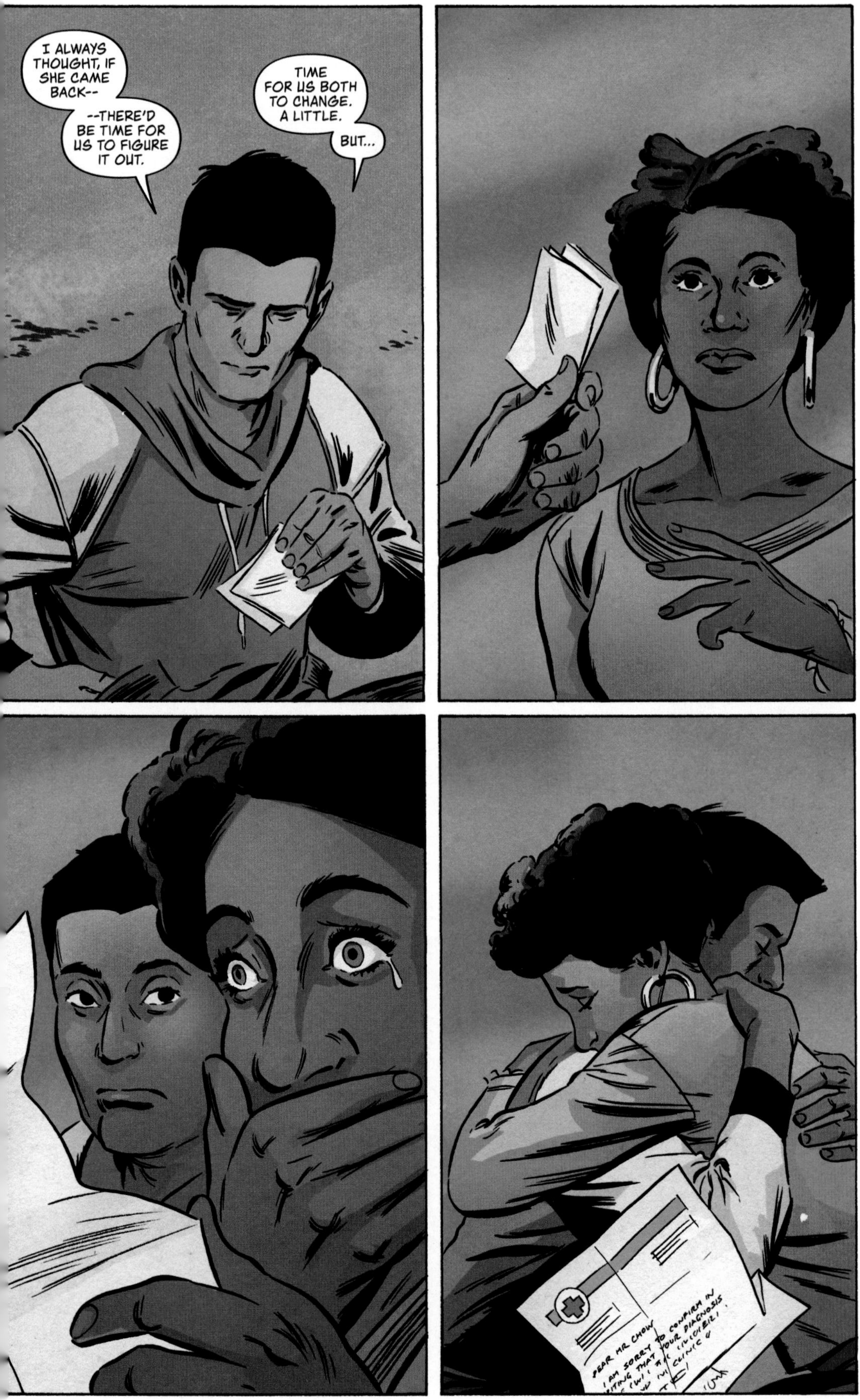
I ALWAYS THOUGHT, IF SHE CAME BACK--
--THERE'D BE TIME FOR US TO FIGURE IT OUT.
TIME FOR US BOTH TO CHANGE. A LITTLE.
BUT...
DEAR MR CHOW
I AM SORRY TO CONFIRM IN

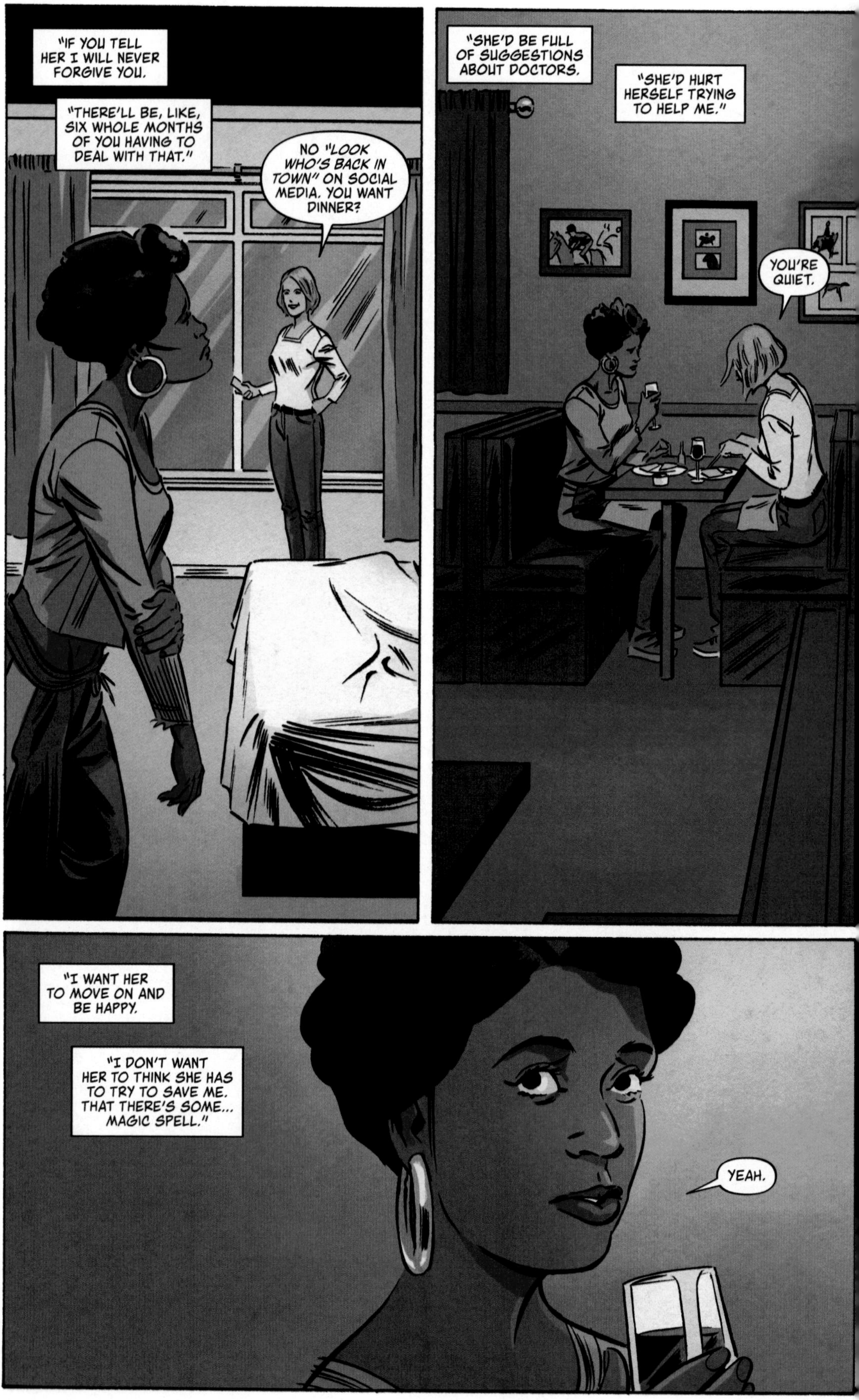
"IF YOU TELL HER I WILL NEVER FORGIVE YOU.
"THERE'LL BE, LIKE, SIX WHOLE MONTHS OF YOU HAVING TO DEAL WITH THAT."
NO "LOOK WHO'S BACK IN TOWN" ON SOCIAL MEDIA. YOU WANT DINNER?
"SHE'D BE FULL OF SUGGESTIONS ABOUT DOCTORS.
"SHE'D HURT HERSELF TRYING TO HELP ME."
YOU'RE QUIET.
"I WANT HER TO MOVE ON AND BE HAPPY.
"I DON'T WANT HER TO THINK SHE HAS TO TRY TO SAVE ME. THAT THERE'S SOME... MAGIC SPELL."
YEAH.

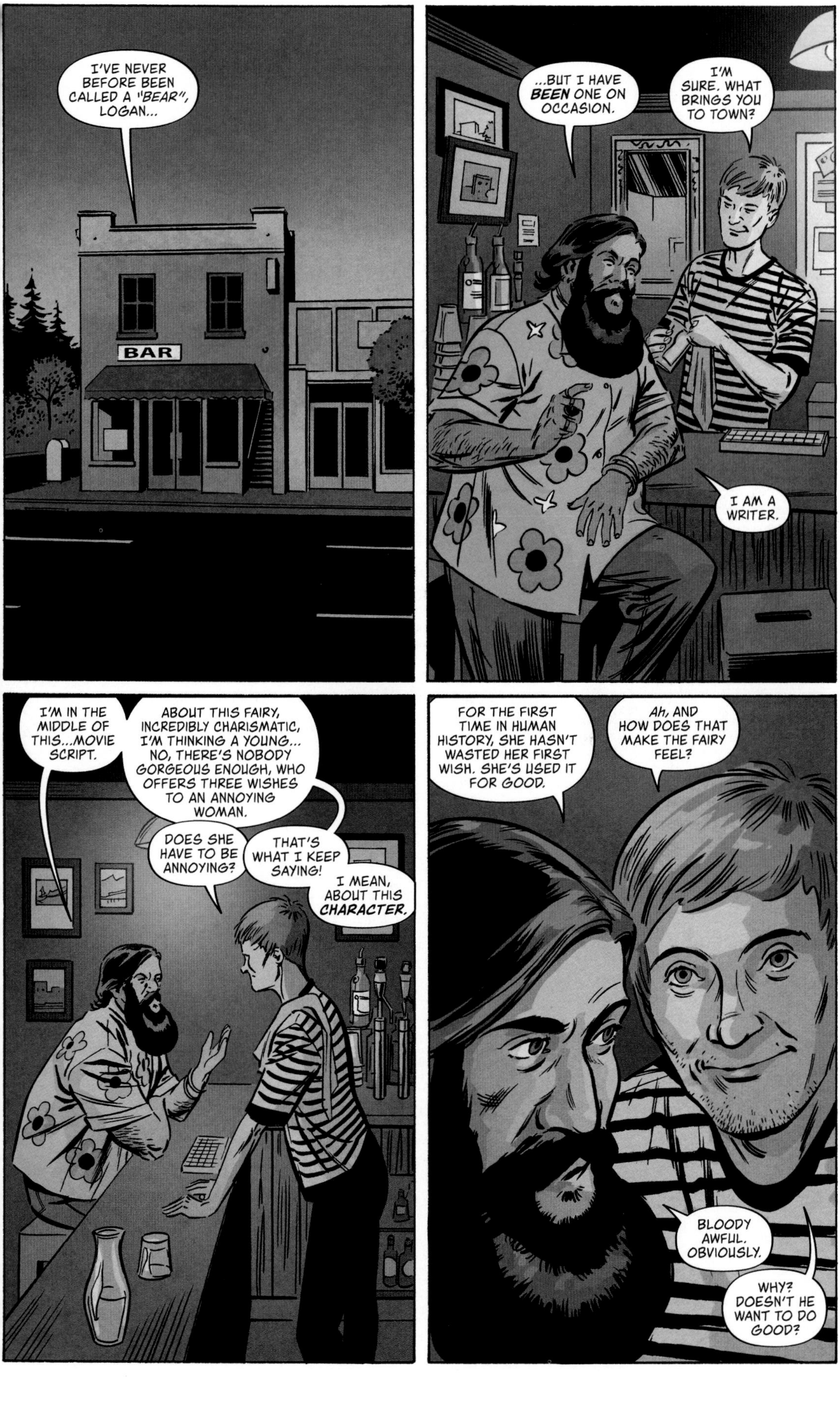
I'VE NEVER BEFORE BEEN CALLED A "BEAR", LOGAN...
...BUT I HAVE BEEN ONE ON OCCASION.
I'M SURE. WHAT BRINGS YOU TO TOWN?
I AM A WRITER.
BAR
I'M IN THE MIDDLE OF THIS...MOVIE SCRIPT.
ABOUT THIS FAIRY, INCREDIBLY CHARISMATIC, I'M THINKING A YOUNG... NO, THERE'S NOBODY GORGEOUS ENOUGH, WHO OFFERS THREE WISHES TO AN ANNOYING WOMAN.
DOES SHE HAVE TO BE ANNOYING?
THAT'S WHAT I KEEP SAYING!
I MEAN, ABOUT THIS CHARACTER.
FOR THE FIRST TIME IN HUMAN HISTORY, SHE HASN'T WASTED HER FIRST WISH. SHE'S USED IT FOR GOOD.
Ah, AND HOW DOES THAT MAKE THE FAIRY FEEL?
BLOODY AWFUL, OBVIOUSLY.
WHY? DOESN'T HE WANT TO DO GOOD?

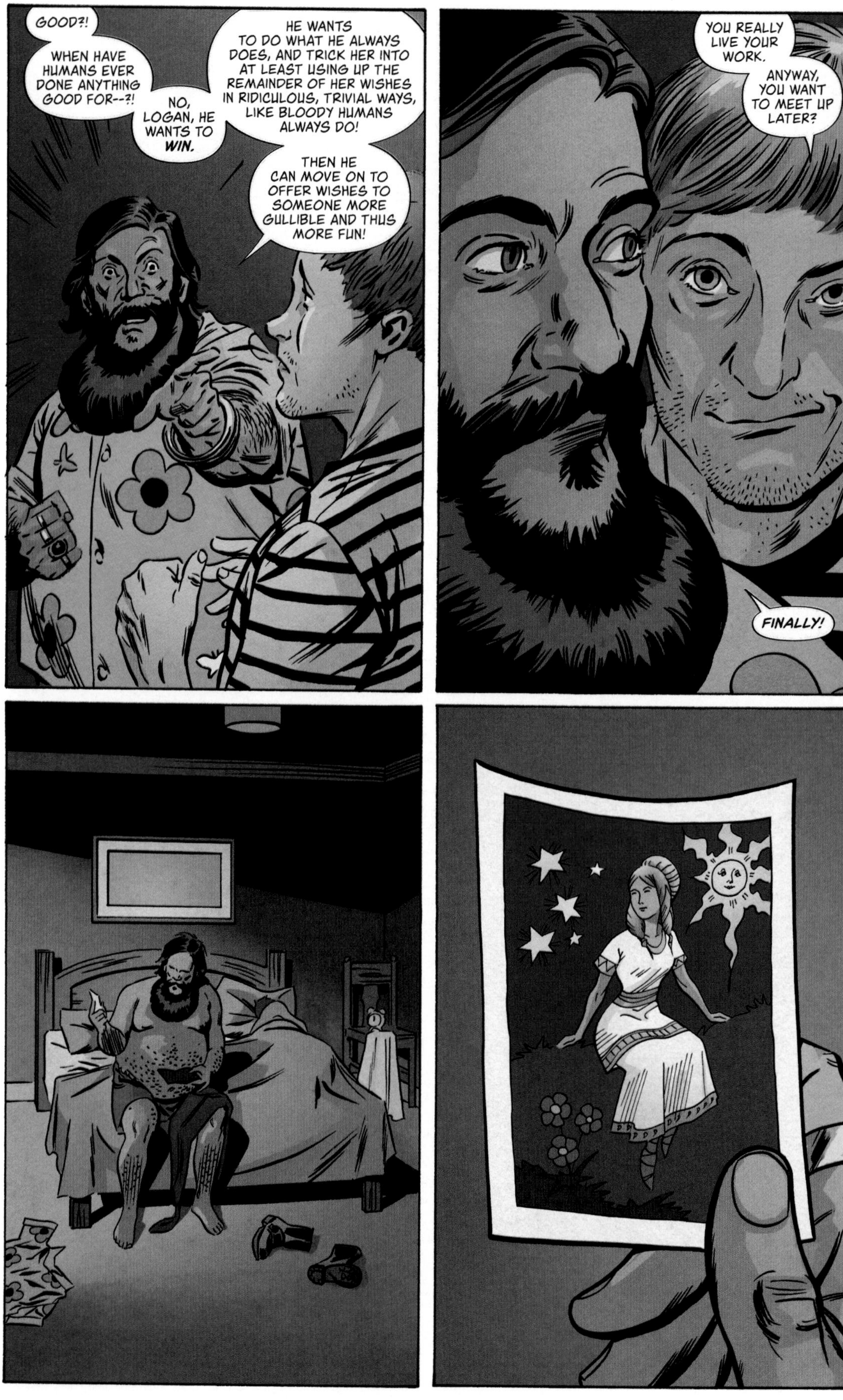

GOOD?!
WHEN HAVE HUMANS EVER DONE ANYTHING GOOD FOR--?!
NO, LOGAN, HE WANTS TO WIN.
HE WANTS TO DO WHAT HE ALWAYS DOES, AND TRICK HER INTO AT LEAST USING UP THE REMAINDER OF HER WISHES IN RIDICULOUS, TRIVIAL WAYS, LIKE BLOODY HUMANS ALWAYS DO!
THEN HE CAN MOVE ON TO OFFER WISHES TO SOMEONE MORE GULLIBLE AND THUS MORE FUN!
YOU REALLY LIVE YOUR WORK.
ANYWAY, YOU WANT TO MEET UP LATER?
FINALLY!

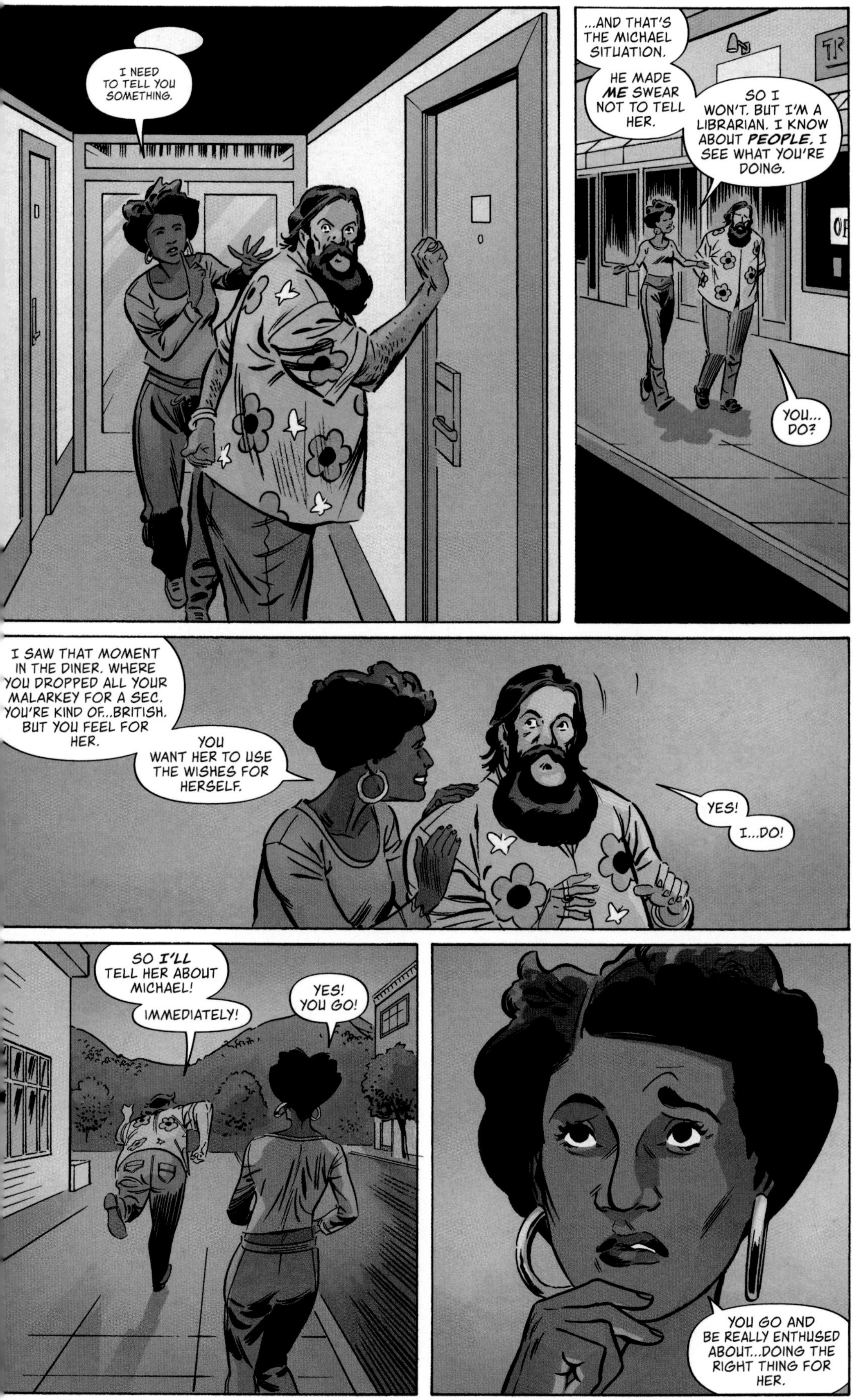
I NEED TO TELL YOU SOMETHING.
...AND THAT'S THE MICHAEL SITUATION.
HE MADE ME SWEAR NOT TO TELL HER.
SO I WON'T. BUT I'M A LIBRARIAN. I KNOW ABOUT PEOPLE. I SEE WHAT YOU'RE DOING.
YOU... DO?
I SAW THAT MOMENT IN THE DINER. WHERE YOU DROPPED ALL YOUR MALARKEY FOR A SEC. YOU'RE KIND OF...BRITISH. BUT YOU FEEL FOR HER.
YOU WANT HER TO USE THE WISHES FOR HERSELF.
YES!
I...DO!
SO I'LL TELL HER ABOUT MICHAEL!
IMMEDIATELY!
YES! YOU GO!
YOU GO AND BE REALLY ENTHUSED ABOUT...DOING THE RIGHT THING FOR HER.

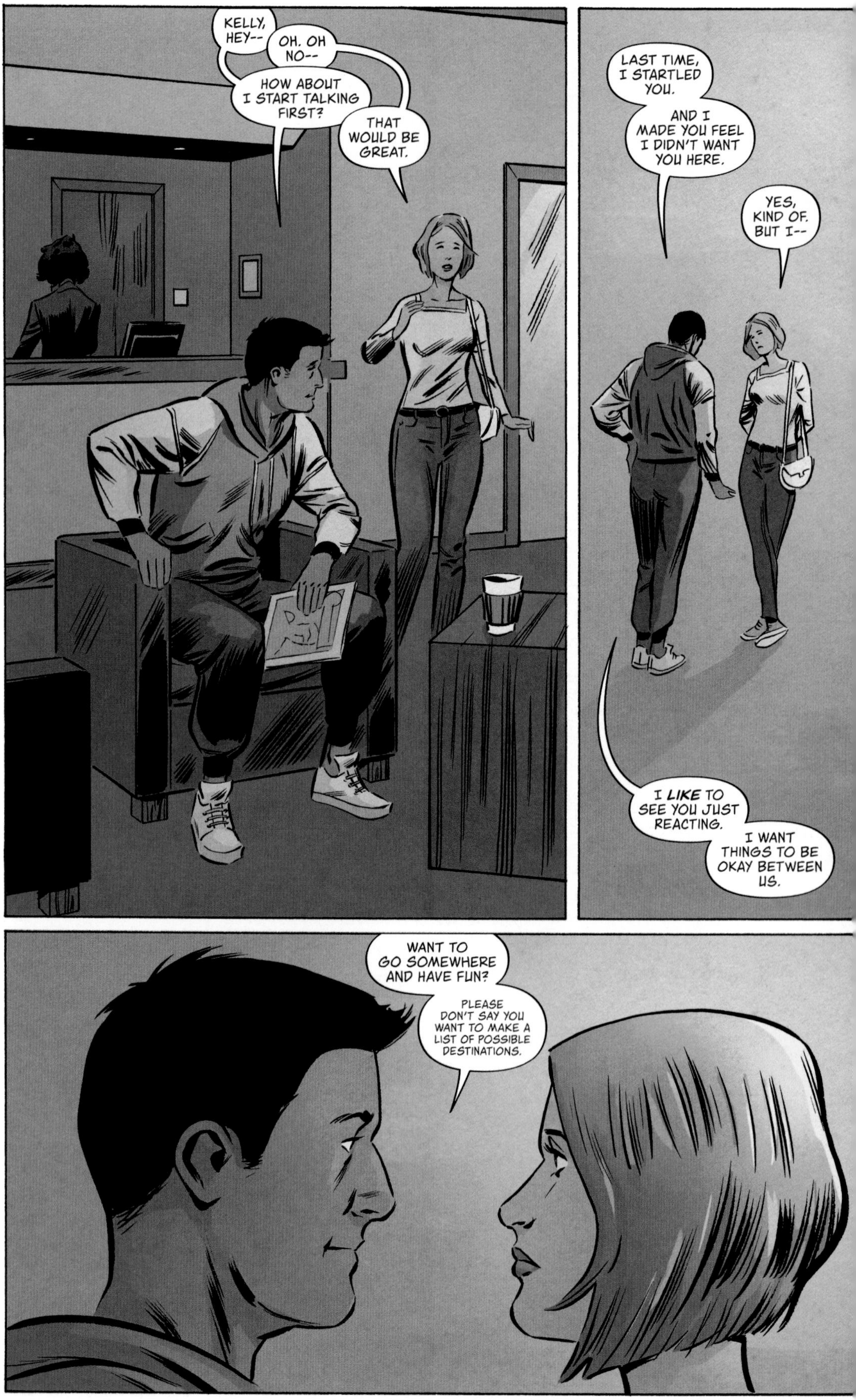
KELLY, HEY--
OH. OH NO--
HOW ABOUT I START TALKING FIRST?
THAT WOULD BE GREAT.
LAST TIME, I STARTLED YOU.
AND I MADE YOU FEEL I DIDN'T WANT YOU HERE.
YES, KIND OF. BUT I--
I LIKE TO SEE YOU JUST REACTING.
I WANT THINGS TO BE OKAY BETWEEN US.
WANT TO GO SOMEWHERE AND HAVE FUN?
PLEASE DON'T SAY YOU WANT TO MAKE A LIST OF POSSIBLE DESTINATIONS.

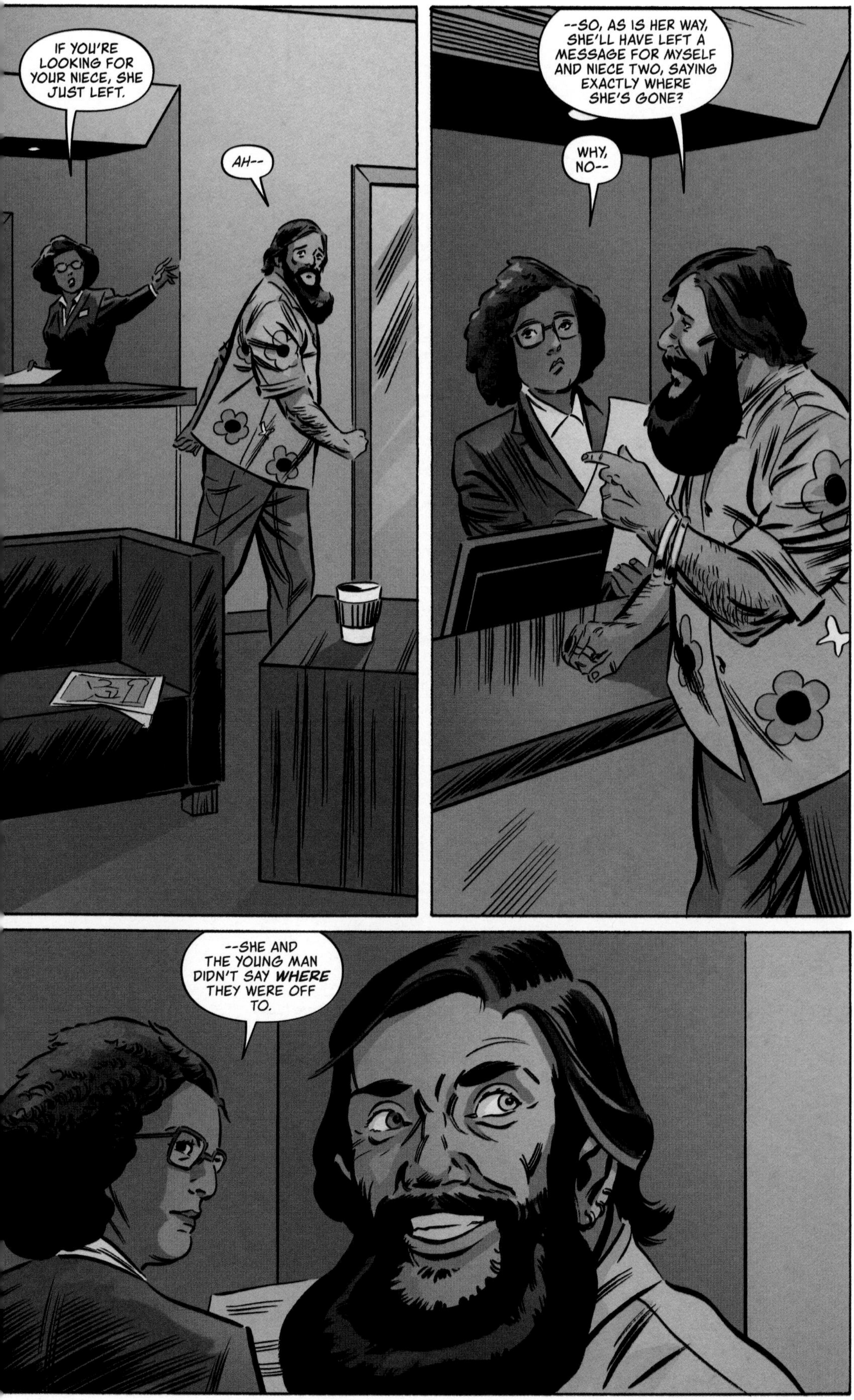
IF YOU'RE LOOKING FOR YOUR NIECE, SHE JUST LEFT.
AH--
--SO, AS IS HER WAY, SHE'LL HAVE LEFT A MESSAGE FOR MYSELF AND NIECE TWO, SAYING EXACTLY WHERE SHE'S GONE?
WHY, NO--
--SHE AND THE YOUNG MAN DIDN'T SAY *WHERE* THEY WERE OFF TO.

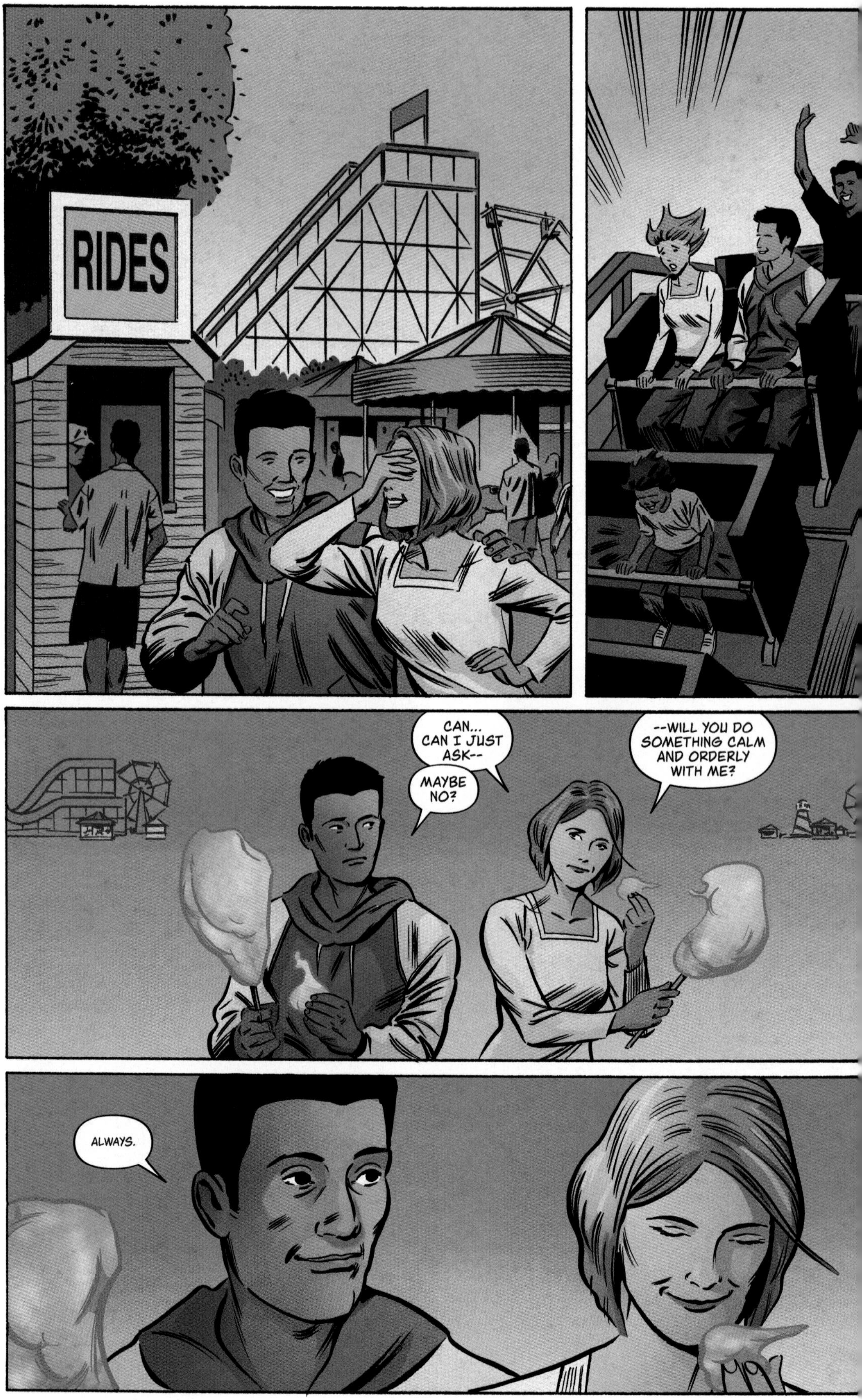
RIDES
CAN... CAN I JUST ASK--
MAYBE NO?
--WILL YOU DO SOMETHING CALM AND ORDERLY WITH ME?
ALWAYS.

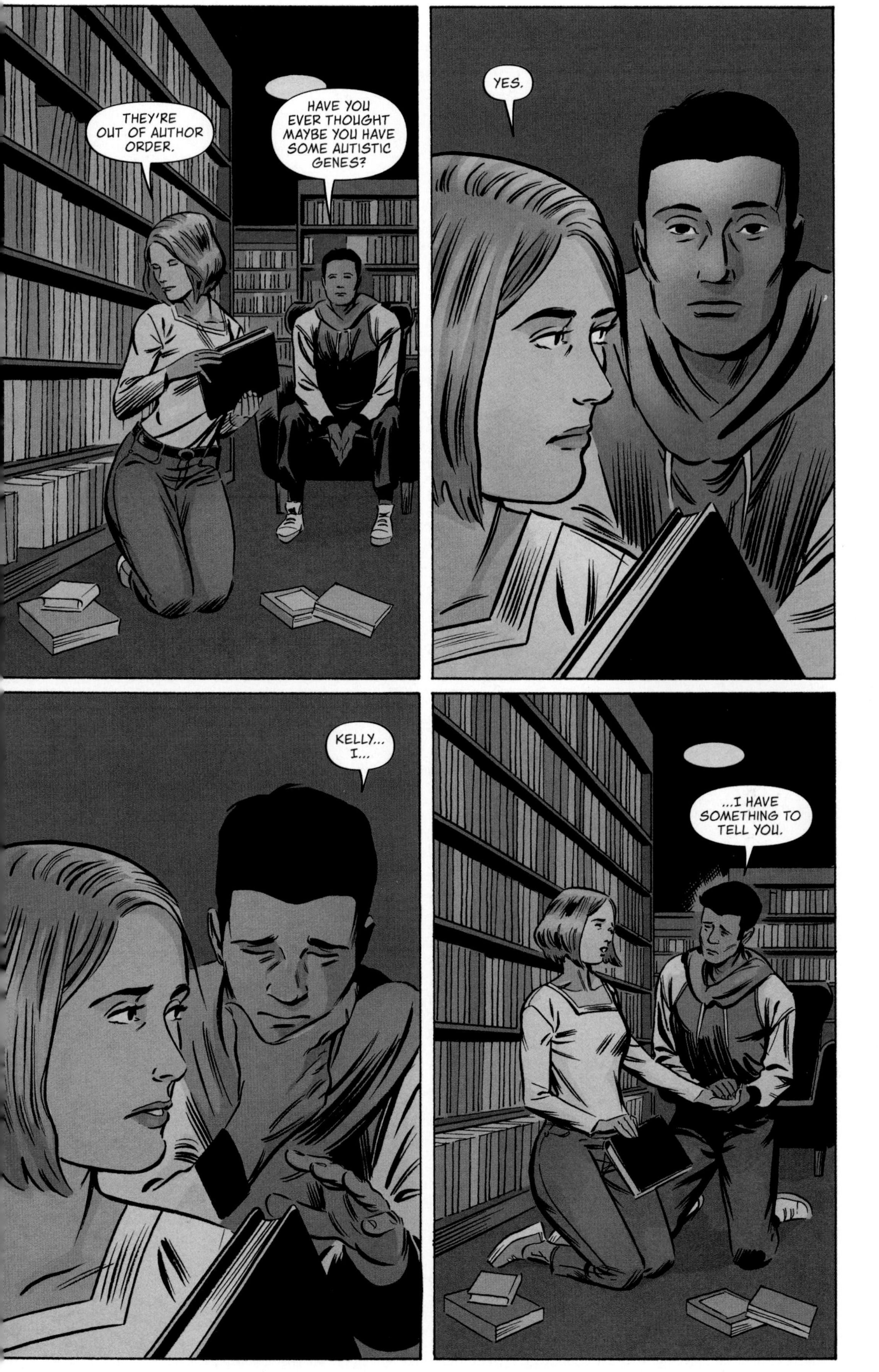

THEY'RE OUT OF AUTHOR ORDER.
HAVE YOU EVER THOUGHT MAYBE YOU HAVE SOME AUTISTIC GENES?
YES.
KELLY... I...
...I HAVE SOMETHING TO TELL YOU.

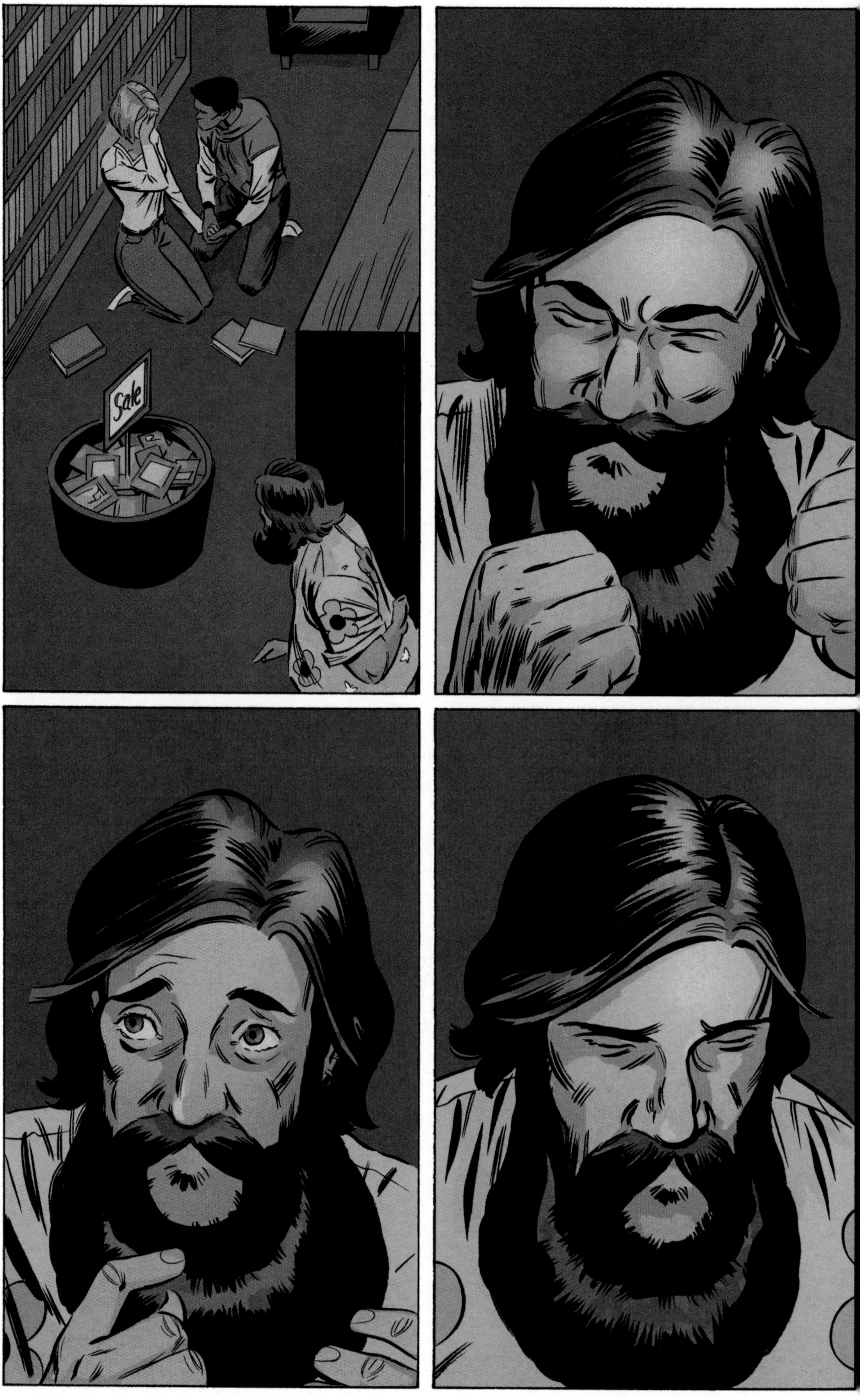
Sale

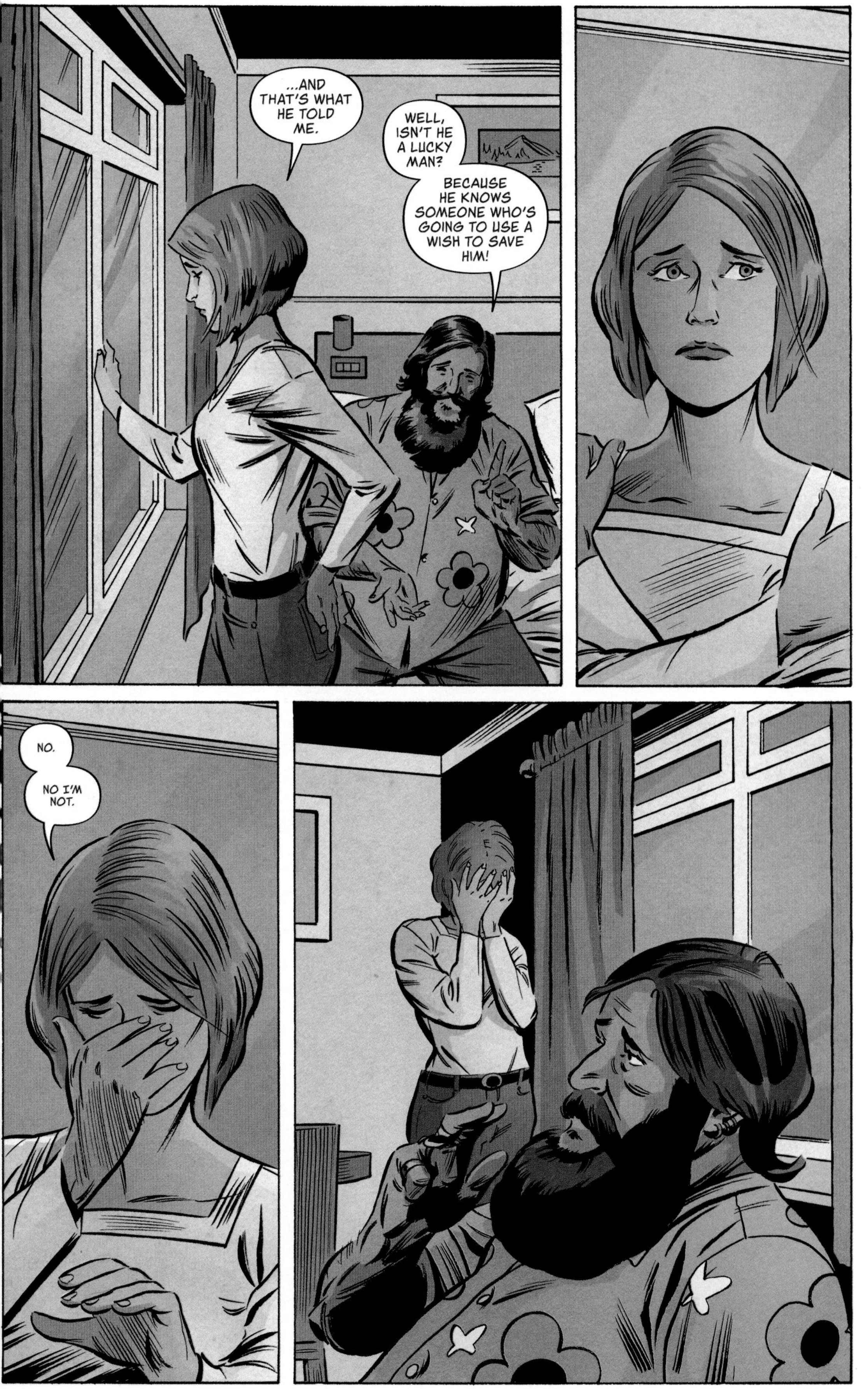
...AND THAT'S WHAT HE TOLD ME.
WELL, ISN'T HE A LUCKY MAN?
BECAUSE HE KNOWS SOMEONE WHO'S GOING TO USE A WISH TO SAVE HIM!
NO.
NO I'M NOT.

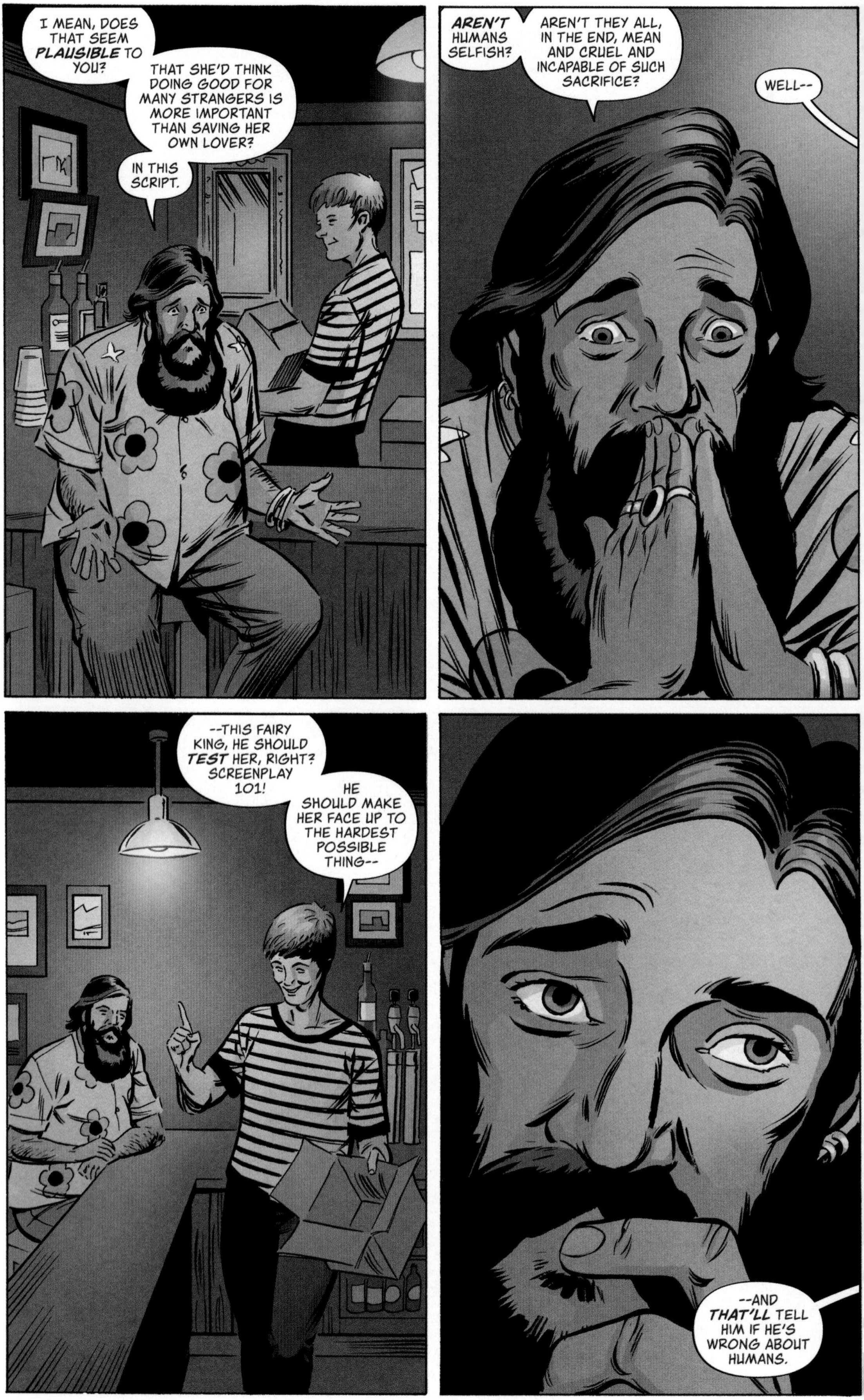
I MEAN, DOES THAT SEEM *PLAUSIBLE* TO YOU?
THAT SHE'D THINK DOING GOOD FOR MANY STRANGERS IS MORE IMPORTANT THAN SAVING HER OWN LOVER?
IN THIS SCRIPT.
AREN'T HUMANS SELFISH?
AREN'T THEY ALL, IN THE END, MEAN AND CRUEL AND INCAPABLE OF SUCH SACRIFICE?
WELL--
--THIS FAIRY KING, HE SHOULD *TEST* HER, RIGHT? SCREENPLAY 101!
HE SHOULD MAKE HER FACE UP TO THE HARDEST POSSIBLE THING--
--AND *THAT'LL* TELL HIM IF HE'S WRONG ABOUT HUMANS.

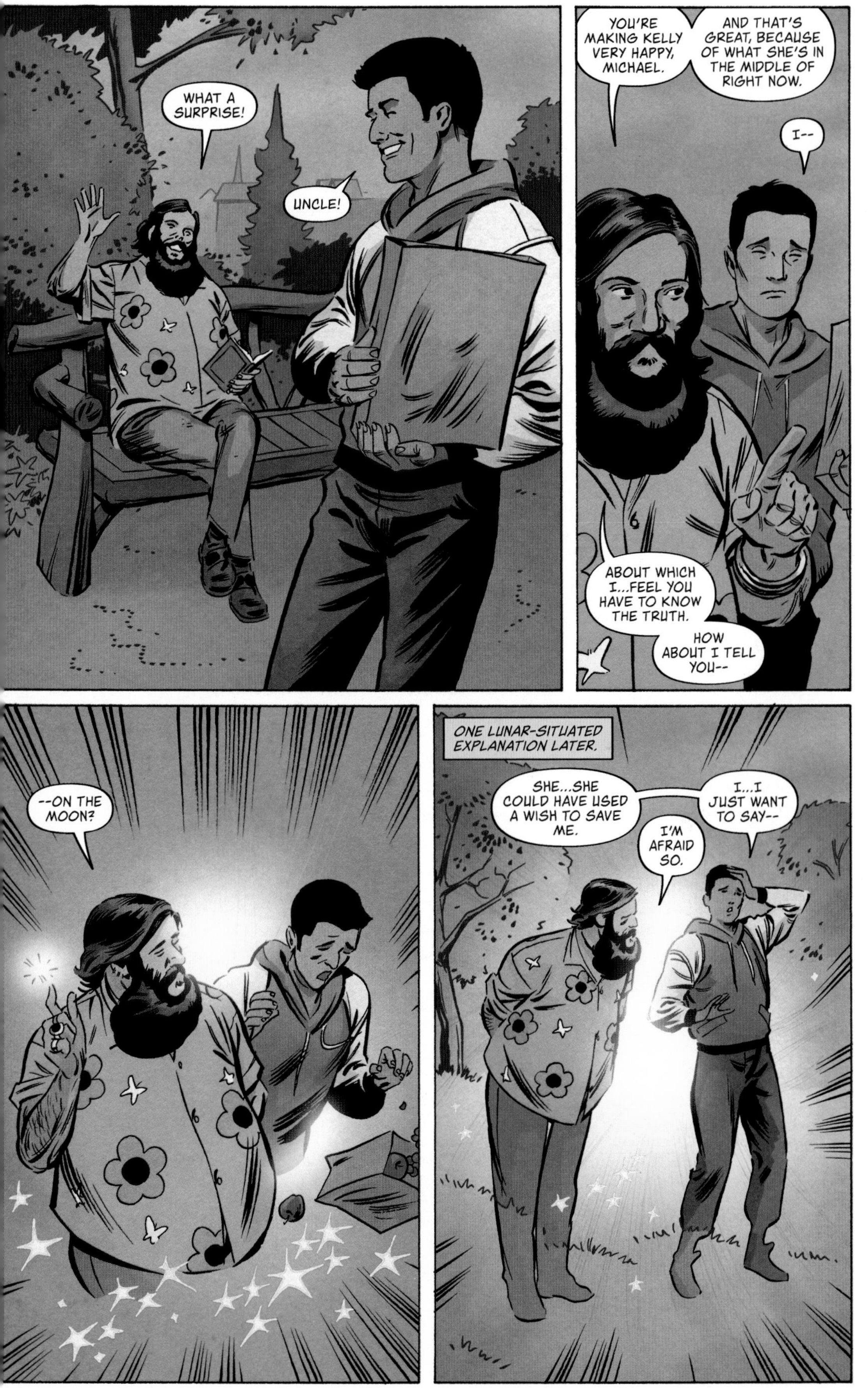
WHAT A SURPRISE!
UNCLE!
YOU'RE MAKING KELLY VERY HAPPY, MICHAEL.
AND THAT'S GREAT, BECAUSE OF WHAT SHE'S IN THE MIDDLE OF RIGHT NOW.
I--
ABOUT WHICH I...FEEL YOU HAVE TO KNOW THE TRUTH.
HOW ABOUT I TELL YOU--
--ON THE MOON?
ONE LUNAR-SITUATED EXPLANATION LATER.
SHE...SHE COULD HAVE USED A WISH TO SAVE ME.
I'M AFRAID SO.
I...I JUST WANT TO SAY--

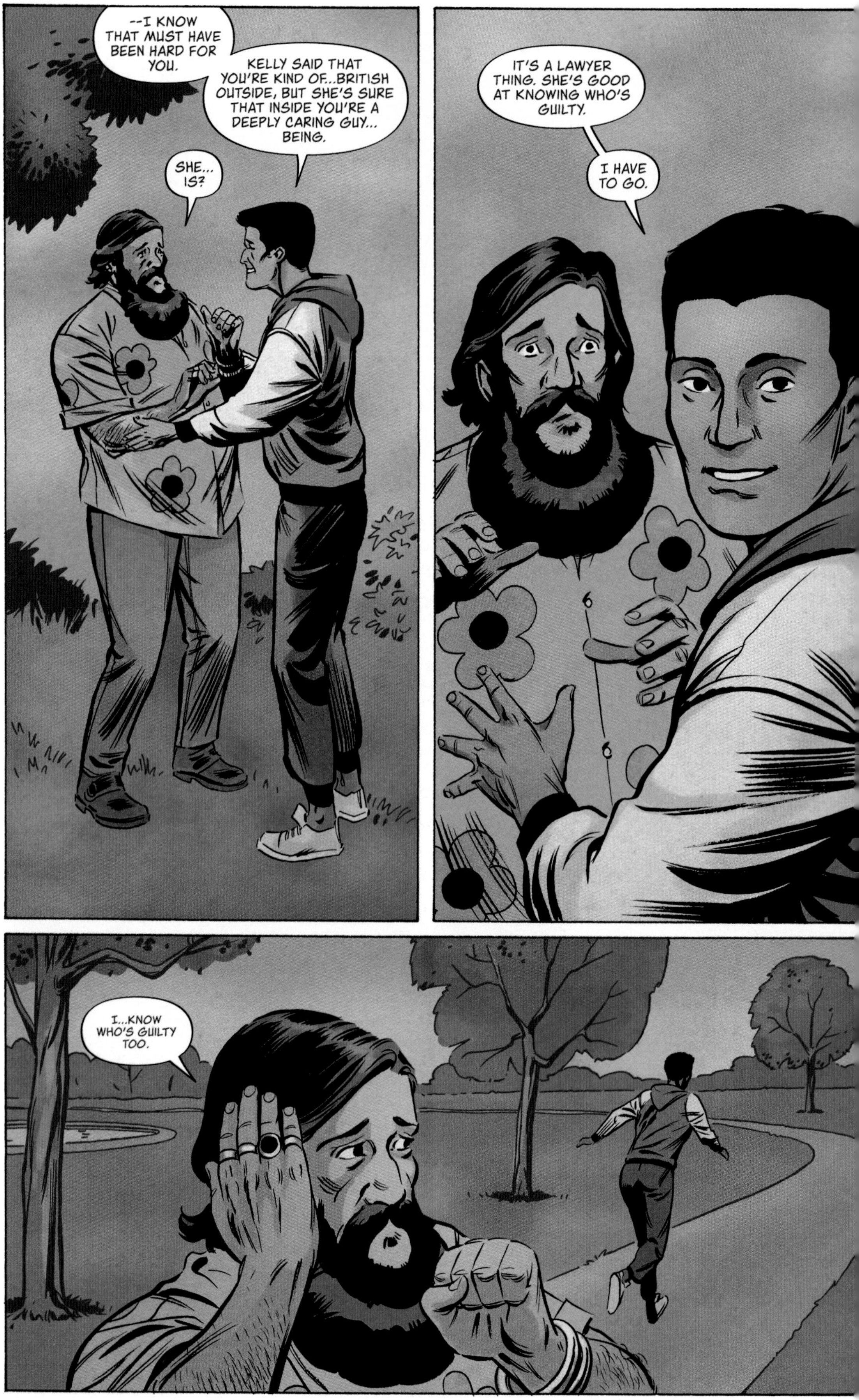
--I KNOW THAT MUST HAVE BEEN HARD FOR YOU.
KELLY SAID THAT YOU'RE KIND OF...BRITISH OUTSIDE, BUT SHE'S SURE THAT INSIDE YOU'RE A DEEPLY CARING GUY... BEING.
SHE... IS?
IT'S A LAWYER THING. SHE'S GOOD AT KNOWING WHO'S GUILTY.
I HAVE TO GO.
I...KNOW WHO'S GUILTY TOO.

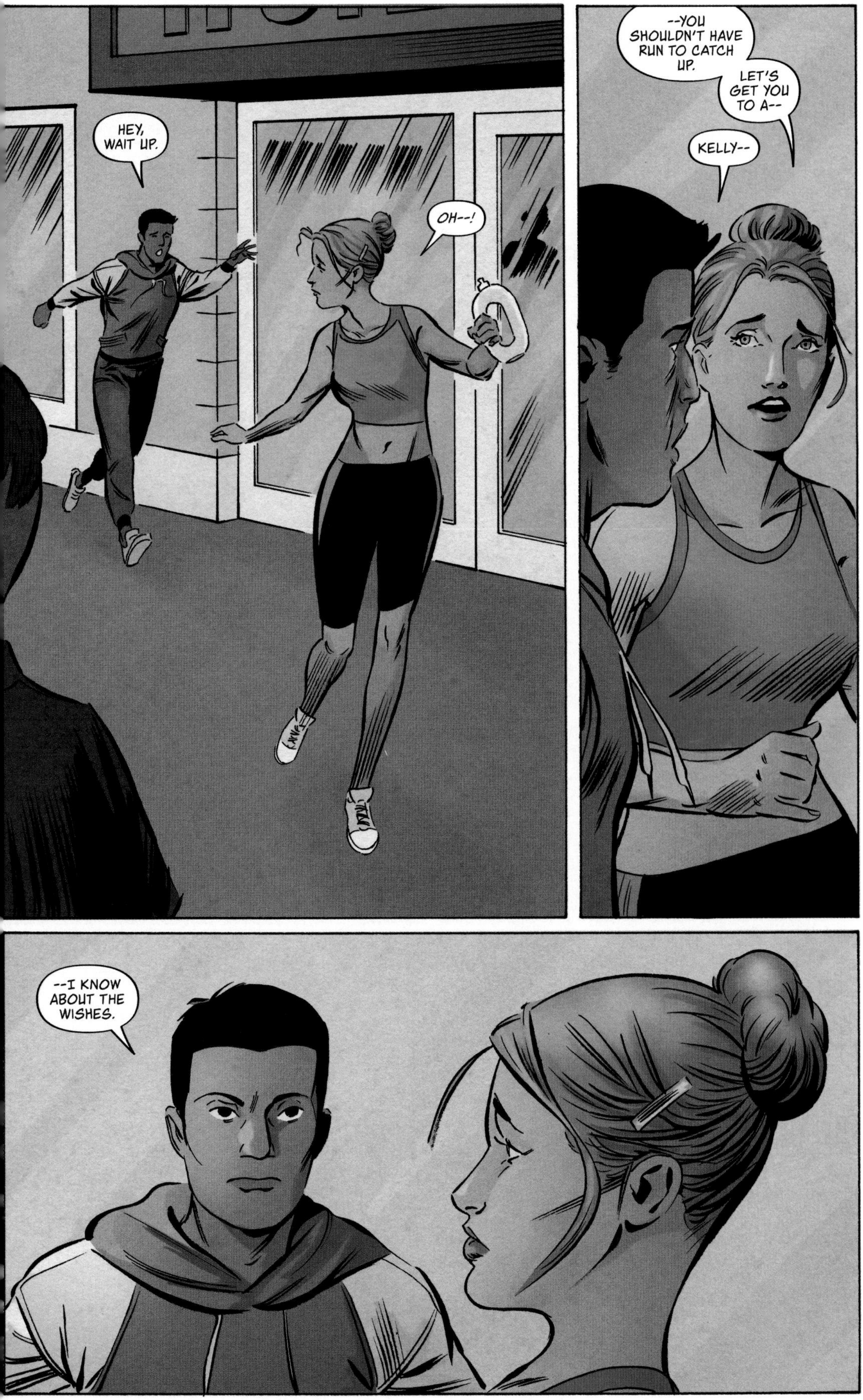
HEY, WAIT UP.
OH--!
--YOU SHOULDN'T HAVE RUN TO CATCH UP.
LET'S GET YOU TO A--
KELLY--
--I KNOW ABOUT THE WISHES.

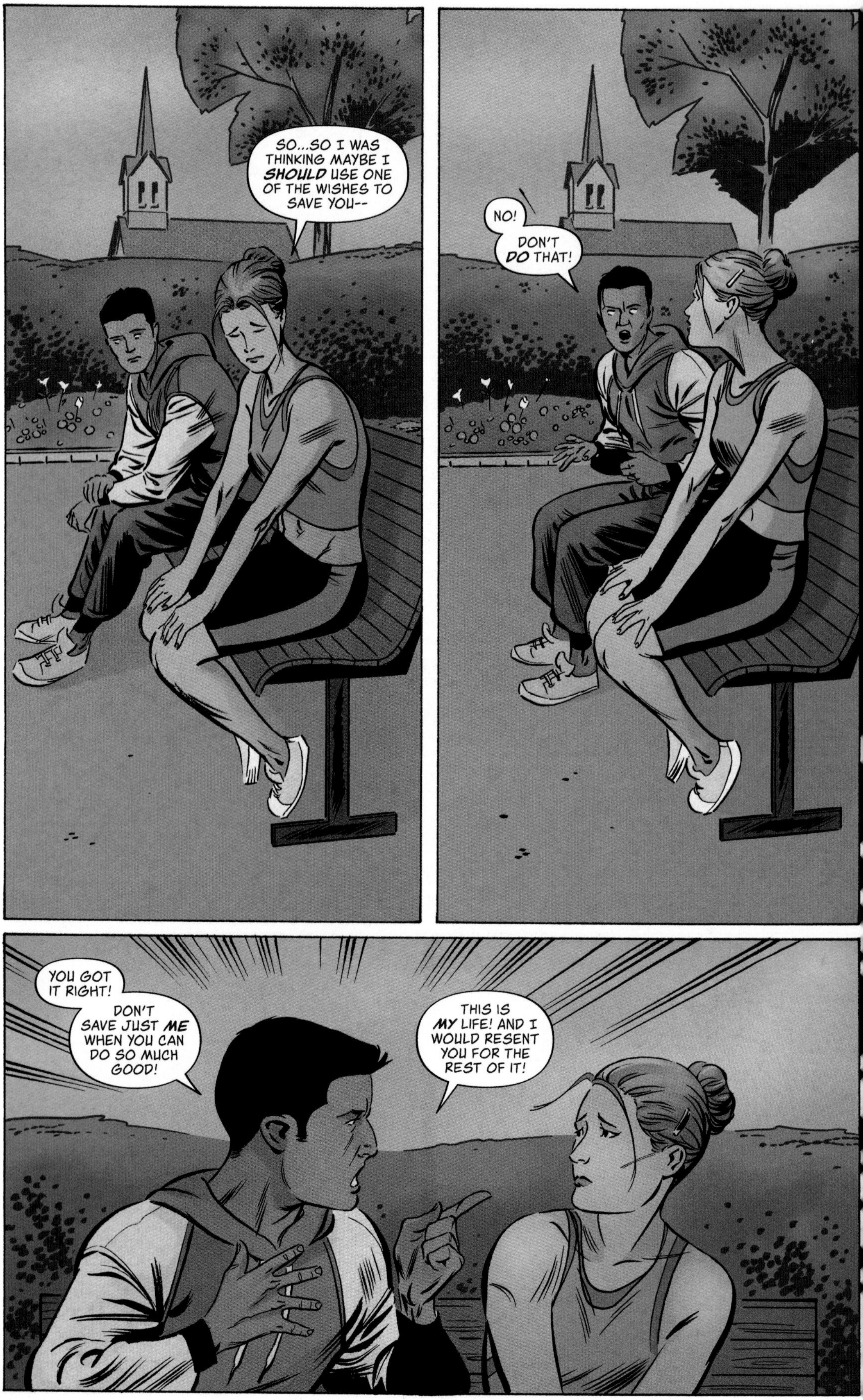
SO...SO I WAS THINKING MAYBE I SHOULD USE ONE OF THE WISHES TO SAVE YOU--
NO!
DON'T DO THAT!
YOU GOT IT RIGHT!
DON'T SAVE JUST ME WHEN YOU CAN DO SO MUCH GOOD!
THIS IS MY LIFE! AND I WOULD RESENT YOU FOR THE REST OF IT!

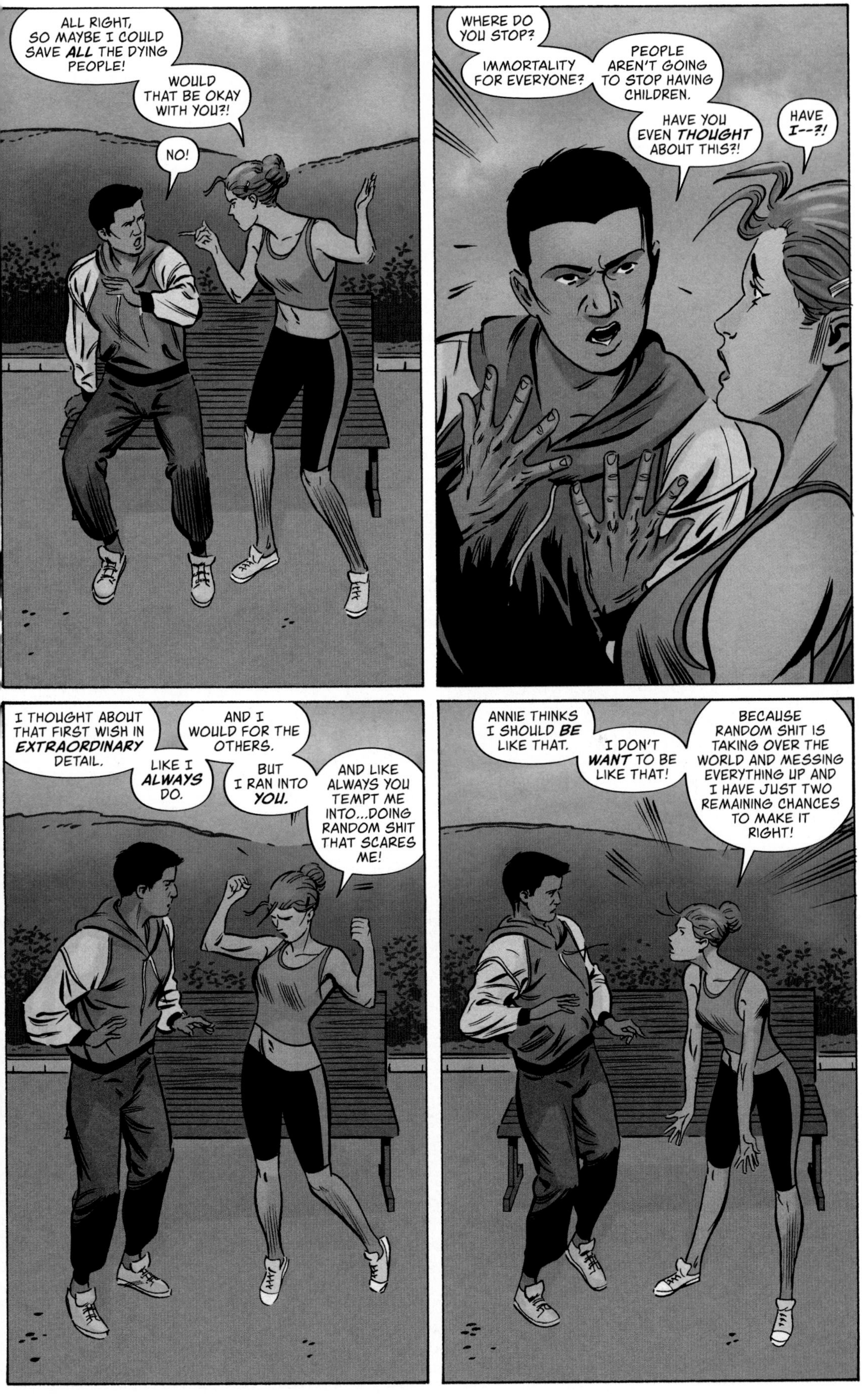
ALL RIGHT, SO MAYBE I COULD SAVE ALL THE DYING PEOPLE!
WOULD THAT BE OKAY WITH YOU?!
NO!
WHERE DO YOU STOP?
IMMORTALITY FOR EVERYONE?
PEOPLE AREN'T GOING TO STOP HAVING CHILDREN.
HAVE YOU EVEN THOUGHT ABOUT THIS?!
HAVE I--?!
I THOUGHT ABOUT THAT FIRST WISH IN EXTRAORDINARY DETAIL.
LIKE I ALWAYS DO.
AND I WOULD FOR THE OTHERS.
BUT I RAN INTO YOU.
AND LIKE ALWAYS YOU TEMPT ME INTO...DOING RANDOM SHIT THAT SCARES ME!
ANNIE THINKS I SHOULD BE LIKE THAT.
I DON'T WANT TO BE LIKE THAT!
BECAUSE RANDOM SHIT IS TAKING OVER THE WORLD AND MESSING EVERYTHING UP AND I HAVE JUST TWO REMAINING CHANCES TO MAKE IT RIGHT!

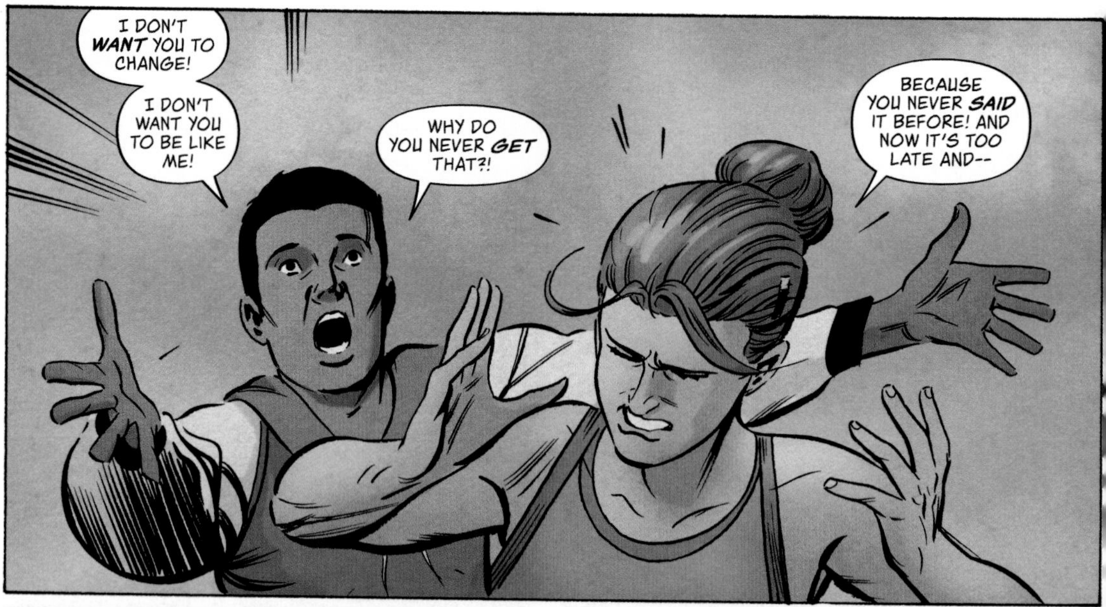
I DON'T *WANT* YOU TO CHANGE!
I DON'T WANT YOU TO BE LIKE ME!
WHY DO YOU NEVER *GET* THAT?!
BECAUSE YOU NEVER *SAID* IT BEFORE! AND NOW IT'S TOO LATE AND--

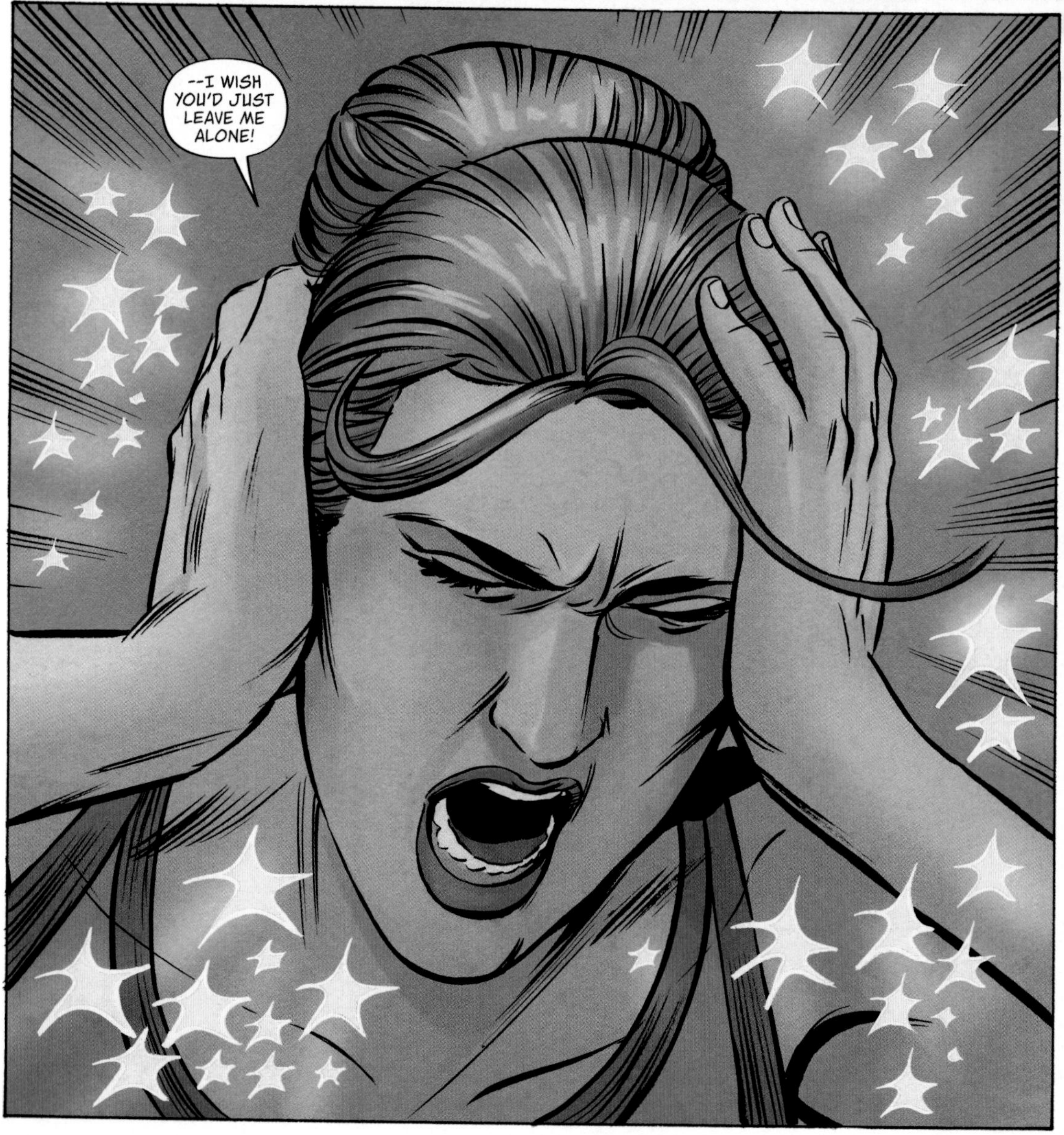
--I WISH YOU'D JUST LEAVE ME ALONE!

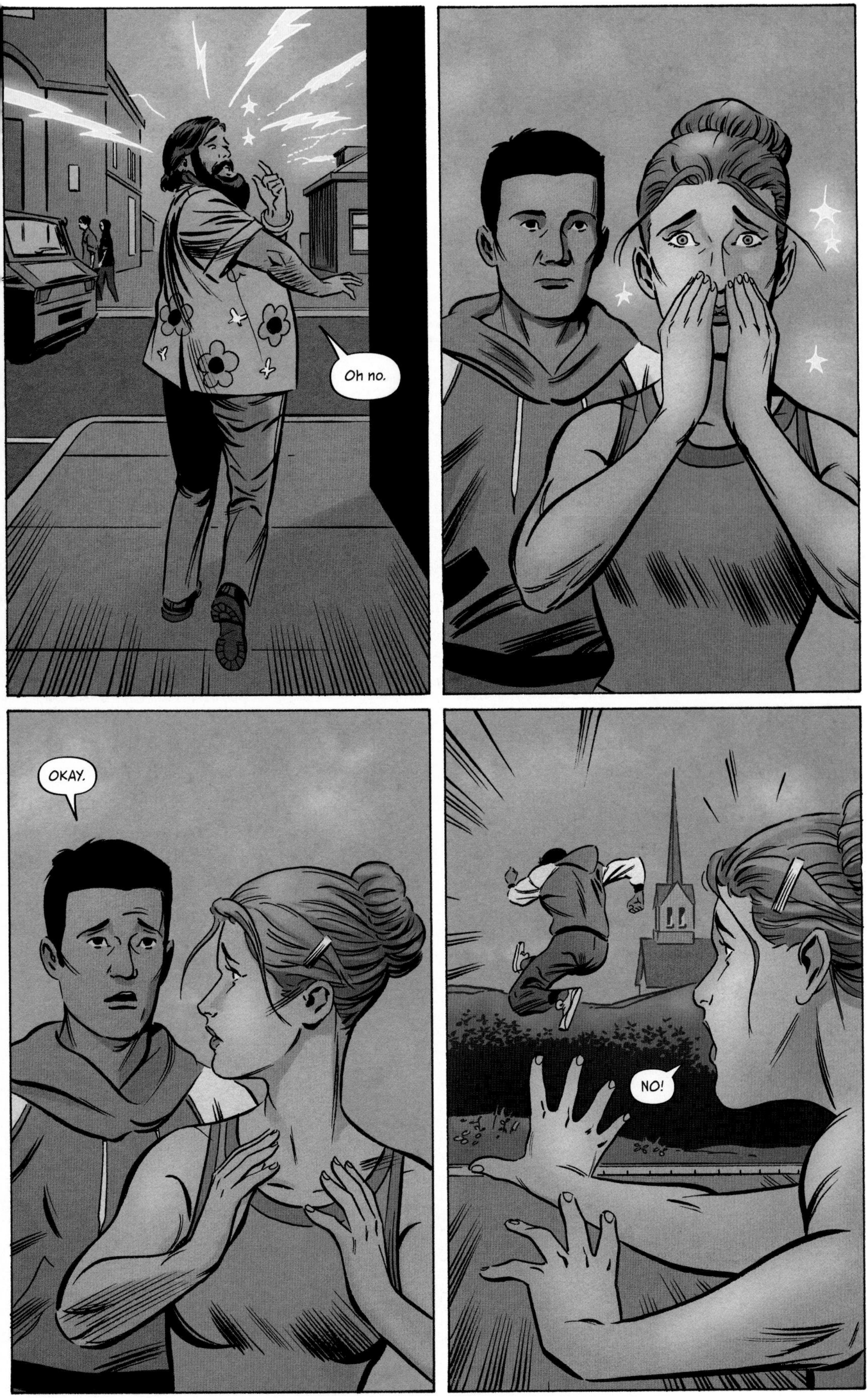
Oh no.
OKAY.
NO!

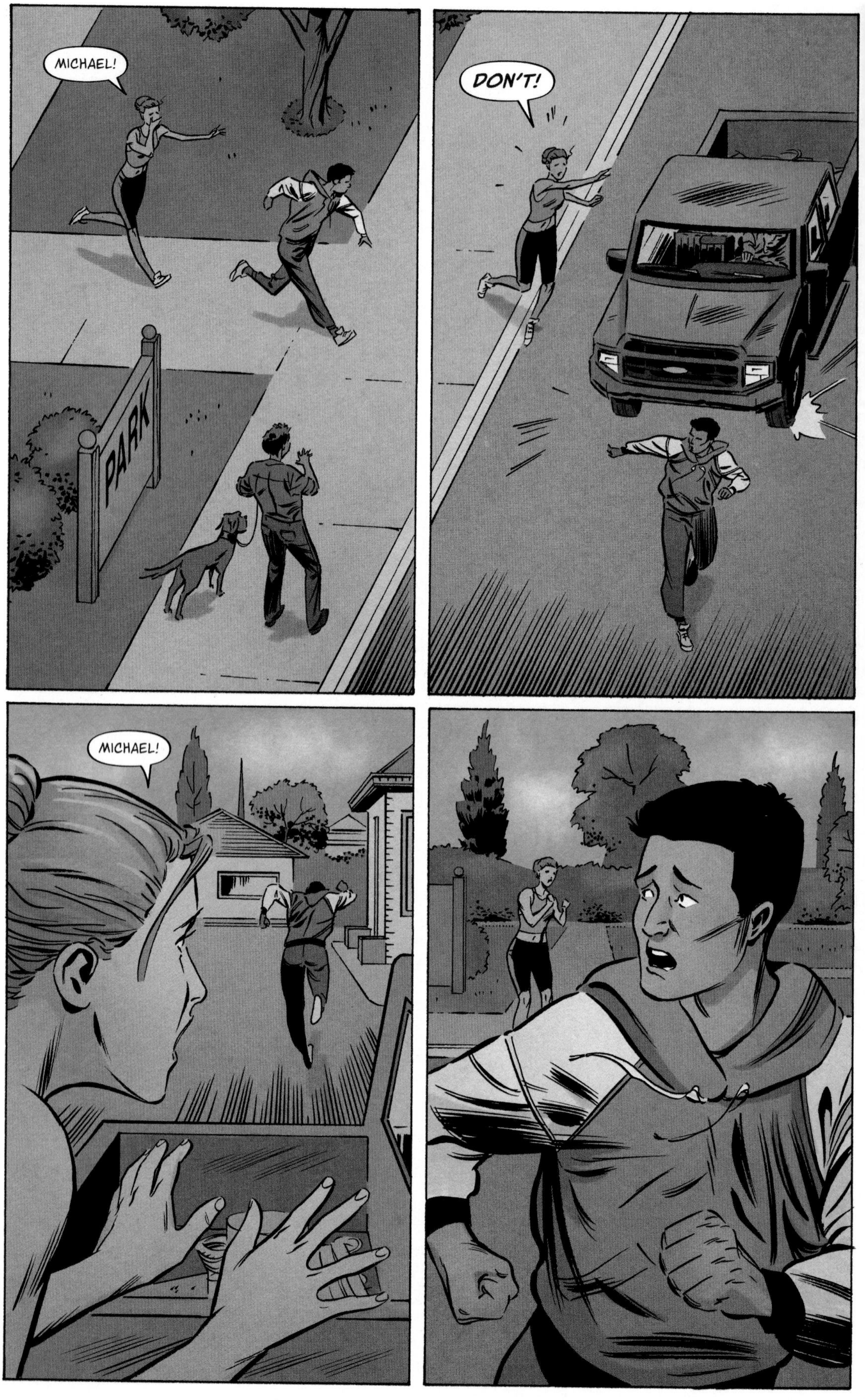
MICHAEL!
PARK
DON'T!
MICHAEL!

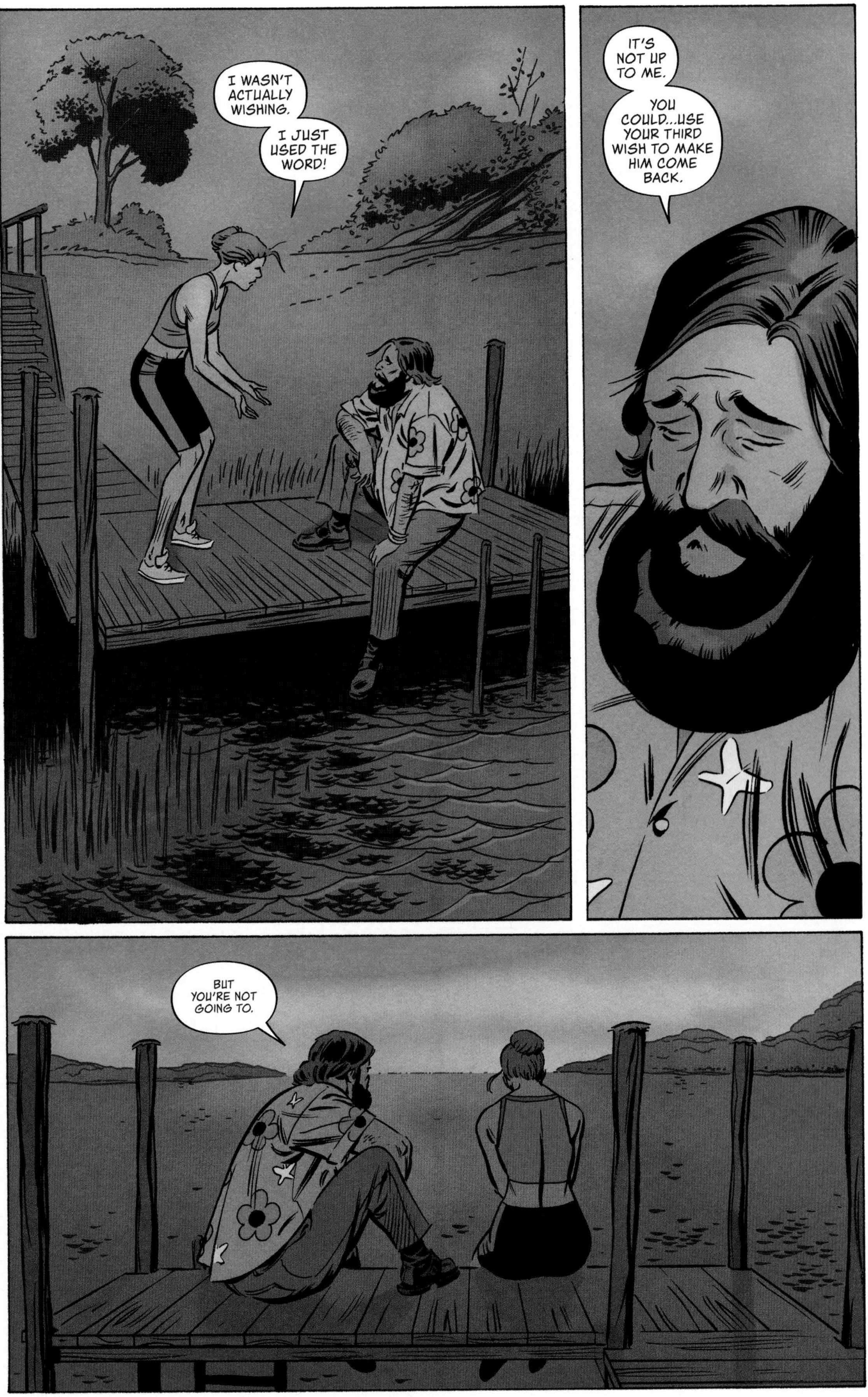
I WASN'T ACTUALLY WISHING.
I JUST USED THE WORD!
IT'S NOT UP TO ME.
YOU COULD...USE YOUR THIRD WISH TO MAKE HIM COME BACK.
BUT YOU'RE NOT GOING TO.

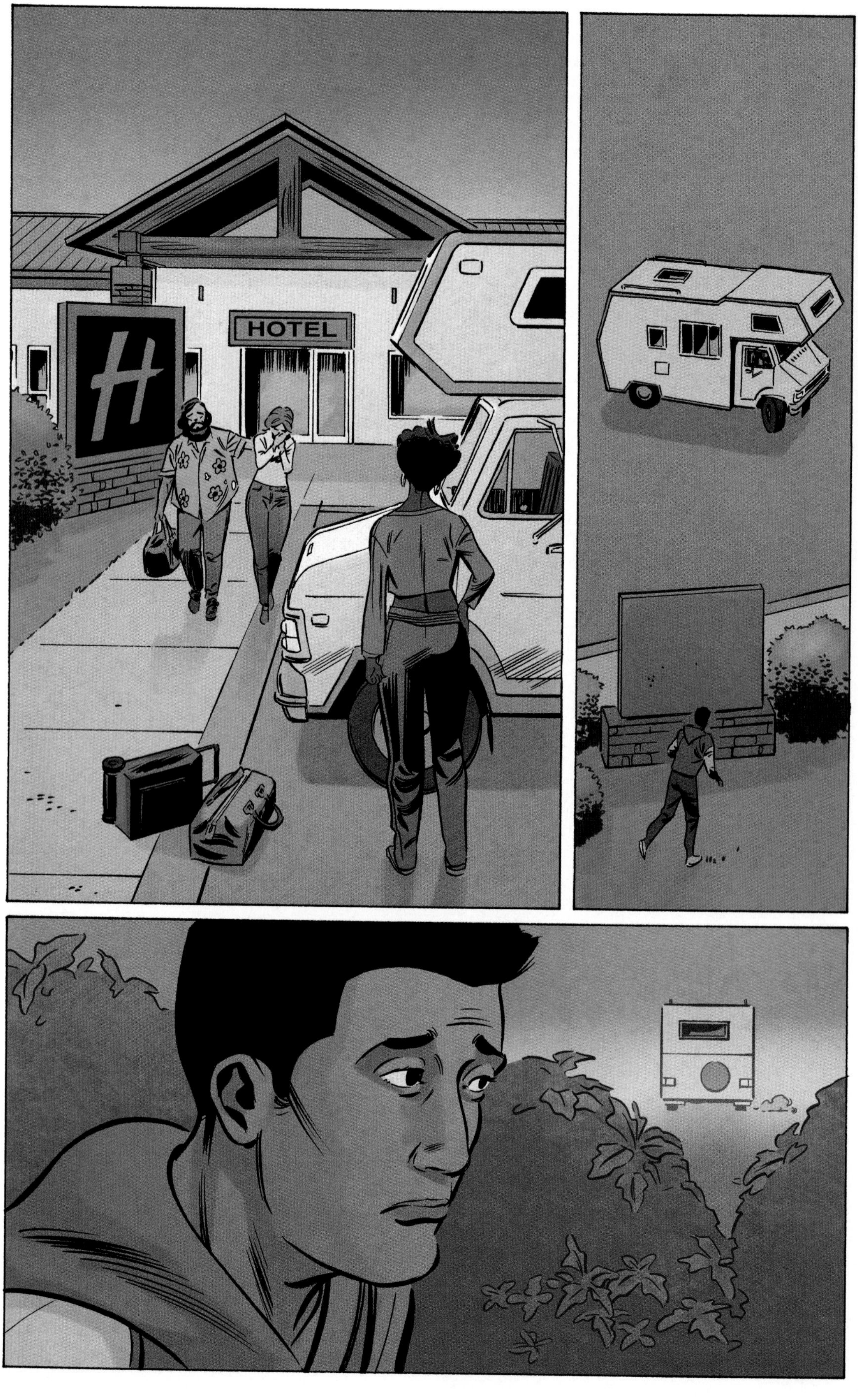
HOTEL

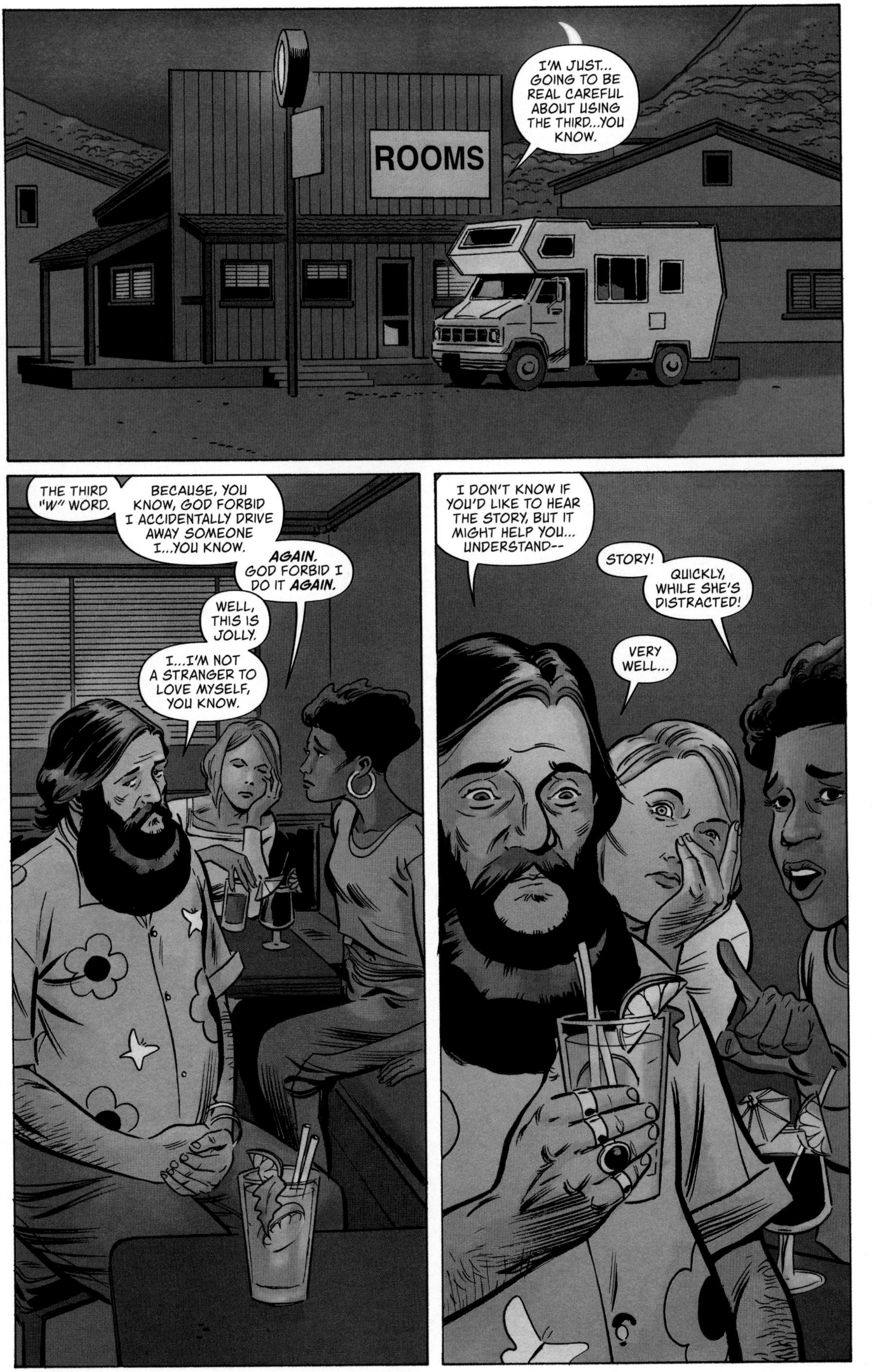
ROOMS
I'M JUST... GOING TO BE REAL CAREFUL ABOUT USING THE THIRD...YOU KNOW.
THE THIRD "W" WORD.
BECAUSE, YOU KNOW, GOD FORBID I ACCIDENTALLY DRIVE AWAY SOMEONE I...YOU KNOW.
AGAIN. GOD FORBID I DO IT AGAIN.
WELL, THIS IS JOLLY.
I...I'M NOT A STRANGER TO LOVE MYSELF, YOU KNOW.
I DON'T KNOW IF YOU'D LIKE TO HEAR THE STORY, BUT IT MIGHT HELP YOU... UNDERSTAND--
STORY!
QUICKLY, WHILE SHE'S DISTRACTED!
VERY WELL...

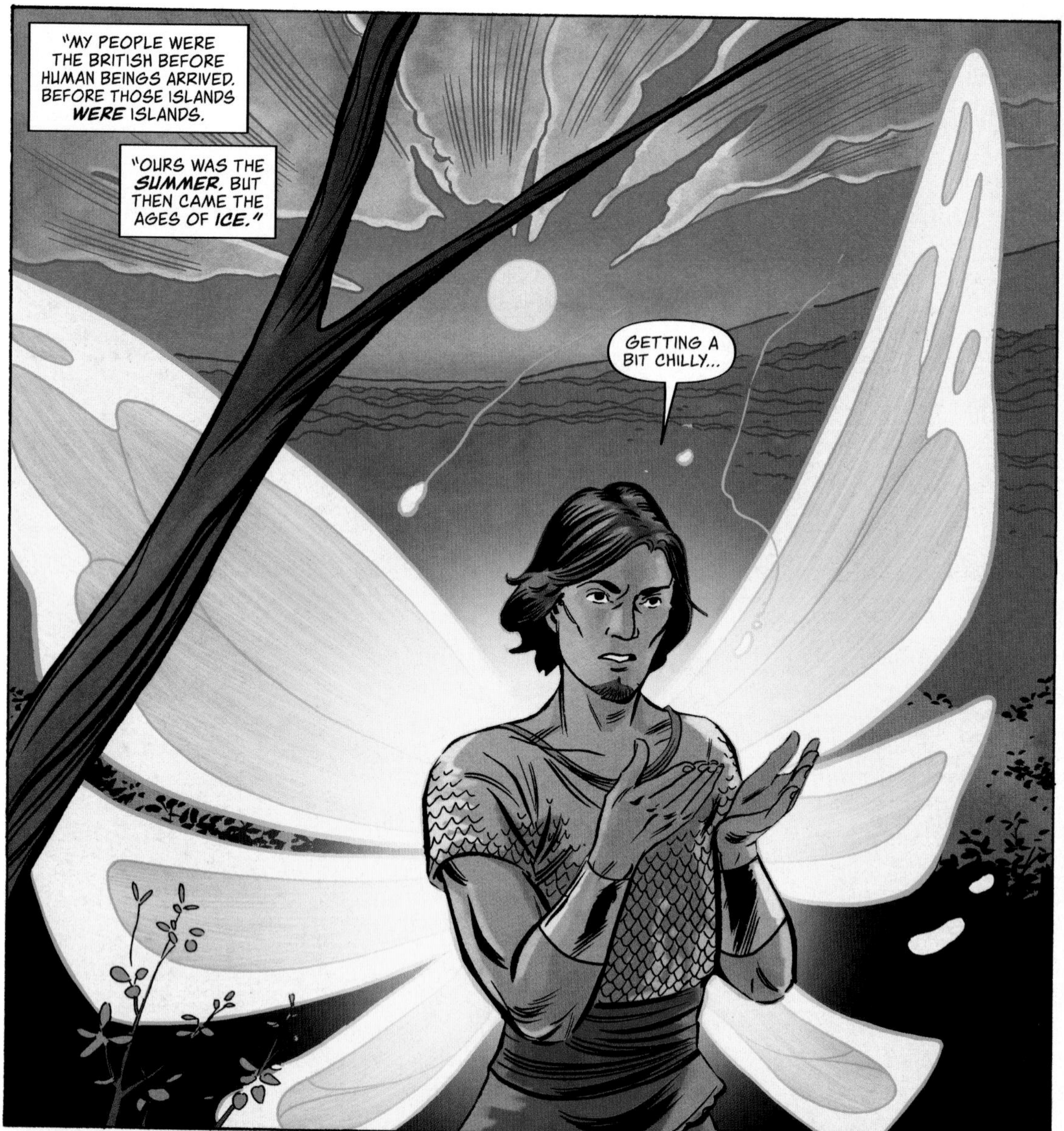
"MY PEOPLE WERE THE BRITISH BEFORE HUMAN BEINGS ARRIVED. BEFORE THOSE ISLANDS *WERE* ISLANDS.
"OURS WAS THE *SUMMER*, BUT THEN CAME THE AGES OF *ICE*."
GETTING A BIT CHILLY...

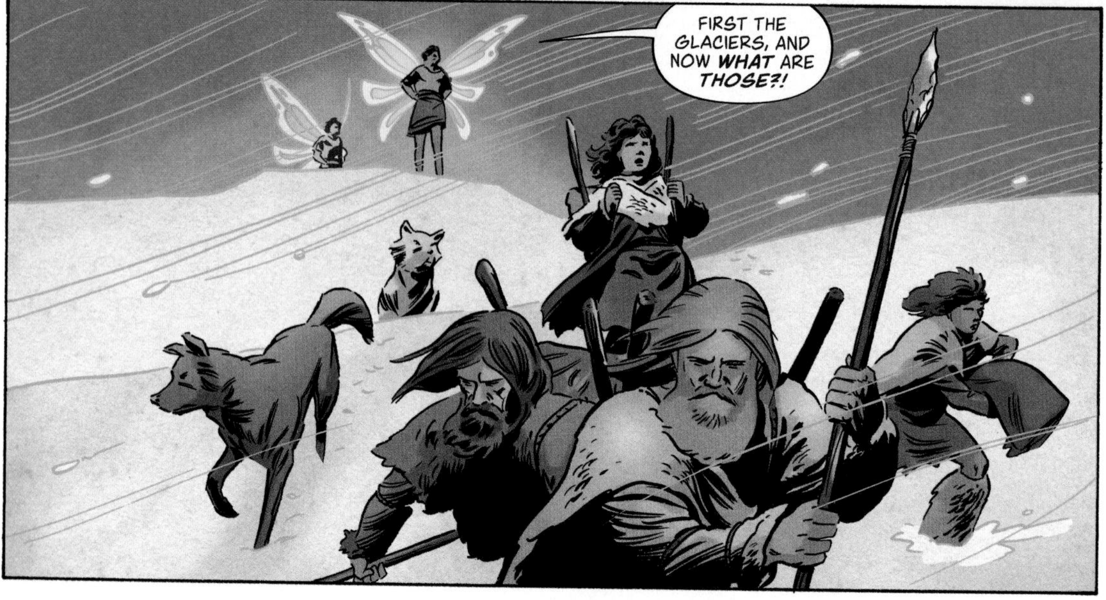
FIRST THE GLACIERS, AND NOW *WHAT* ARE *THOSE?!*

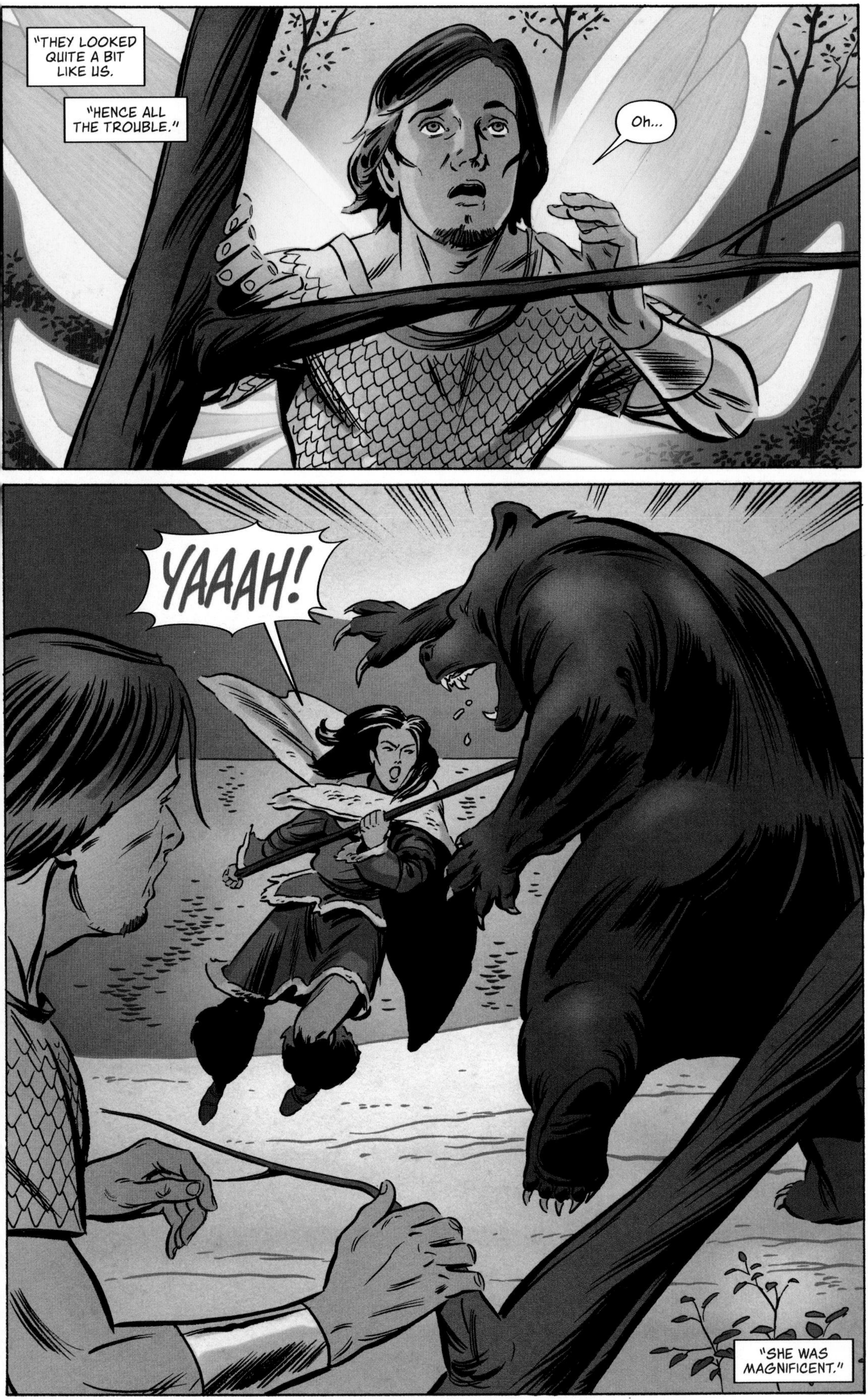
"THEY LOOKED QUITE A BIT LIKE US.
"HENCE ALL THE TROUBLE."
Oh...
YAAAH!
"SHE WAS MAGNIFICENT."

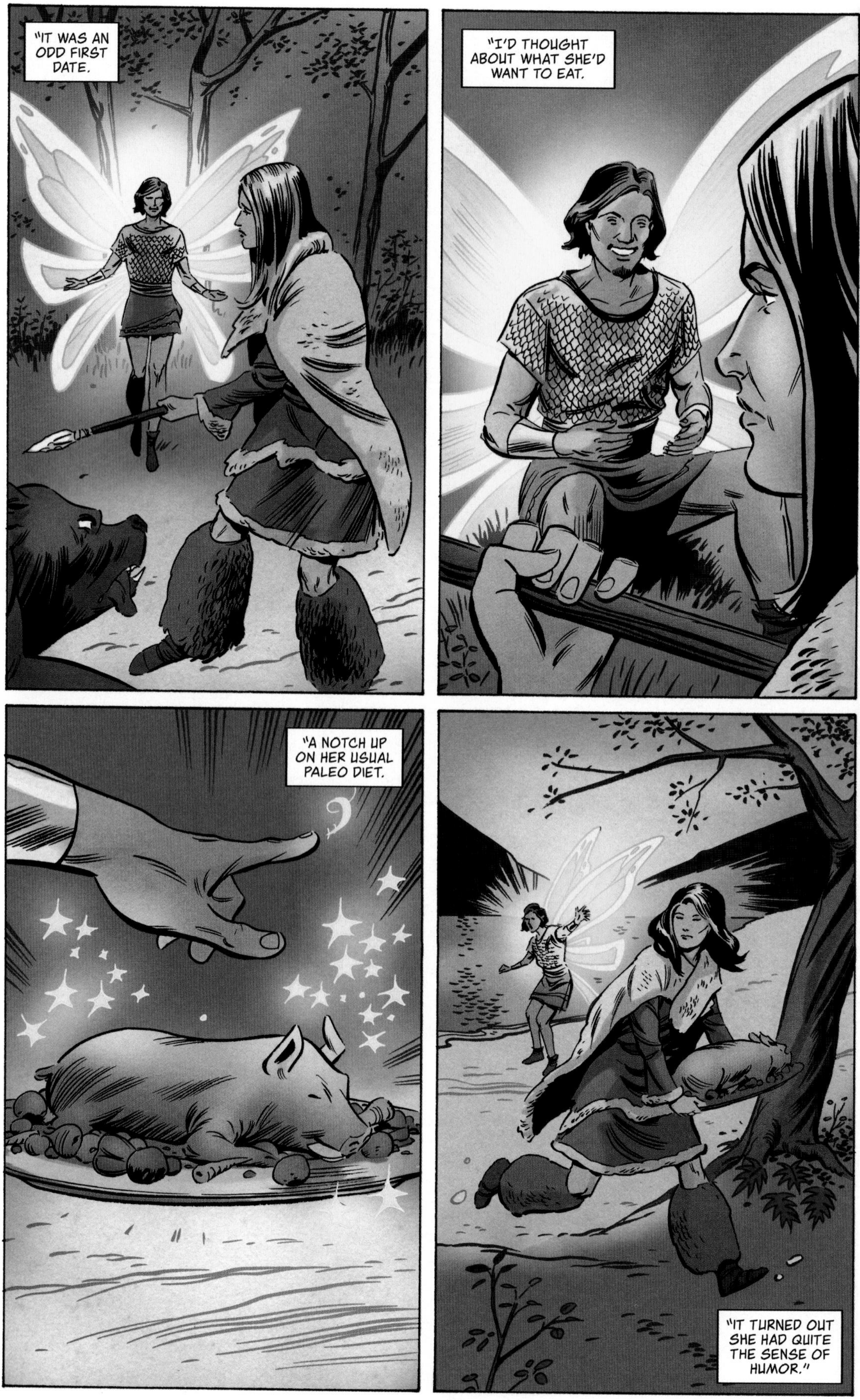
"IT WAS AN ODD FIRST DATE.
"I'D THOUGHT ABOUT WHAT SHE'D WANT TO EAT.
"A NOTCH UP ON HER USUAL PALEO DIET.
"IT TURNED OUT SHE HAD QUITE THE SENSE OF HUMOR."

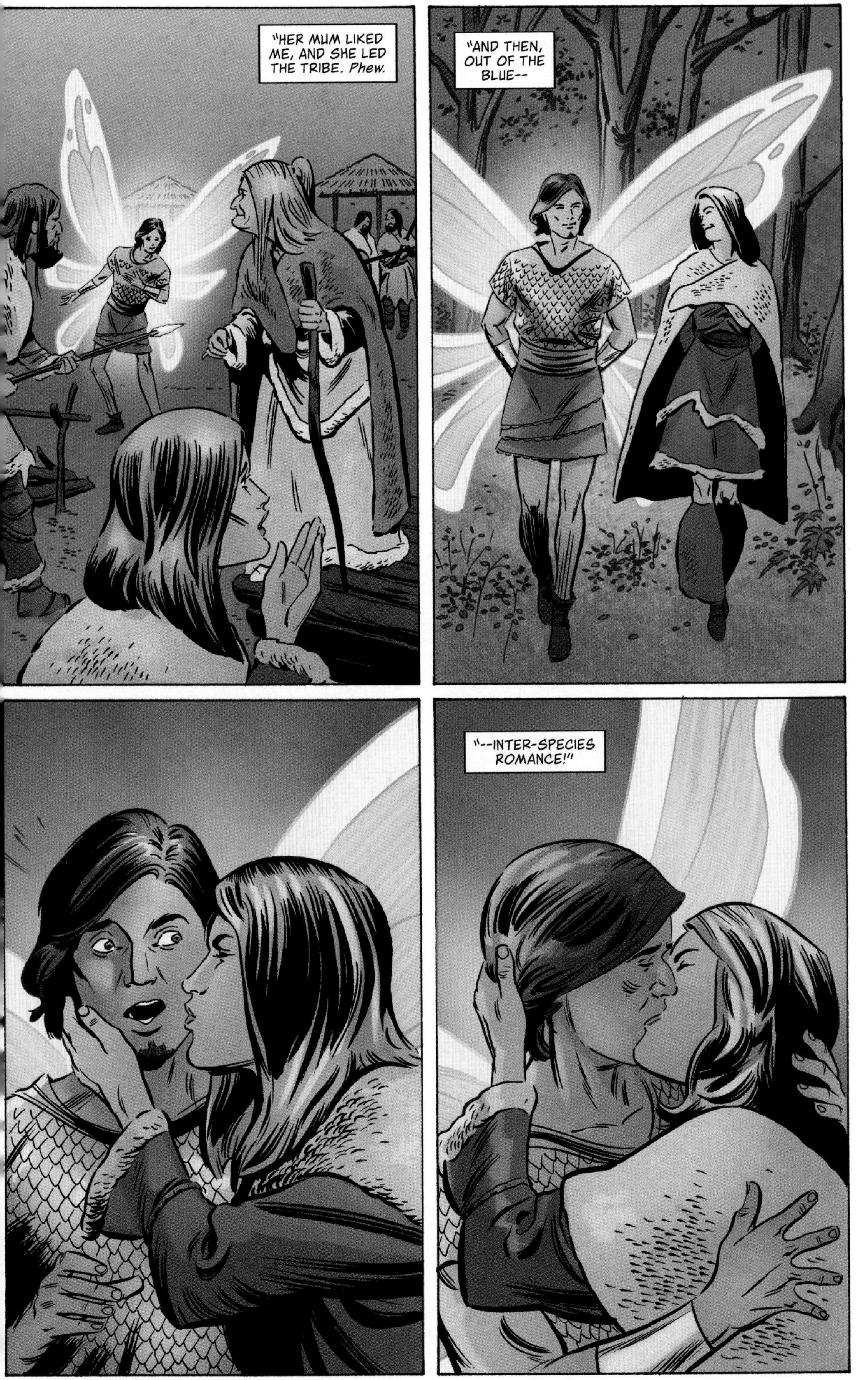
"HER MUM LIKED ME, AND SHE LED THE TRIBE. *Phew.*
"AND THEN, OUT OF THE BLUE--
"--INTER-SPECIES ROMANCE!"

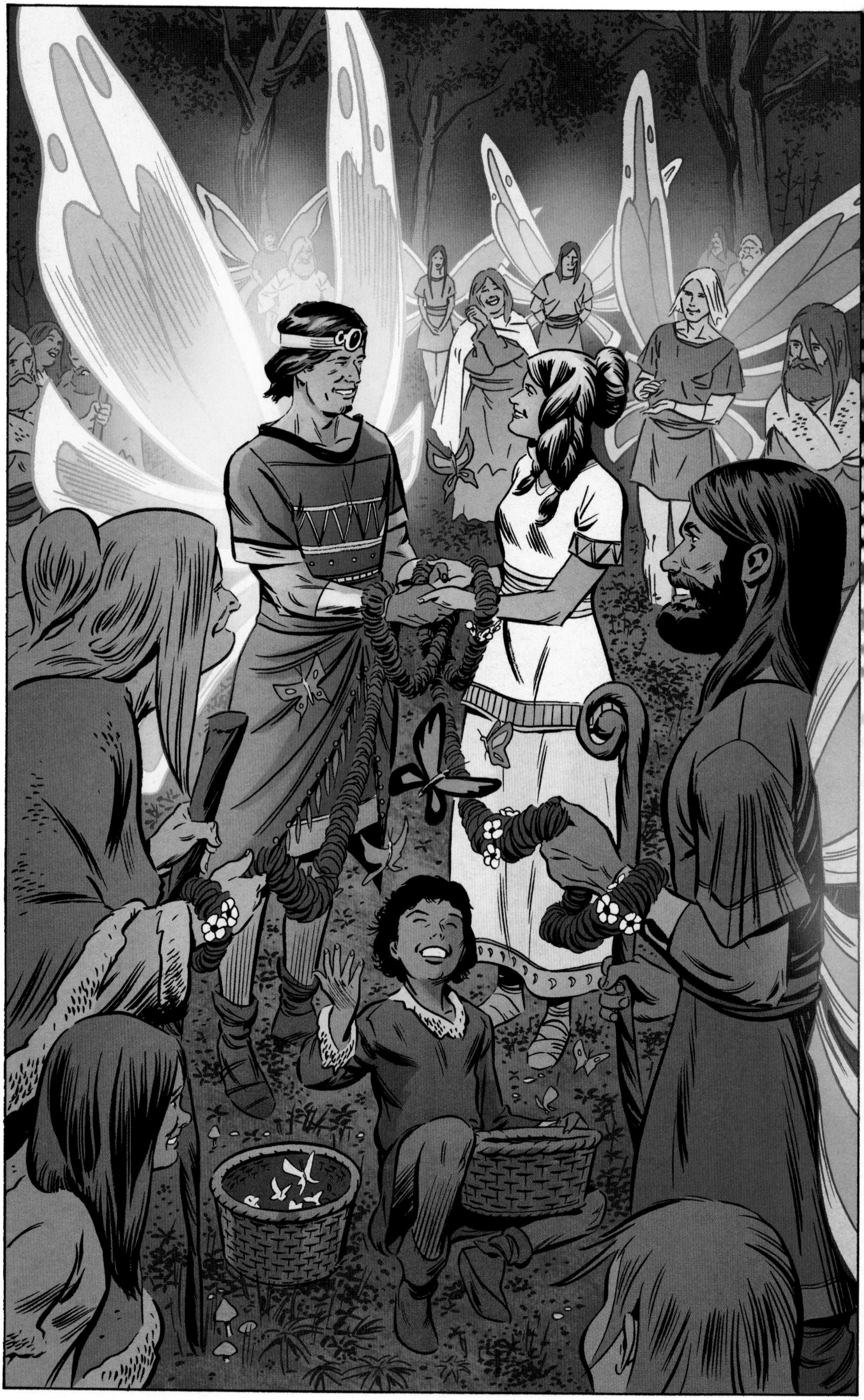

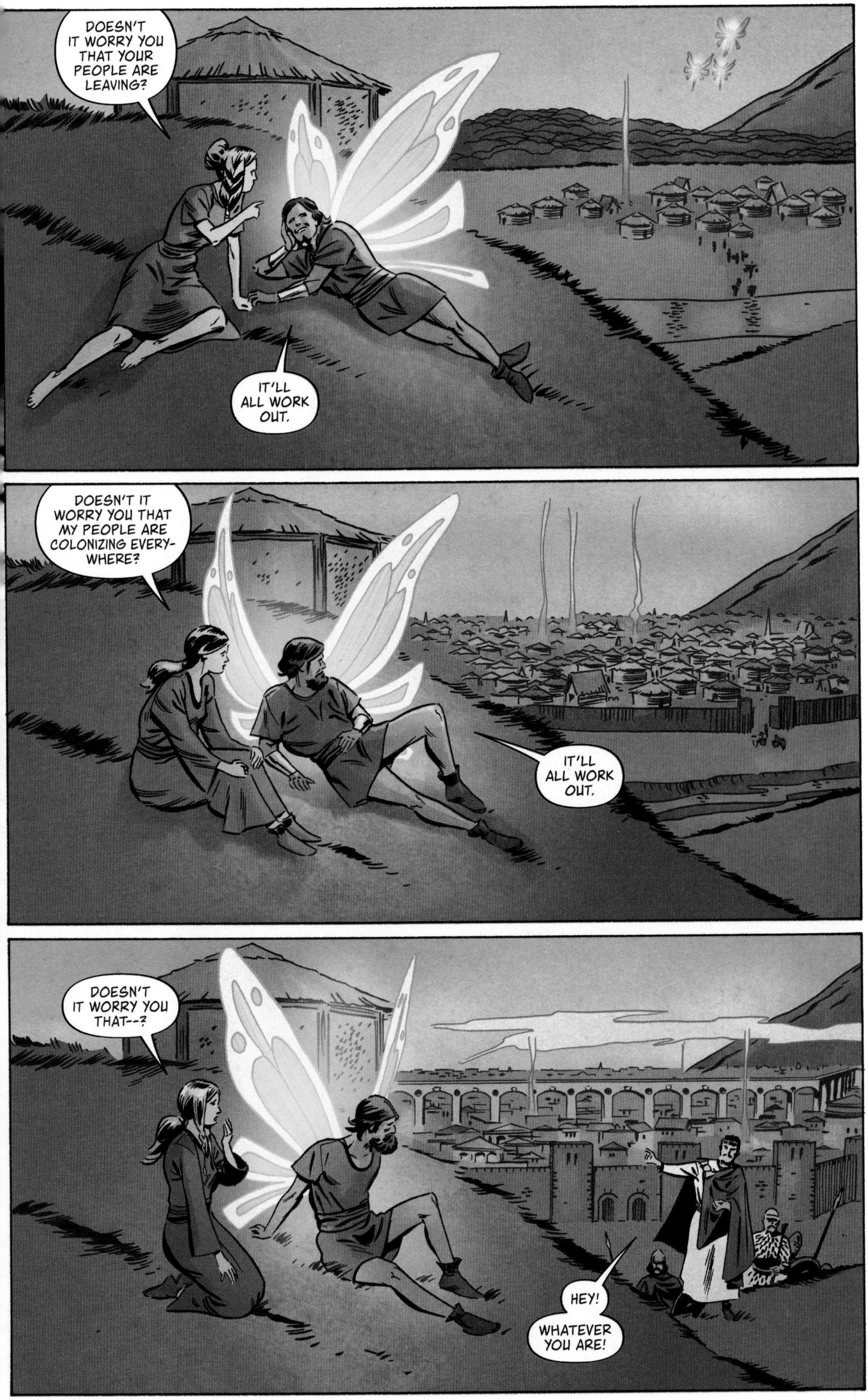
DOESN'T IT WORRY YOU THAT YOUR PEOPLE ARE LEAVING?
IT'LL ALL WORK OUT.
DOESN'T IT WORRY YOU THAT MY PEOPLE ARE COLONIZING EVERY-WHERE?
IT'LL ALL WORK OUT.
DOESN'T IT WORRY YOU THAT--?
HEY! WHATEVER YOU ARE!

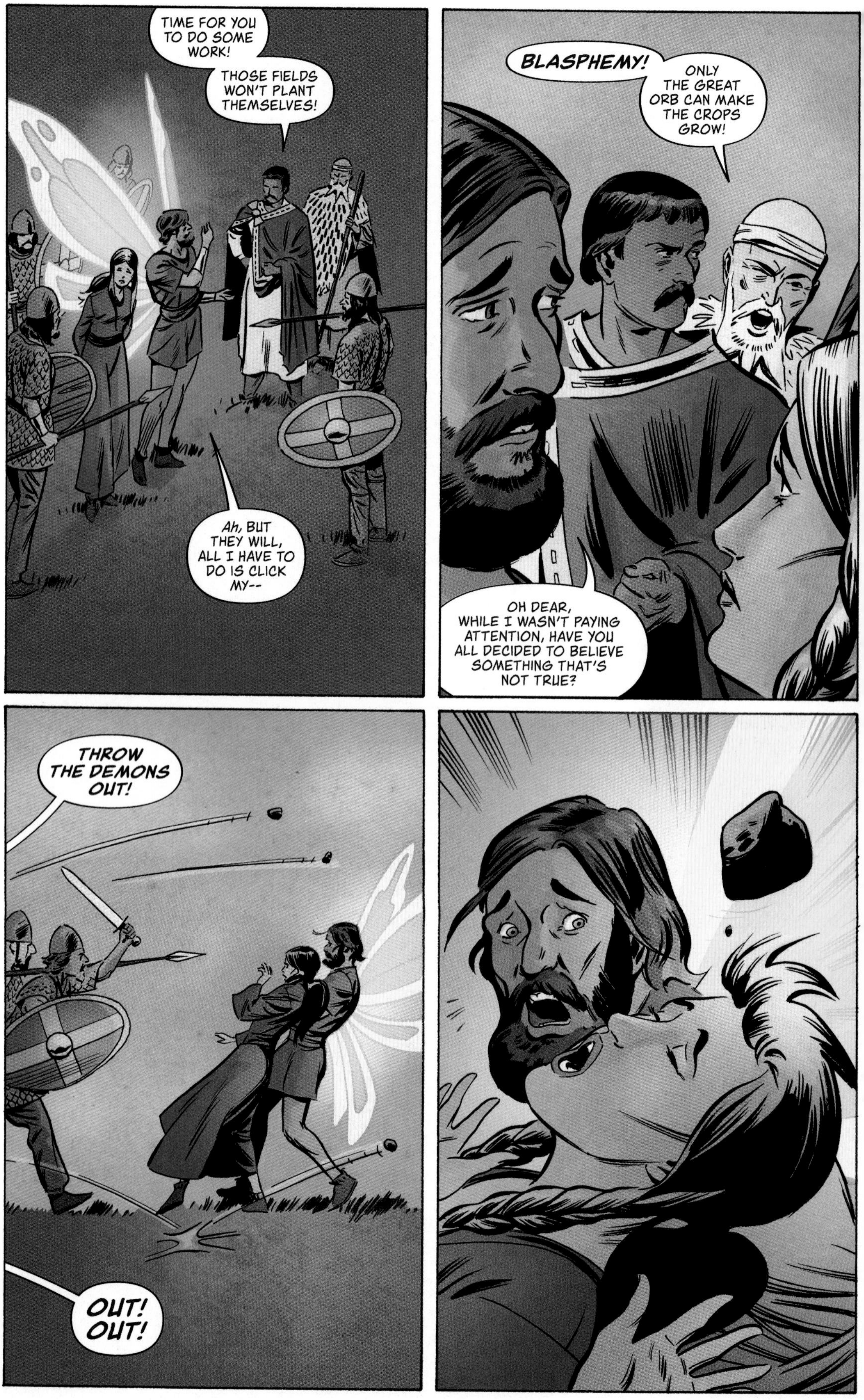
TIME FOR YOU TO DO SOME WORK!
THOSE FIELDS WON'T PLANT THEMSELVES!
Ah, BUT THEY WILL, ALL I HAVE TO DO IS CLICK MY--
BLASPHEMY!
ONLY THE GREAT ORB CAN MAKE THE CROPS GROW!
OH DEAR, WHILE I WASN'T PAYING ATTENTION, HAVE YOU ALL DECIDED TO BELIEVE SOMETHING THAT'S NOT TRUE?
THROW THE DEMONS OUT!
OUT! OUT!

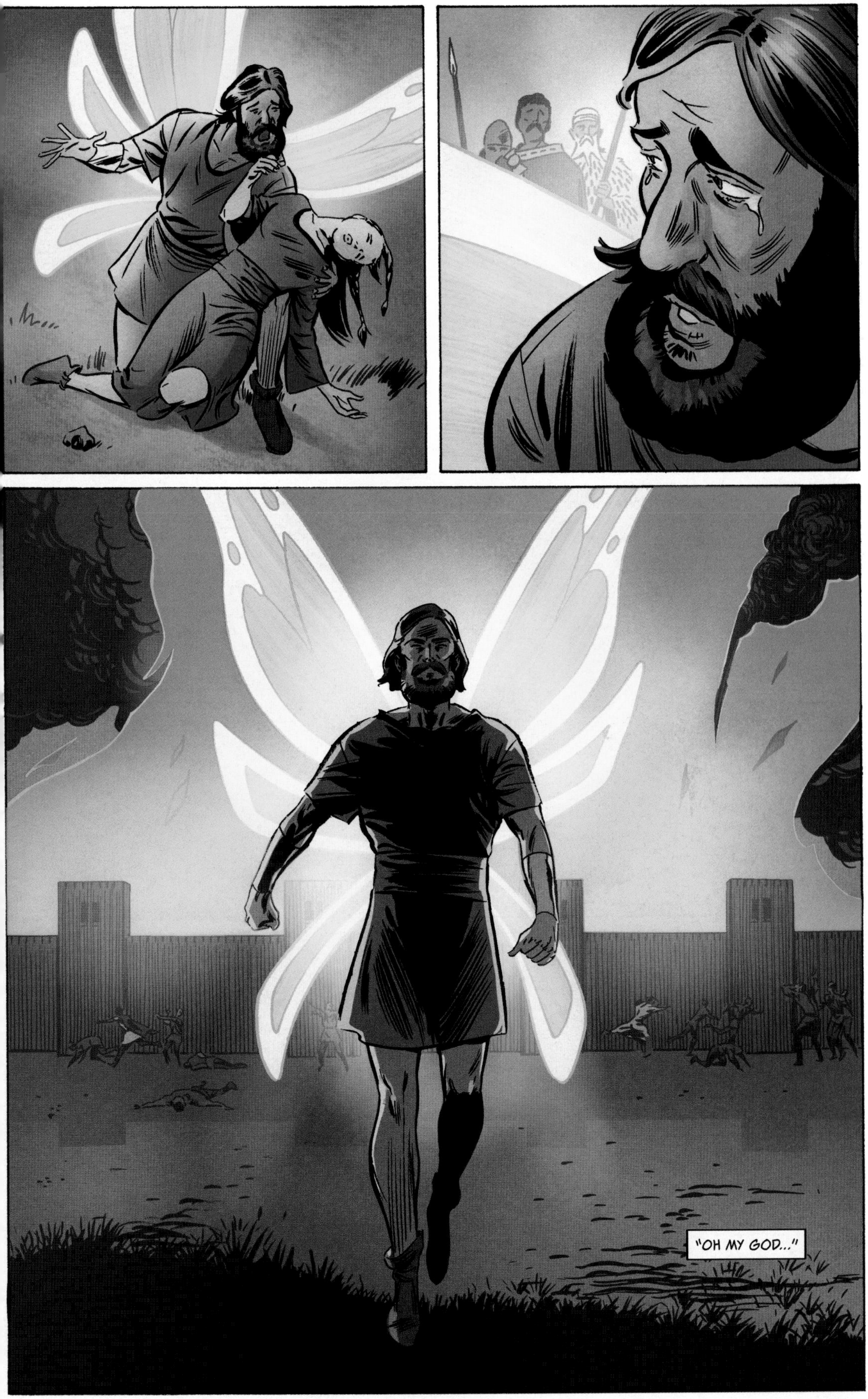
"OH MY GOD..."

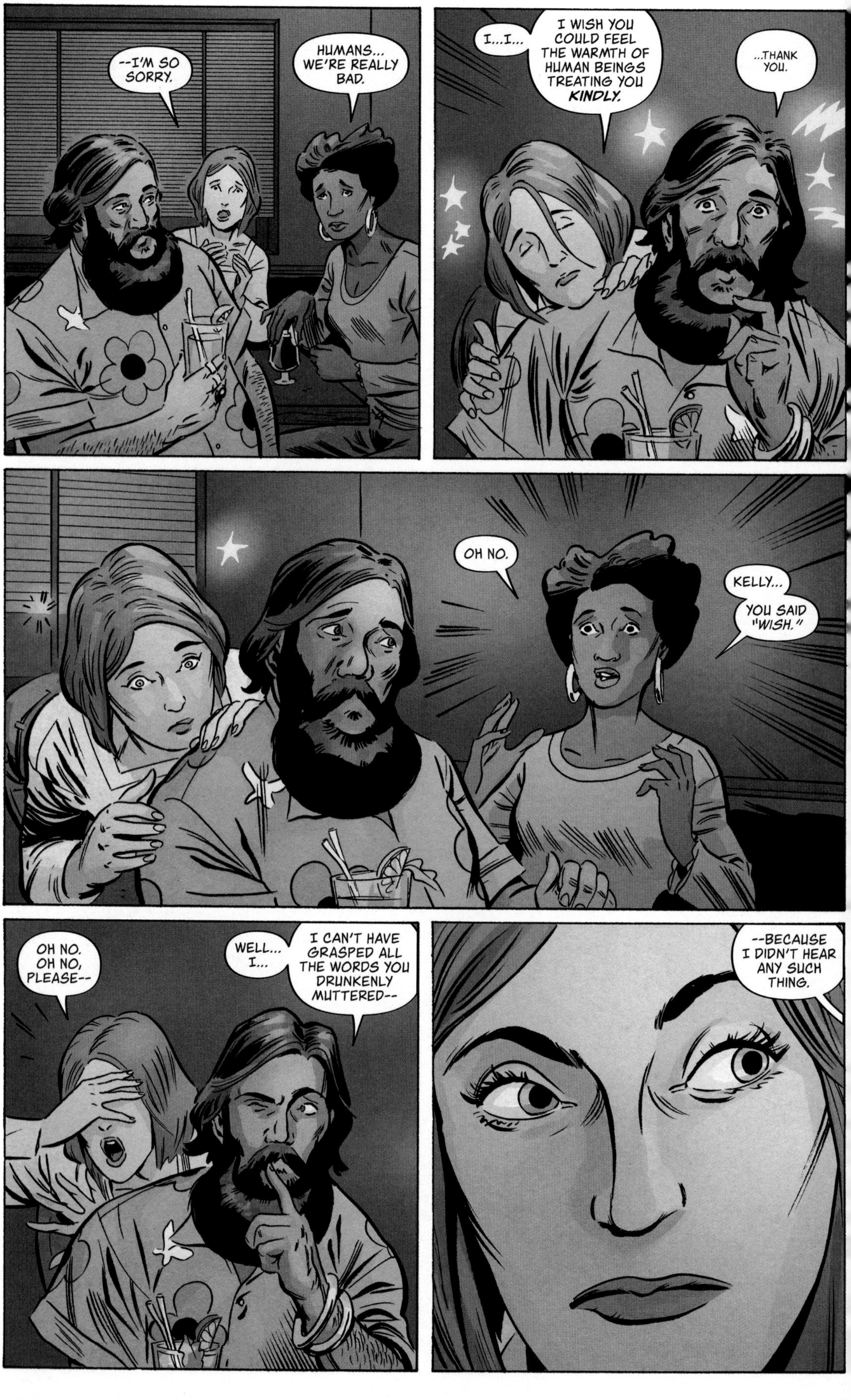
--I'M SO SORRY.
HUMANS... WE'RE REALLY BAD.
I...I...
I WISH YOU COULD FEEL THE WARMTH OF HUMAN BEINGS TREATING YOU KINDLY.
...THANK YOU.
OH NO.
KELLY...
YOU SAID "WISH."
OH NO. OH NO, PLEASE--
WELL... I...
I CAN'T HAVE GRASPED ALL THE WORDS YOU DRUNKENLY MUTTERED--
--BECAUSE I DIDN'T HEAR ANY SUCH THING.

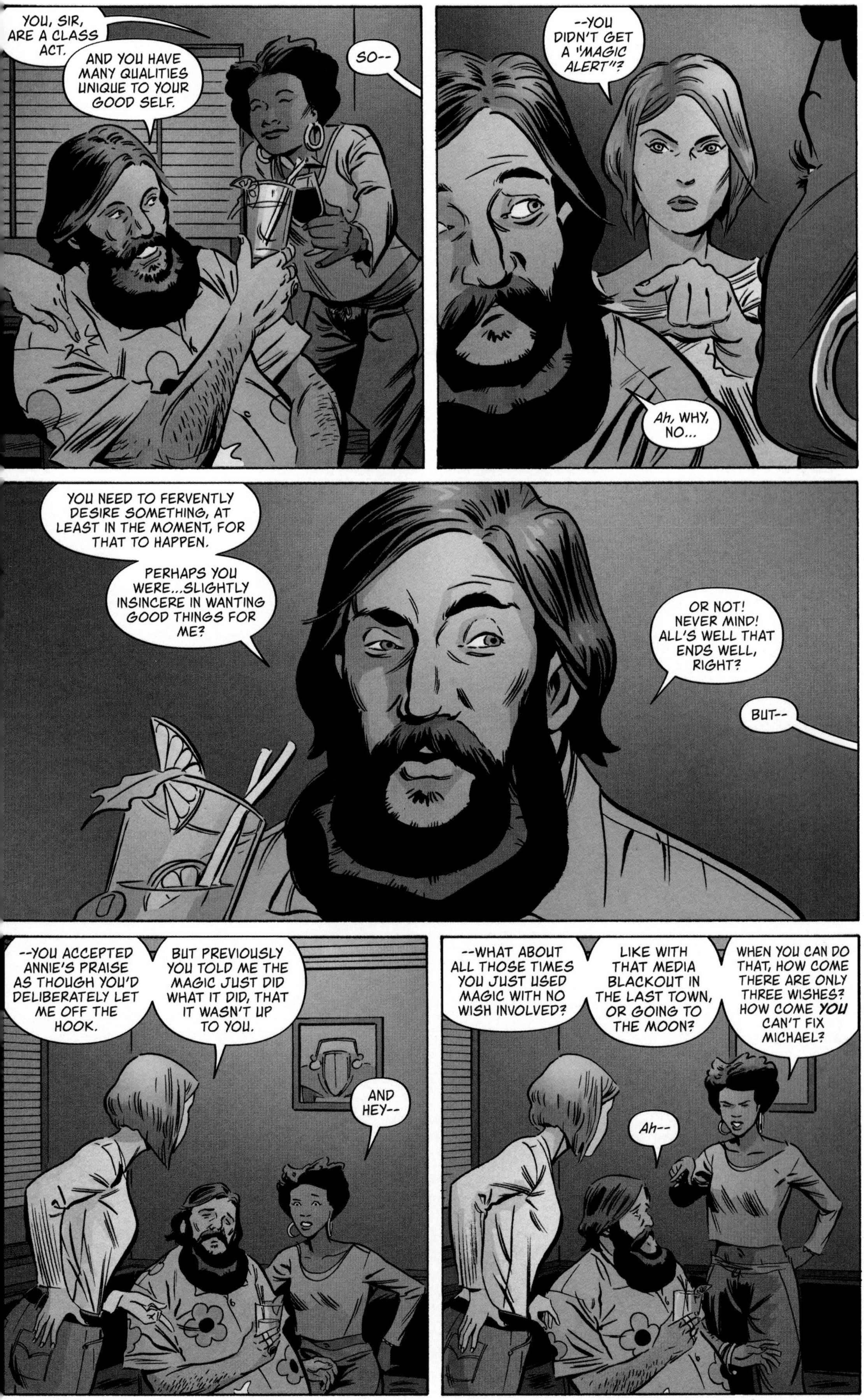
YOU, SIR, ARE A CLASS ACT.
AND YOU HAVE MANY QUALITIES UNIQUE TO YOUR GOOD SELF.
SO--
--YOU DIDN'T GET A "MAGIC ALERT"?
Ah, WHY, NO...
YOU NEED TO FERVENTLY DESIRE SOMETHING, AT LEAST IN THE MOMENT, FOR THAT TO HAPPEN.
PERHAPS YOU WERE...SLIGHTLY INSINCERE IN WANTING GOOD THINGS FOR ME?
OR NOT! NEVER MIND! ALL'S WELL THAT ENDS WELL, RIGHT?
BUT--
--YOU ACCEPTED ANNIE'S PRAISE AS THOUGH YOU'D DELIBERATELY LET ME OFF THE HOOK.
BUT PREVIOUSLY YOU TOLD ME THE MAGIC JUST DID WHAT IT DID, THAT IT WASN'T UP TO YOU.
AND HEY--
--WHAT ABOUT ALL THOSE TIMES YOU JUST USED MAGIC WITH NO WISH INVOLVED?
LIKE WITH THAT MEDIA BLACKOUT IN THE LAST TOWN, OR GOING TO THE MOON?
WHEN YOU CAN DO THAT, HOW COME THERE ARE ONLY THREE WISHES? HOW COME *YOU* CAN'T FIX MICHAEL?
Ah--

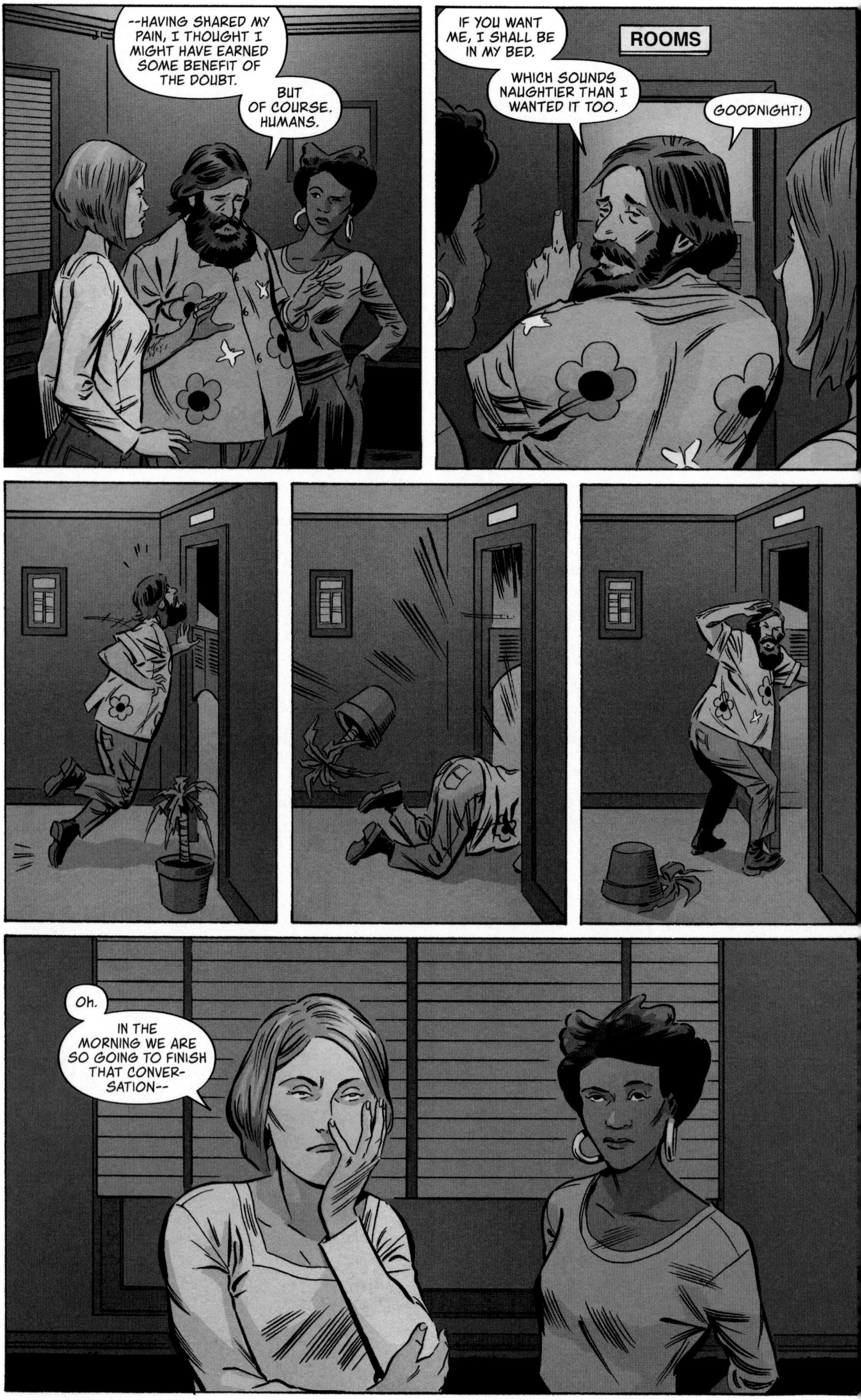
--HAVING SHARED MY PAIN, I THOUGHT I MIGHT HAVE EARNED SOME BENEFIT OF THE DOUBT.
BUT OF COURSE. HUMANS.
IF YOU WANT ME, I SHALL BE IN MY BED.
ROOMS
WHICH SOUNDS NAUGHTIER THAN I WANTED IT TOO.
GOODNIGHT!
Oh.
IN THE MORNING WE ARE SO GOING TO FINISH THAT CONVER-SATION--

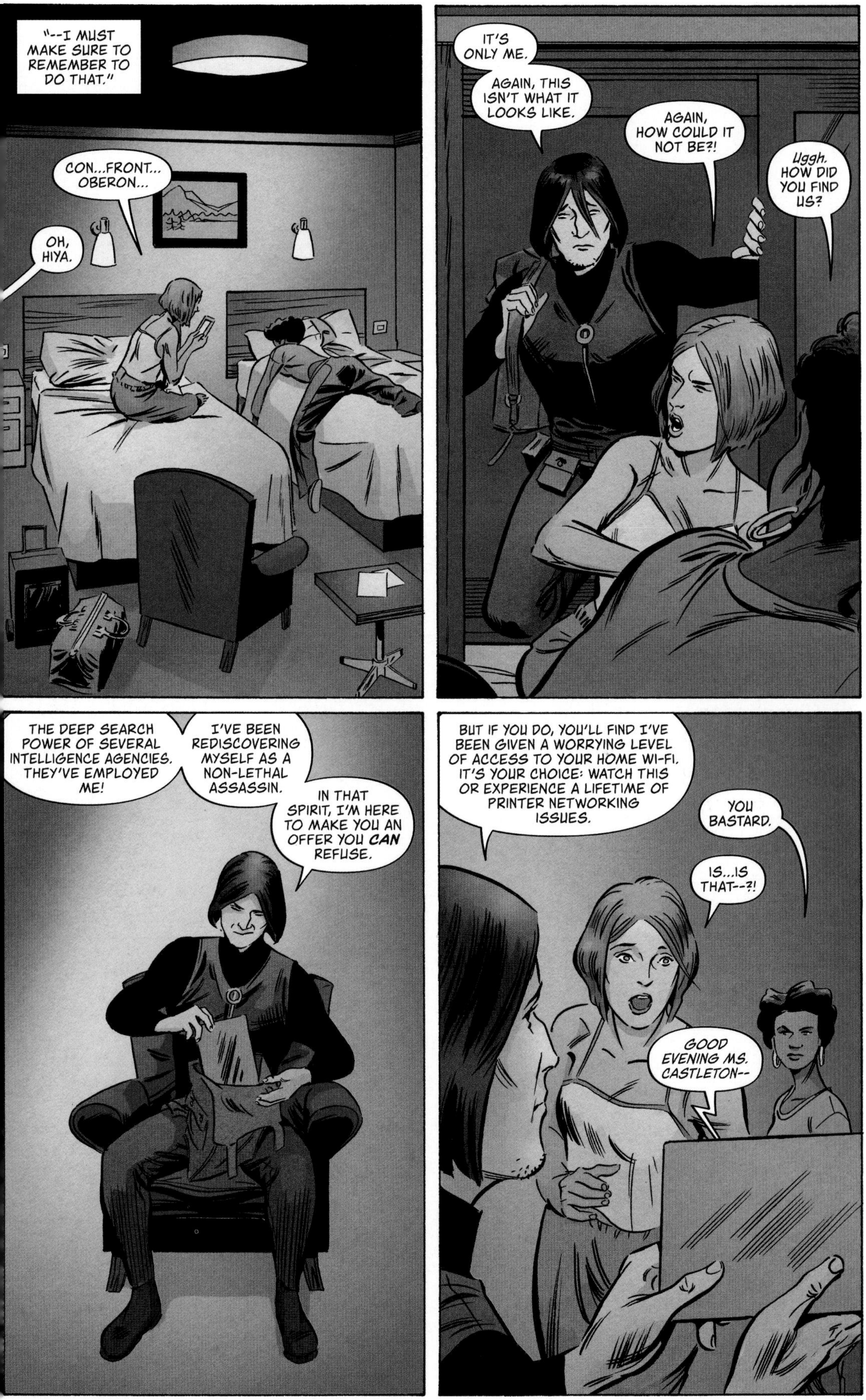
"--I MUST MAKE SURE TO REMEMBER TO DO THAT."
CON...FRONT... OBERON...
OH, HIYA.
IT'S ONLY ME.
AGAIN, THIS ISN'T WHAT IT LOOKS LIKE.
AGAIN, HOW COULD IT NOT BE?!
Uggh. HOW DID YOU FIND US?
THE DEEP SEARCH POWER OF SEVERAL INTELLIGENCE AGENCIES. THEY'VE EMPLOYED ME!
I'VE BEEN REDISCOVERING MYSELF AS A NON-LETHAL ASSASSIN.
IN THAT SPIRIT, I'M HERE TO MAKE YOU AN OFFER YOU CAN REFUSE.
BUT IF YOU DO, YOU'LL FIND I'VE BEEN GIVEN A WORRYING LEVEL OF ACCESS TO YOUR HOME WI-FI. IT'S YOUR CHOICE: WATCH THIS OR EXPERIENCE A LIFETIME OF PRINTER NETWORKING ISSUES.
YOU BASTARD.
IS...IS THAT--?!
GOOD EVENING MS. CASTLETON--

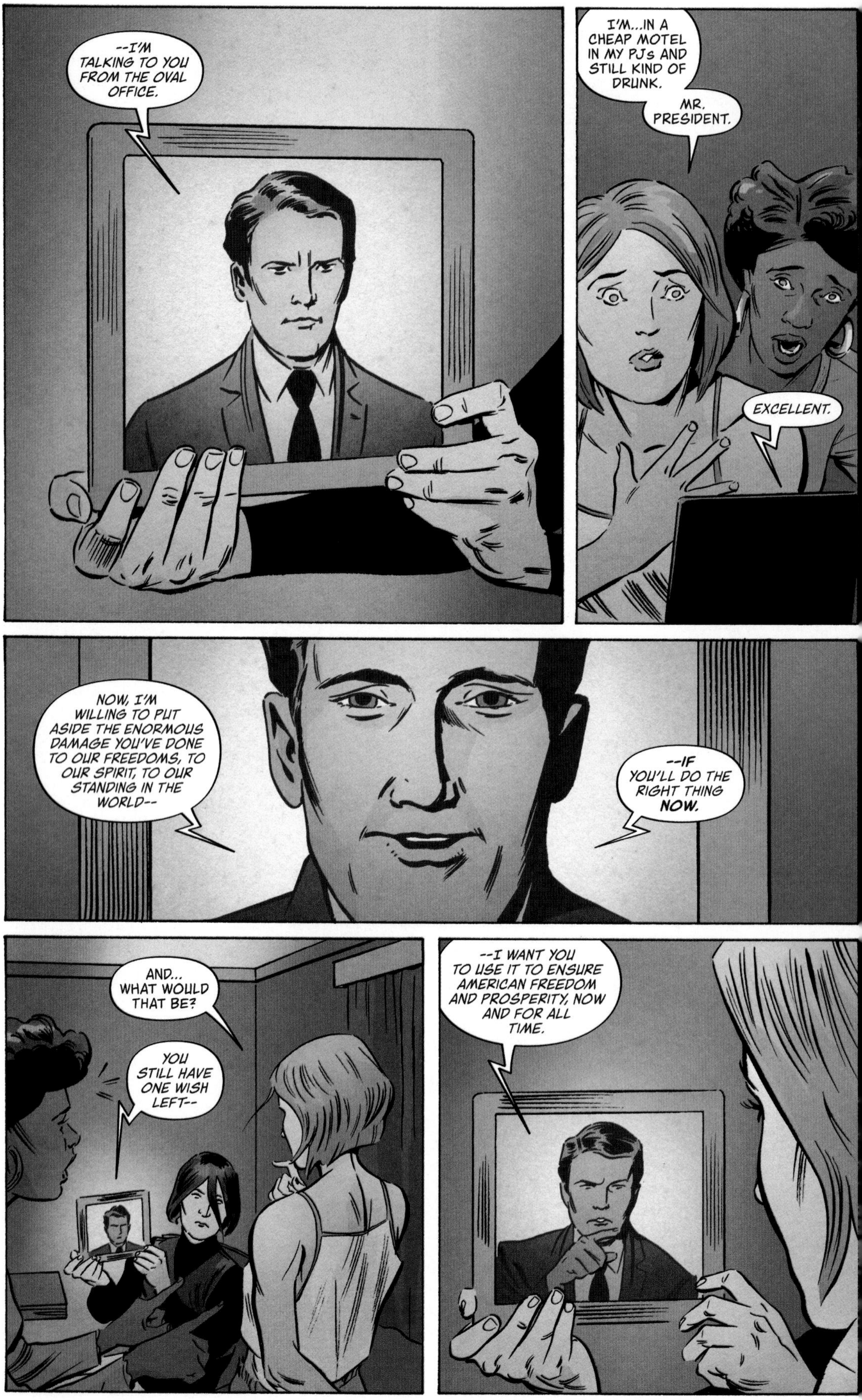
--I'M TALKING TO YOU FROM THE OVAL OFFICE.
I'M...IN A CHEAP MOTEL IN MY PJs AND STILL KIND OF DRUNK.
MR. PRESIDENT.
EXCELLENT.
NOW, I'M WILLING TO PUT ASIDE THE ENORMOUS DAMAGE YOU'VE DONE TO OUR FREEDOMS, TO OUR SPIRIT, TO OUR STANDING IN THE WORLD--
--IF YOU'LL DO THE RIGHT THING **NOW.**
AND... WHAT WOULD THAT BE?
YOU STILL HAVE ONE WISH LEFT--
--I WANT YOU TO USE IT TO ENSURE AMERICAN FREEDOM AND PROSPERITY, NOW AND FOR ALL TIME.

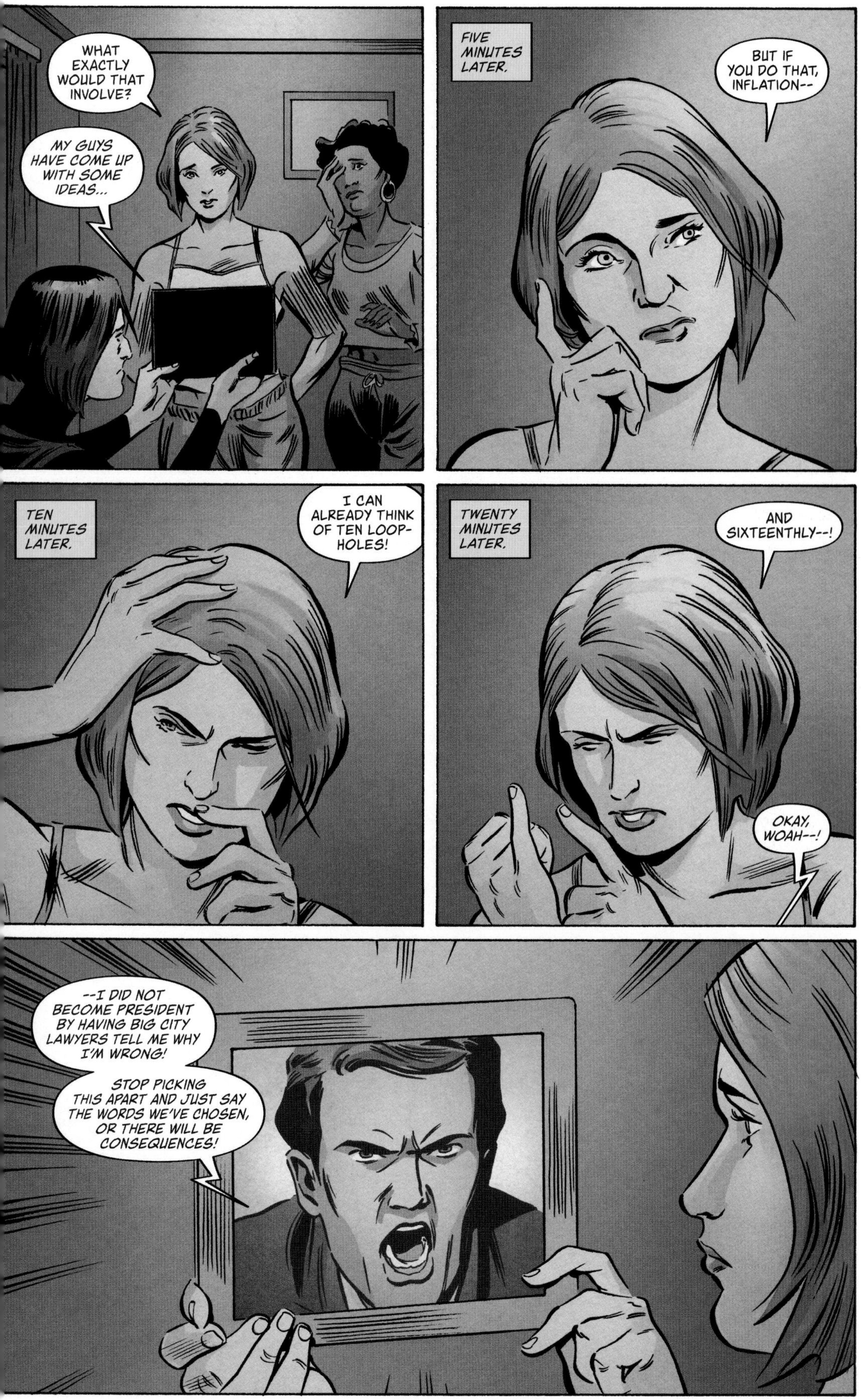
WHAT EXACTLY WOULD THAT INVOLVE?
MY GUYS HAVE COME UP WITH SOME IDEAS...
FIVE MINUTES LATER.
BUT IF YOU DO THAT, INFLATION--
TEN MINUTES LATER.
I CAN ALREADY THINK OF TEN LOOP-HOLES!
TWENTY MINUTES LATER.
AND SIXTEENTHLY--!
OKAY, WOAH--!
--I DID NOT BECOME PRESIDENT BY HAVING BIG CITY LAWYERS TELL ME WHY I'M WRONG!
STOP PICKING THIS APART AND JUST SAY THE WORDS WE'VE CHOSEN, OR THERE WILL BE CONSEQUENCES!

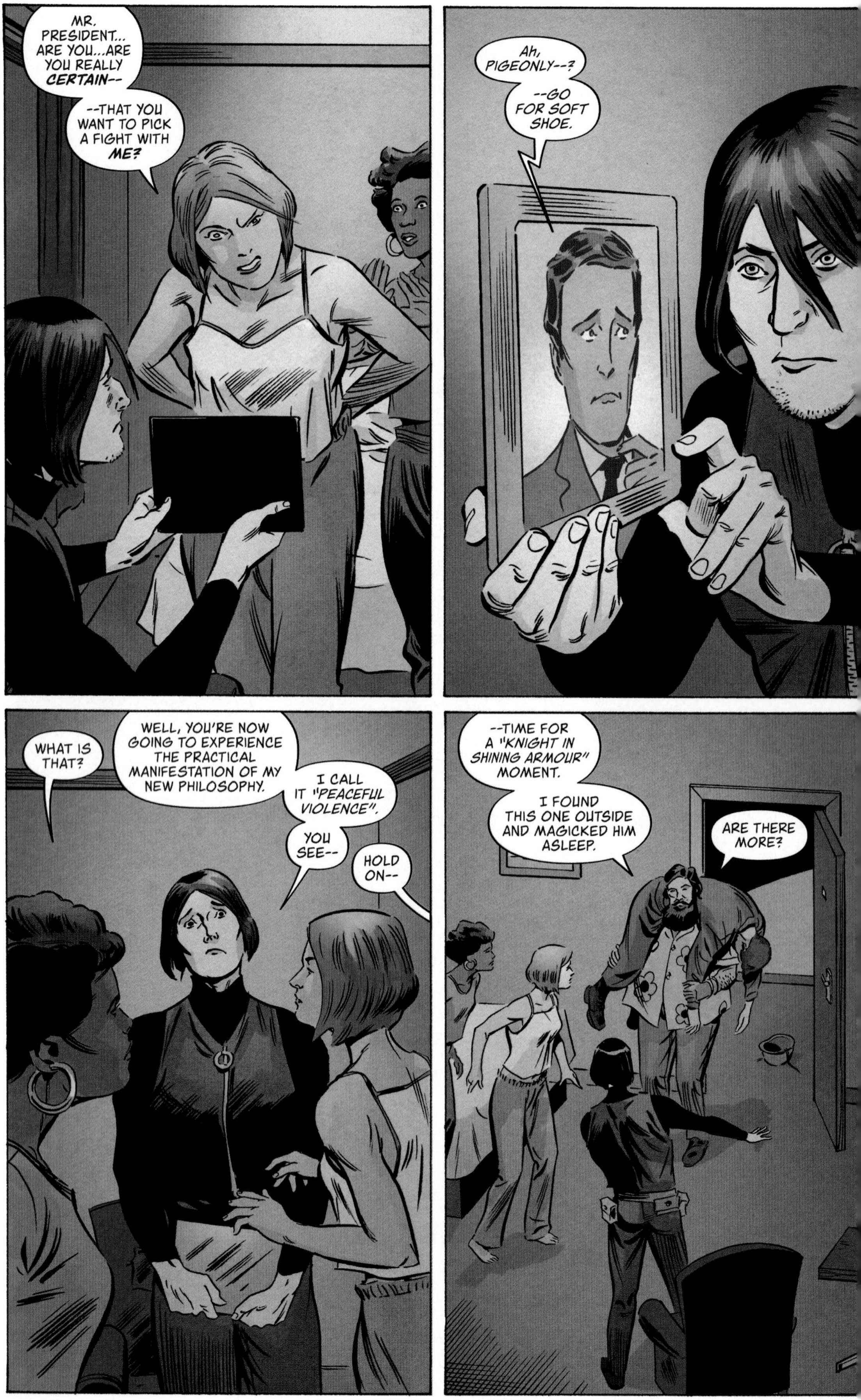
MR. PRESIDENT... ARE YOU...ARE YOU REALLY CERTAIN--
--THAT YOU WANT TO PICK A FIGHT WITH ME?
Ah, PIGEONLY--?
--GO FOR SOFT SHOE.
WHAT IS THAT?
WELL, YOU'RE NOW GOING TO EXPERIENCE THE PRACTICAL MANIFESTATION OF MY NEW PHILOSOPHY.
I CALL IT "PEACEFUL VIOLENCE".
YOU SEE--
HOLD ON--
--TIME FOR A "KNIGHT IN SHINING ARMOUR" MOMENT.
I FOUND THIS ONE OUTSIDE AND MAGICKED HIM ASLEEP.
ARE THERE MORE?

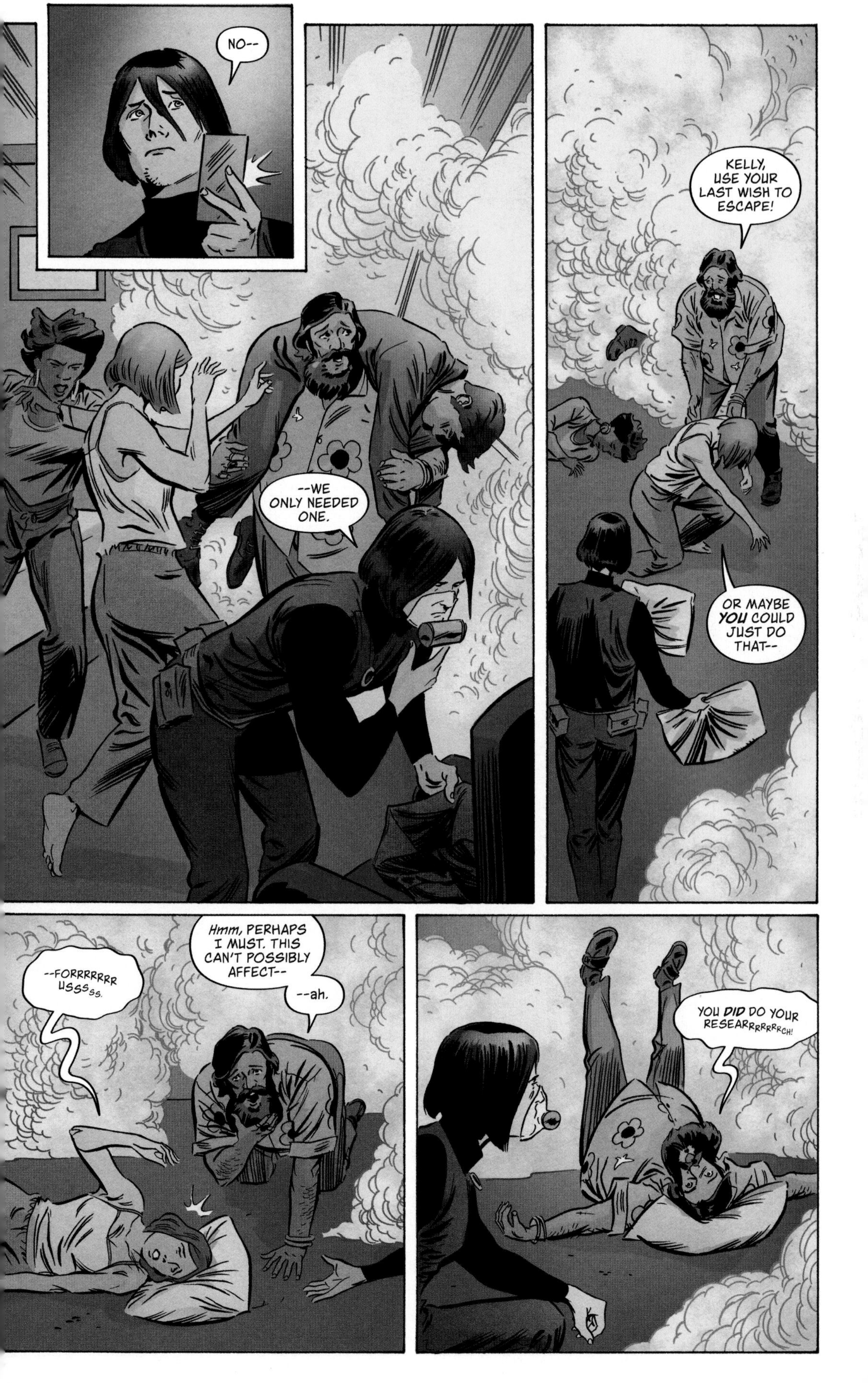
NO--
--WE ONLY NEEDED ONE.
KELLY, USE YOUR LAST WISH TO ESCAPE!
OR MAYBE YOU COULD JUST DO THAT--
Hmm, PERHAPS I MUST. THIS CAN'T POSSIBLY AFFECT--
--ah.
--FORRRRRRR USSSSS.
YOU DID DO YOUR RESEARRRRRRCH!

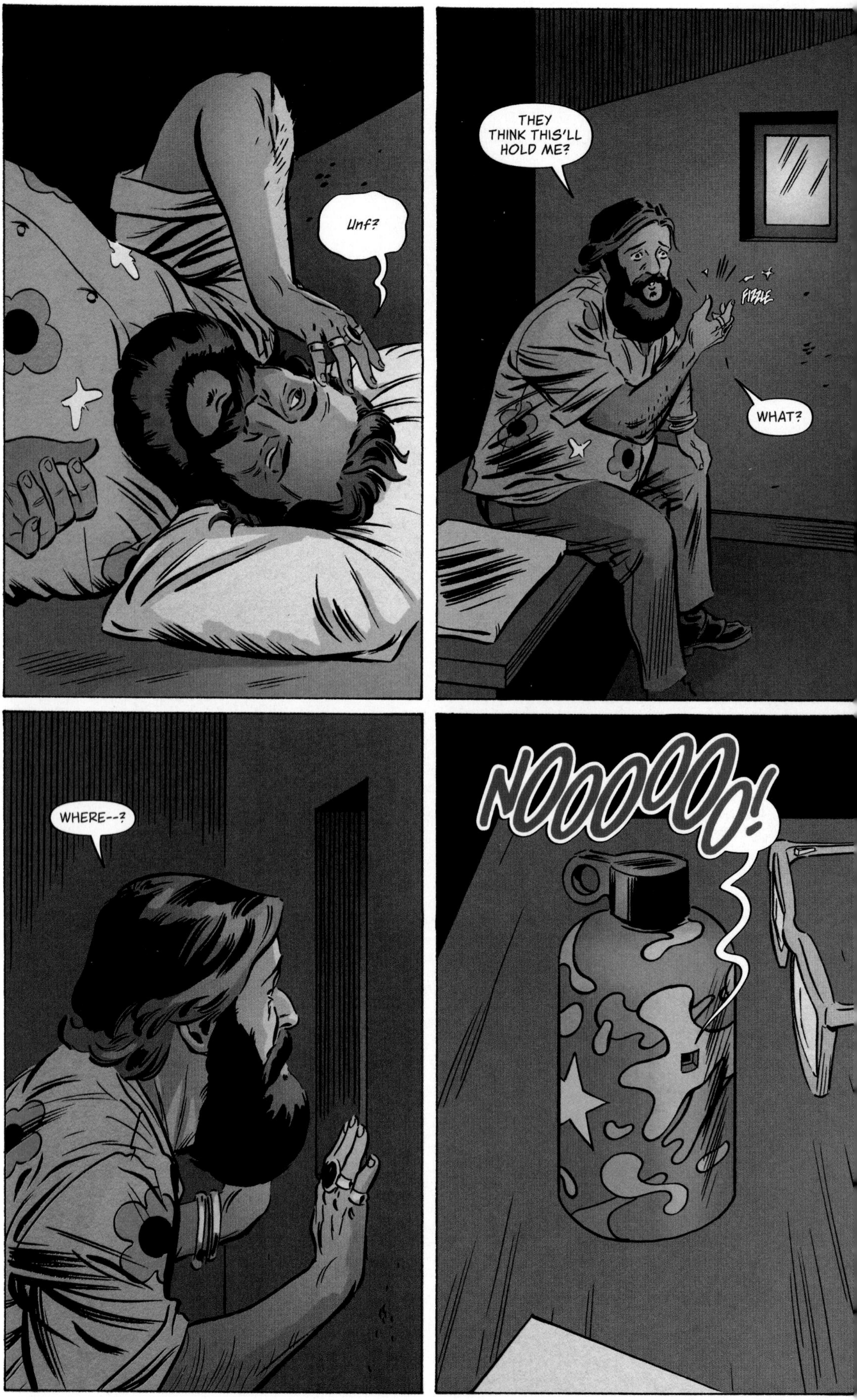
Unf?
THEY THINK THIS'LL HOLD ME?
FIZZLE
WHAT?
WHERE--?
NOOOOOO!

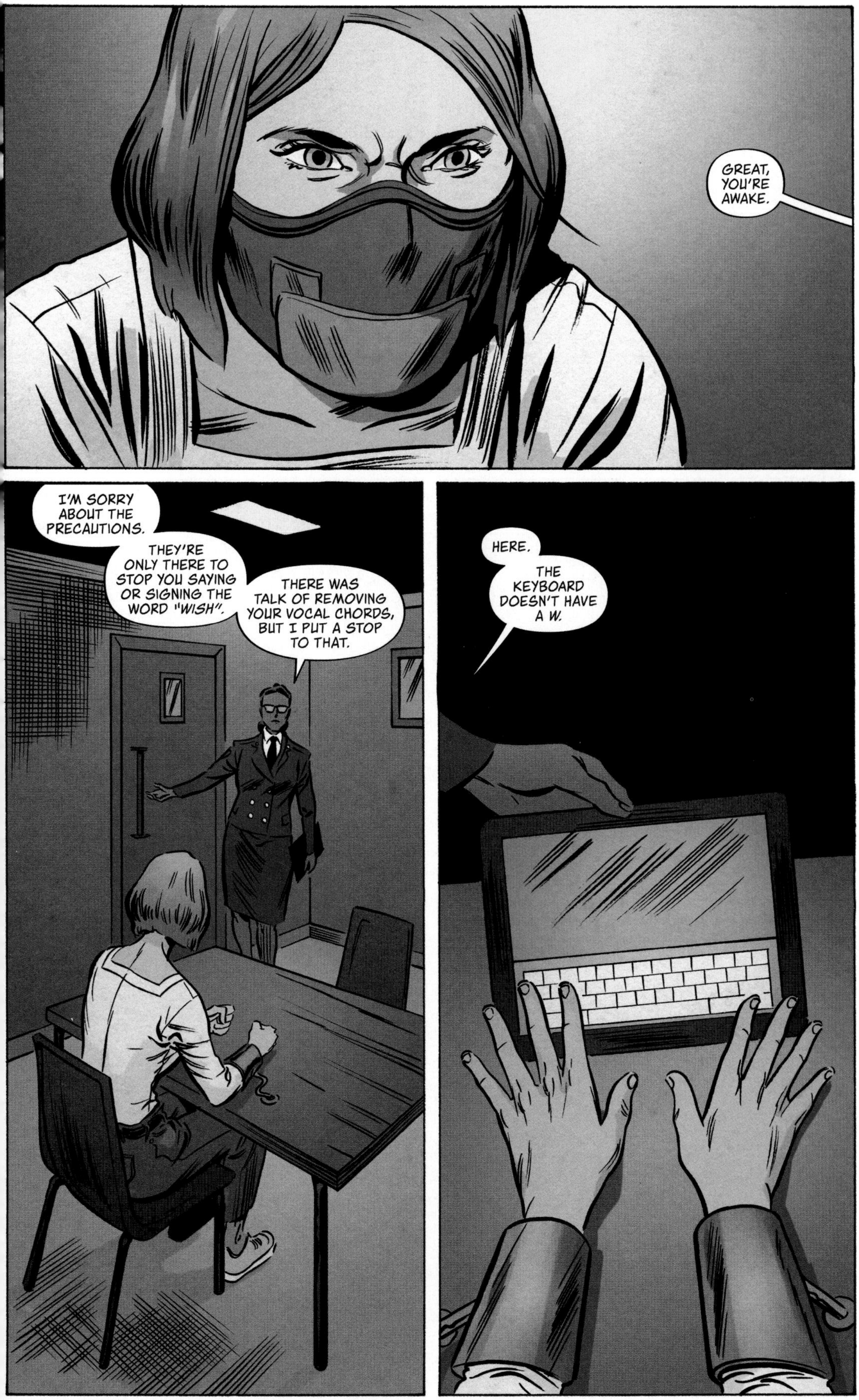
GREAT, YOU'RE AWAKE.
I'M SORRY ABOUT THE PRECAUTIONS.
THEY'RE ONLY THERE TO STOP YOU SAYING OR SIGNING THE WORD "WISH".
THERE WAS TALK OF REMOVING YOUR VOCAL CHORDS, BUT I PUT A STOP TO THAT.
HERE.
THE KEYBOARD DOESN'T HAVE A W.

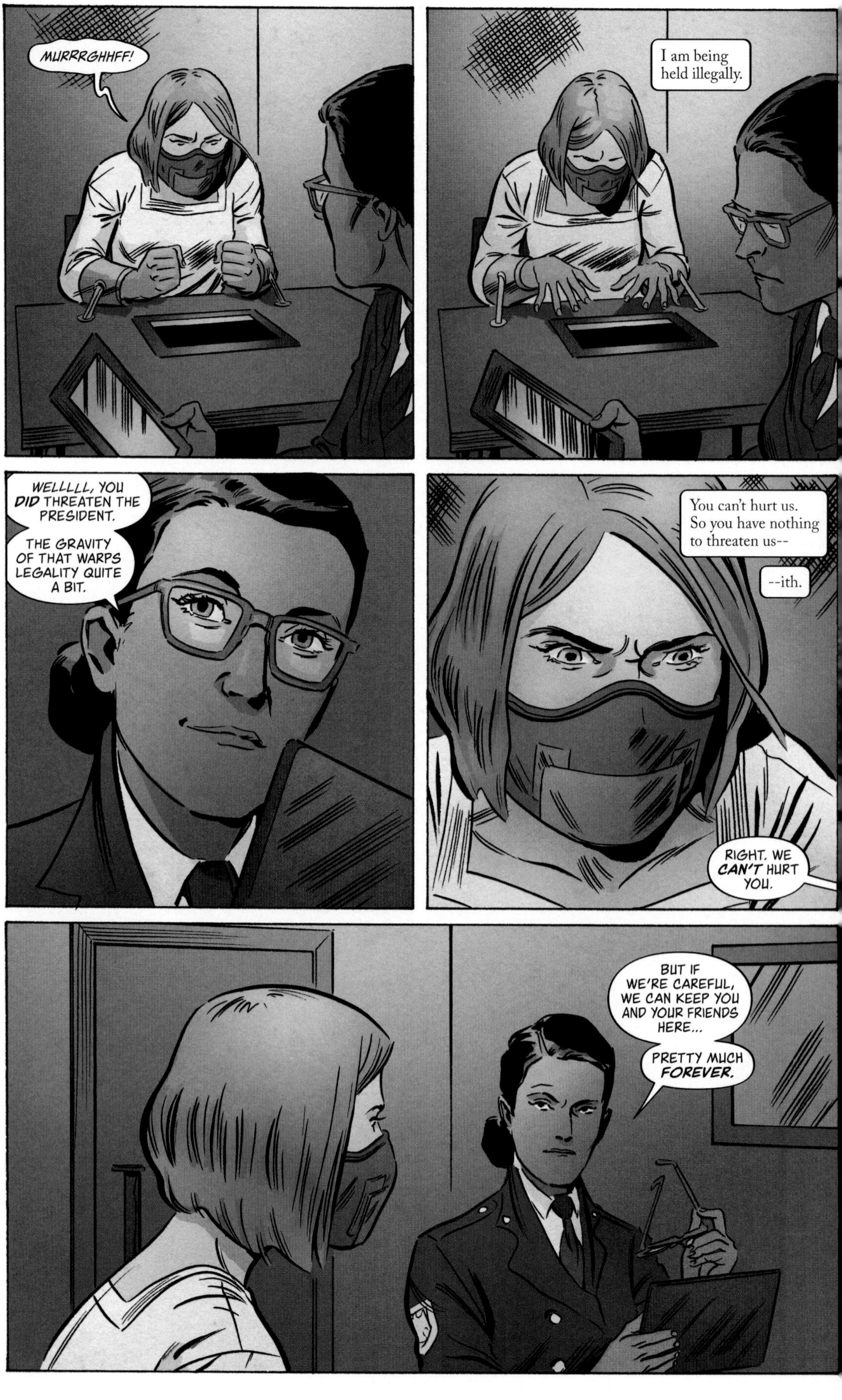
MURRRGHHFF!
I am being held illegally.
WELLLLL, YOU **DID** THREATEN THE PRESIDENT.
THE GRAVITY OF THAT WARPS LEGALITY QUITE A BIT.
You can't hurt us. So you have nothing to threaten us--
--ith.
RIGHT. WE **CAN'T** HURT YOU.
BUT IF WE'RE CAREFUL, WE CAN KEEP YOU AND YOUR FRIENDS HERE...
PRETTY MUCH **FOREVER.**

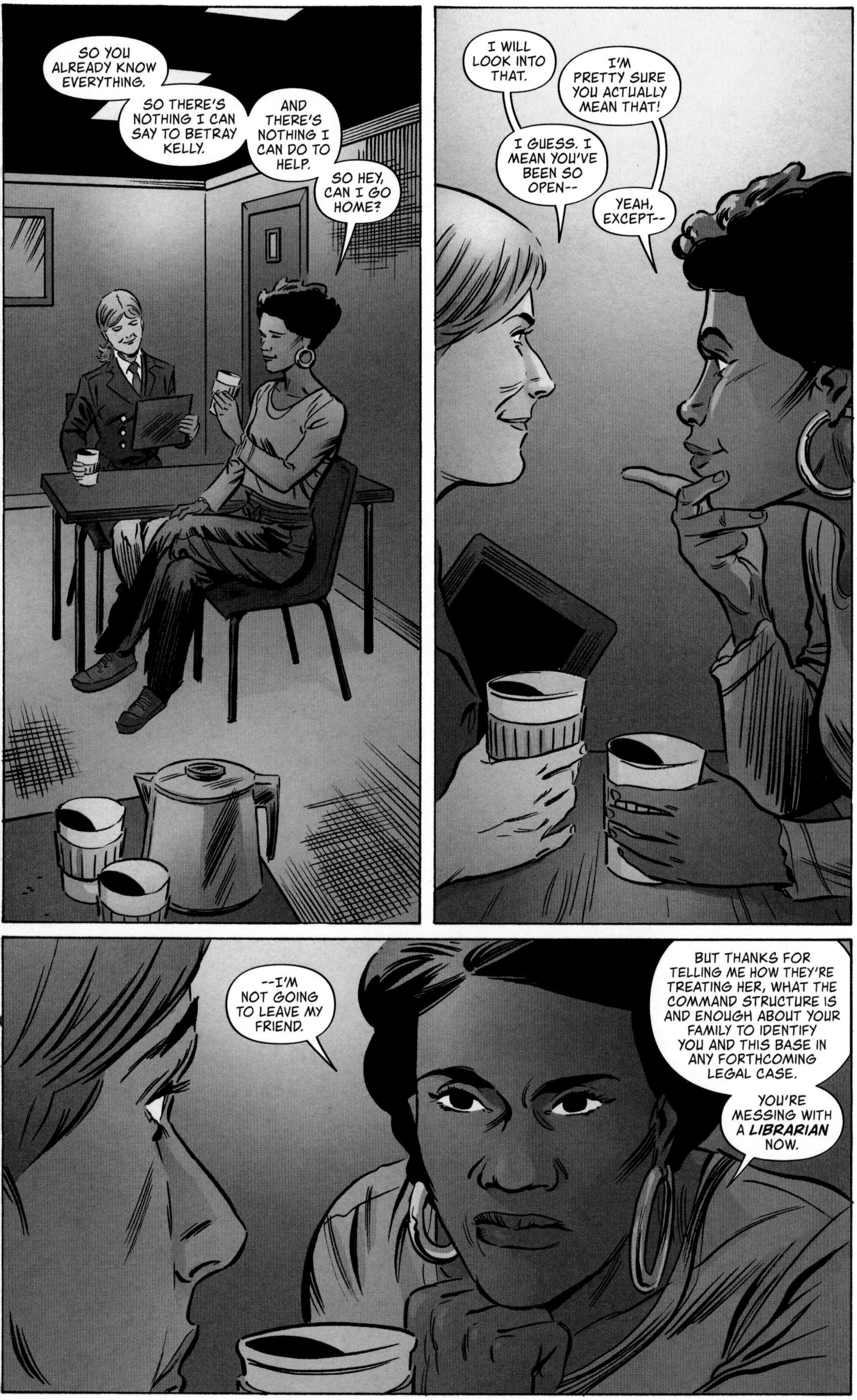
SO YOU ALREADY KNOW EVERYTHING.
SO THERE'S NOTHING I CAN SAY TO BETRAY KELLY.
AND THERE'S NOTHING I CAN DO TO HELP.
SO HEY, CAN I GO HOME?
I WILL LOOK INTO THAT.
I'M PRETTY SURE YOU ACTUALLY MEAN THAT!
I GUESS. I MEAN YOU'VE BEEN SO OPEN--
YEAH, EXCEPT--
--I'M NOT GOING TO LEAVE MY FRIEND.
BUT THANKS FOR TELLING ME HOW THEY'RE TREATING HER, WHAT THE COMMAND STRUCTURE IS AND ENOUGH ABOUT YOUR FAMILY TO IDENTIFY YOU AND THIS BASE IN ANY FORTHCOMING LEGAL CASE.
YOU'RE MESSING WITH A ***LIBRARIAN*** NOW.

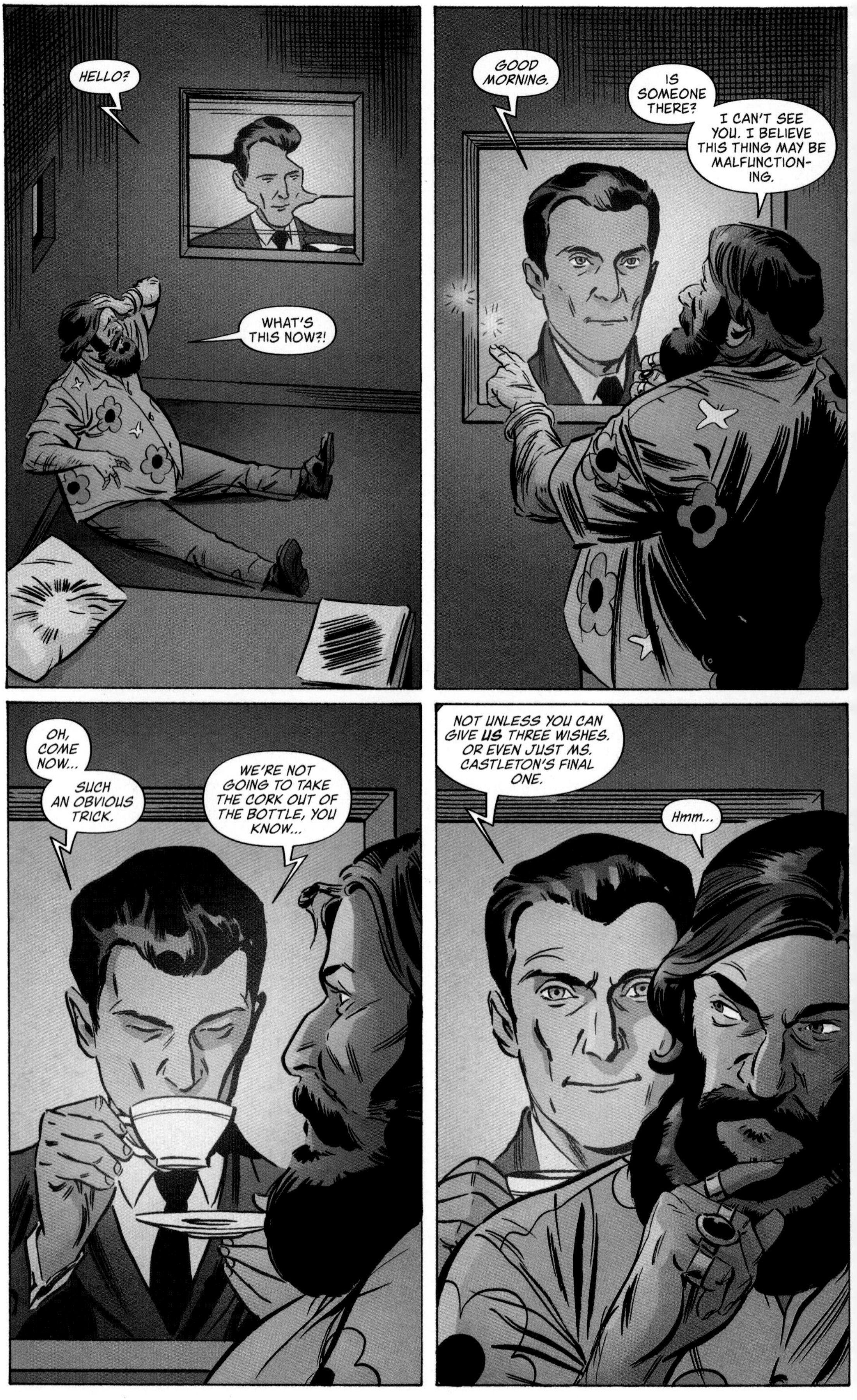
HELLO?
WHAT'S THIS NOW?!
GOOD MORNING.
IS SOMEONE THERE?
I CAN'T SEE YOU. I BELIEVE THIS THING MAY BE MALFUNCTION-ING.
OH, COME NOW...
SUCH AN OBVIOUS TRICK.
WE'RE NOT GOING TO TAKE THE CORK OUT OF THE BOTTLE, YOU KNOW...
NOT UNLESS YOU CAN GIVE US THREE WISHES. OR EVEN JUST MS. CASTLETON'S FINAL ONE.
Hmm...

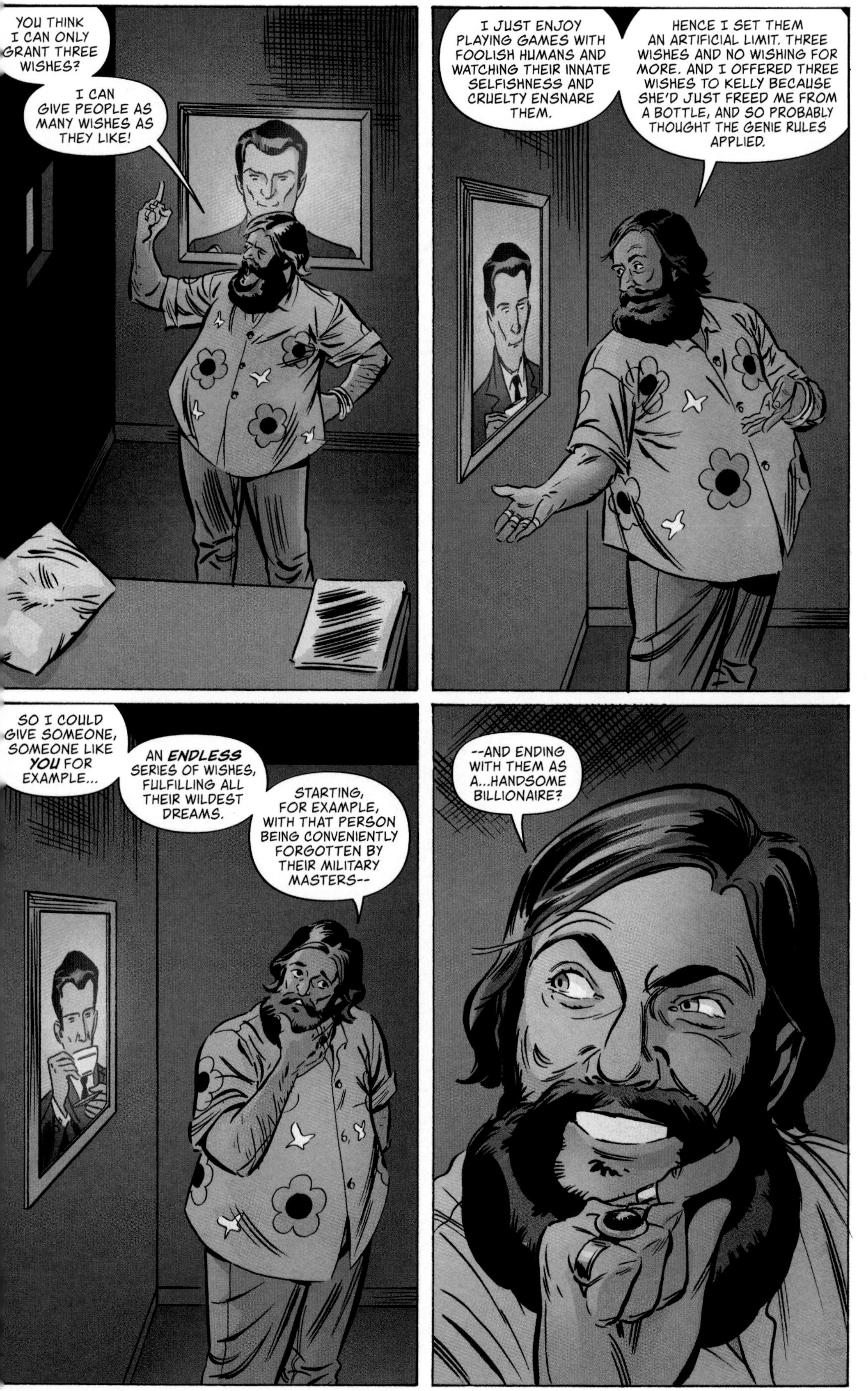
YOU THINK I CAN ONLY GRANT THREE WISHES?
I CAN GIVE PEOPLE AS MANY WISHES AS THEY LIKE!
I JUST ENJOY PLAYING GAMES WITH FOOLISH HUMANS AND WATCHING THEIR INNATE SELFISHNESS AND CRUELTY ENSNARE THEM.
HENCE I SET THEM AN ARTIFICIAL LIMIT. THREE WISHES AND NO WISHING FOR MORE. AND I OFFERED THREE WISHES TO KELLY BECAUSE SHE'D JUST FREED ME FROM A BOTTLE, AND SO PROBABLY THOUGHT THE GENIE RULES APPLIED.
SO I COULD GIVE SOMEONE, SOMEONE LIKE ***YOU*** FOR EXAMPLE...
AN ***ENDLESS*** SERIES OF WISHES, FULFILLING ALL THEIR WILDEST DREAMS.
STARTING, FOR EXAMPLE, WITH THAT PERSON BEING CONVENIENTLY FORGOTTEN BY THEIR MILITARY MASTERS--
--AND ENDING WITH THEM AS A...HANDSOME BILLIONAIRE?

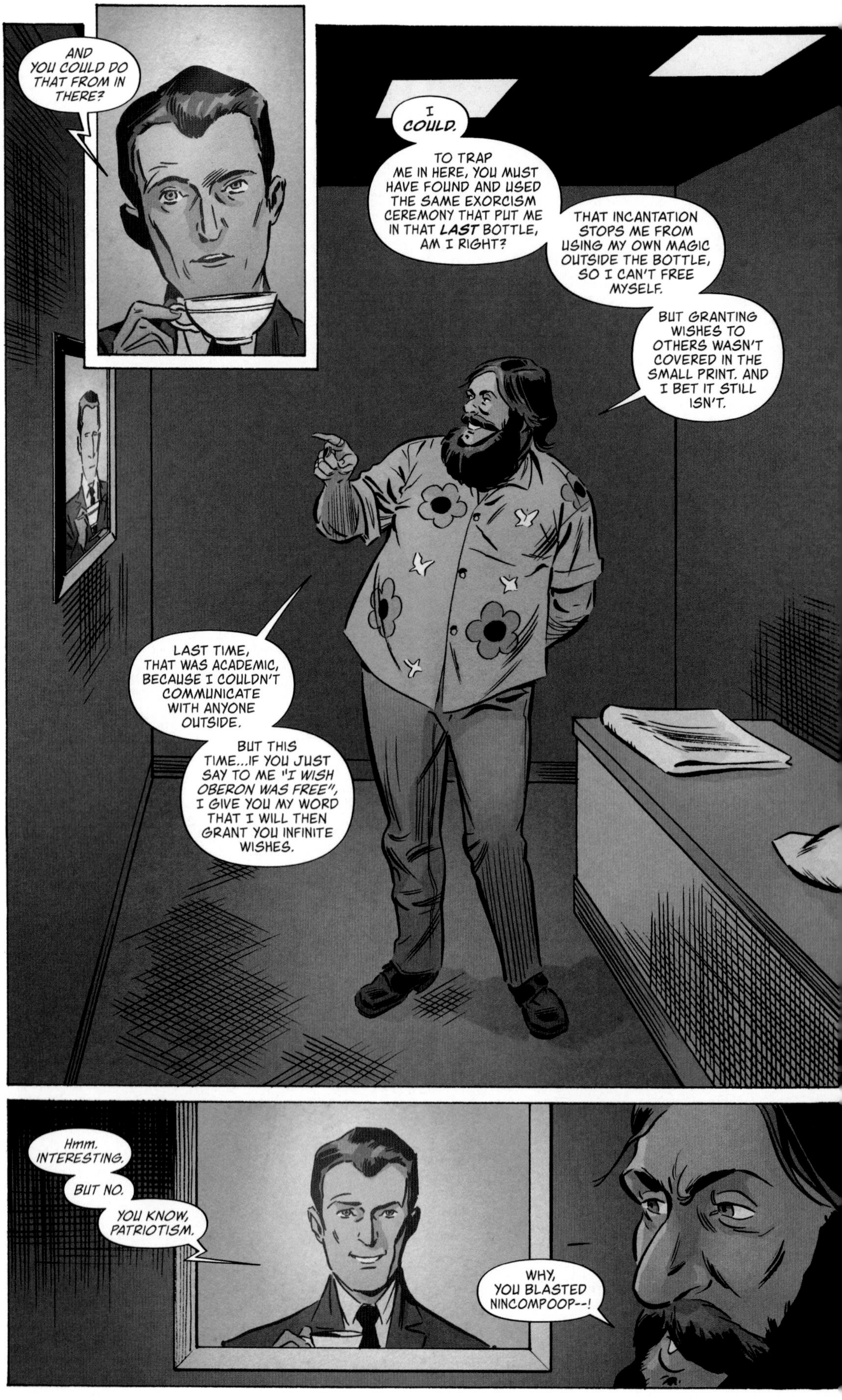
AND YOU COULD DO THAT FROM IN THERE?
I COULD.
TO TRAP ME IN HERE, YOU MUST HAVE FOUND AND USED THE SAME EXORCISM CEREMONY THAT PUT ME IN THAT LAST BOTTLE, AM I RIGHT?
THAT INCANTATION STOPS ME FROM USING MY OWN MAGIC OUTSIDE THE BOTTLE, SO I CAN'T FREE MYSELF.
BUT GRANTING WISHES TO OTHERS WASN'T COVERED IN THE SMALL PRINT. AND I BET IT STILL ISN'T.
LAST TIME, THAT WAS ACADEMIC, BECAUSE I COULDN'T COMMUNICATE WITH ANYONE OUTSIDE.
BUT THIS TIME...IF YOU JUST SAY TO ME "I WISH OBERON WAS FREE", I GIVE YOU MY WORD THAT I WILL THEN GRANT YOU INFINITE WISHES.
Hmm. INTERESTING.
BUT NO.
YOU KNOW, PATRIOTISM.
WHY, YOU BLASTED NINCOMPOOP--!

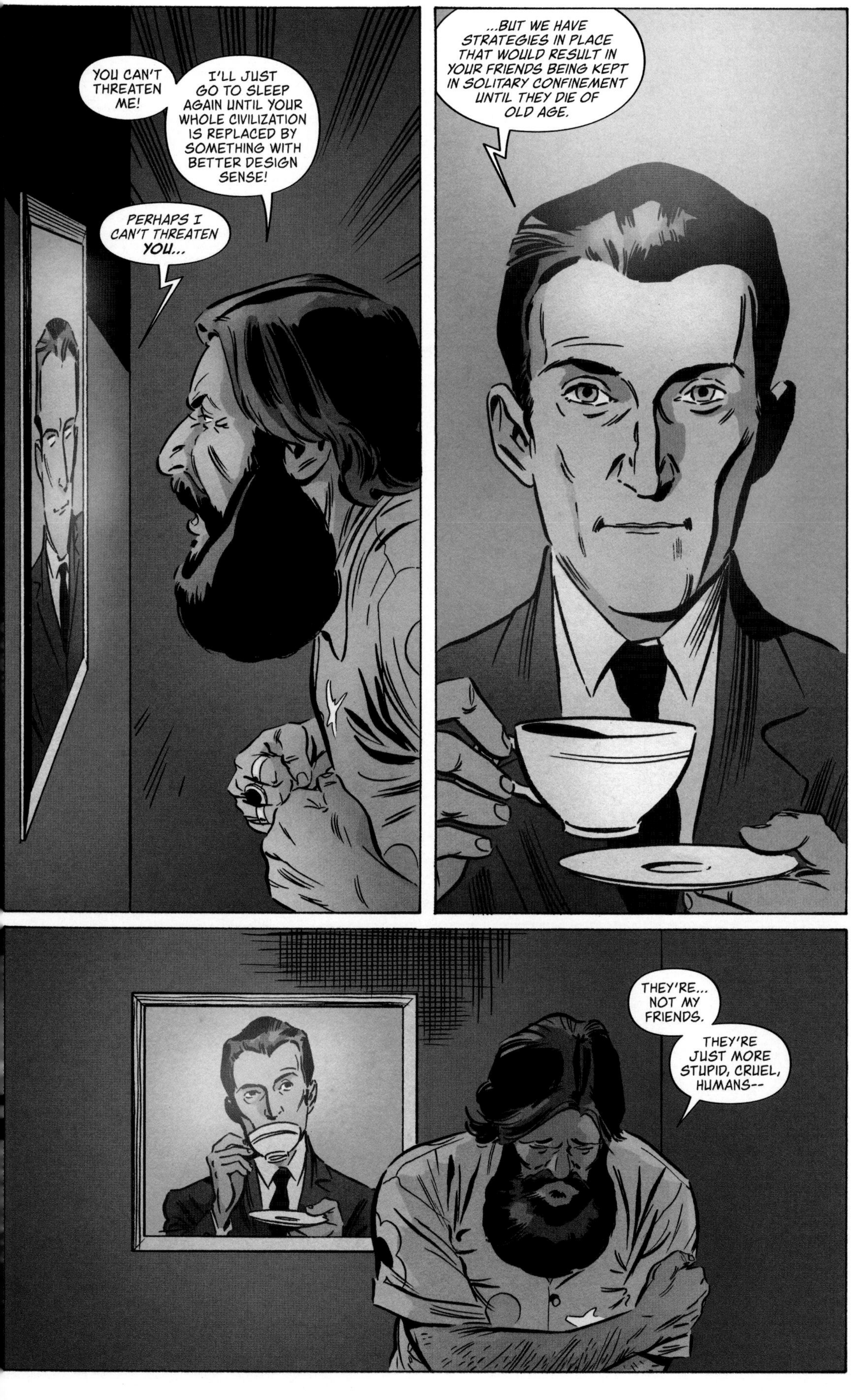
YOU CAN'T THREATEN ME!
I'LL JUST GO TO SLEEP AGAIN UNTIL YOUR WHOLE CIVILIZATION IS REPLACED BY SOMETHING WITH BETTER DESIGN SENSE!
PERHAPS I CAN'T THREATEN YOU...
...BUT WE HAVE STRATEGIES IN PLACE THAT WOULD RESULT IN YOUR FRIENDS BEING KEPT IN SOLITARY CONFINEMENT UNTIL THEY DIE OF OLD AGE.
THEY'RE... NOT MY FRIENDS.
THEY'RE JUST MORE STUPID, CRUEL, HUMANS--

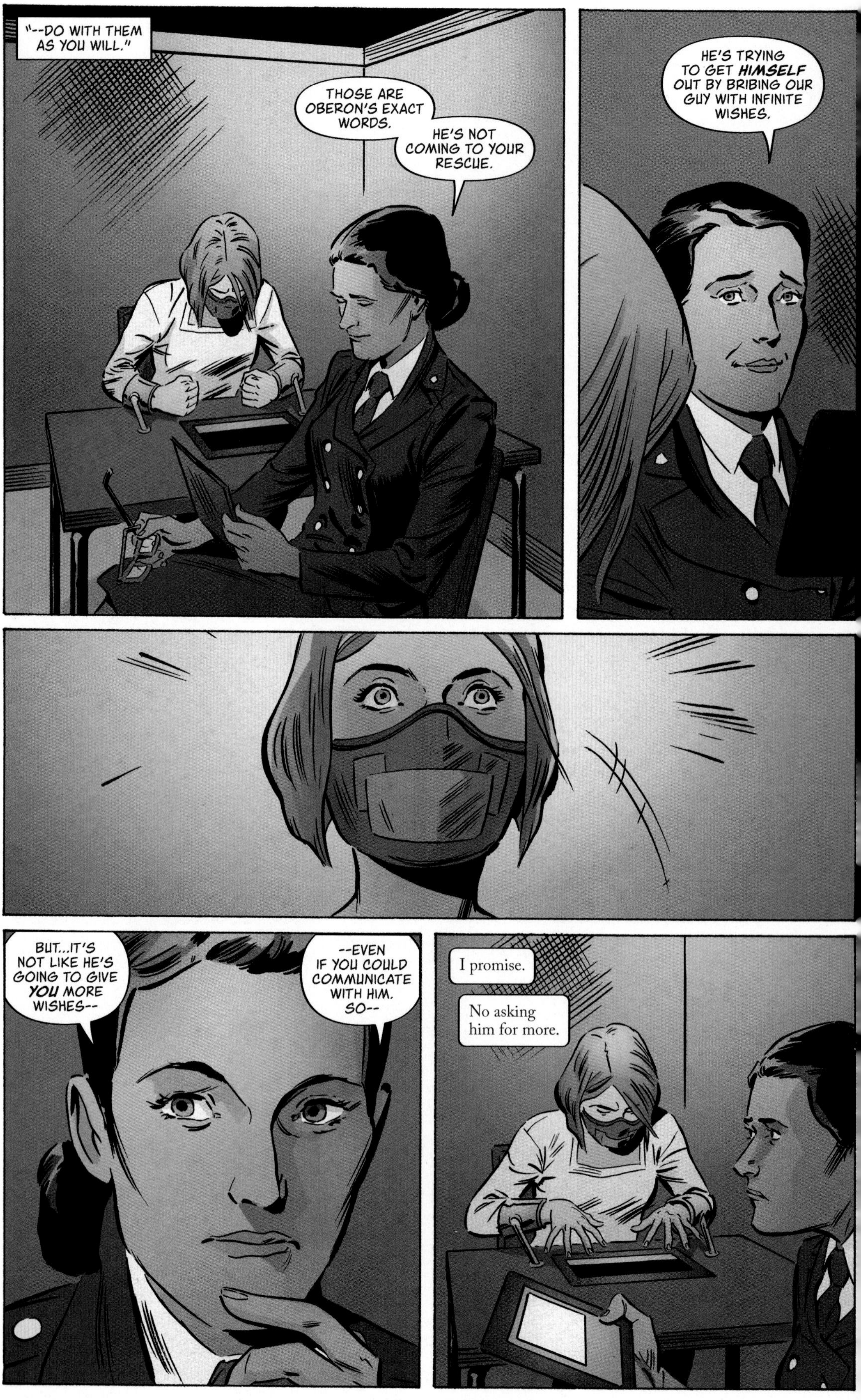
"--DO WITH THEM AS YOU WILL."
THOSE ARE OBERON'S EXACT WORDS.
HE'S NOT COMING TO YOUR RESCUE.
HE'S TRYING TO GET HIMSELF OUT BY BRIBING OUR GUY WITH INFINITE WISHES.
BUT...IT'S NOT LIKE HE'S GOING TO GIVE YOU MORE WISHES--
--EVEN IF YOU COULD COMMUNICATE WITH HIM. SO--
I promise.
No asking him for more.

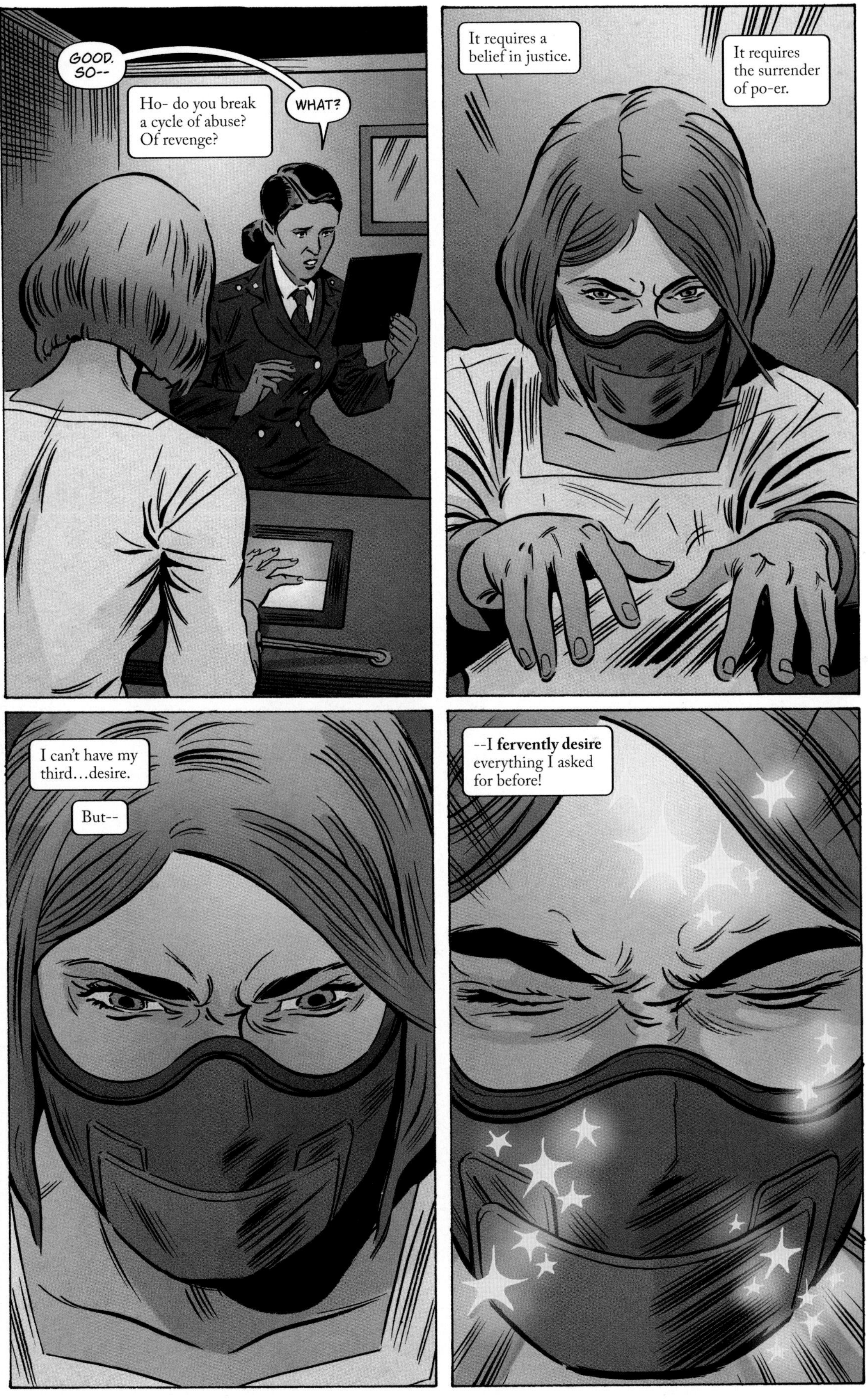
GOOD. SO--
Ho- do you break a cycle of abuse? Of revenge?
WHAT?
It requires a belief in justice.
It requires the surrender of po-er.
I can't have my third…desire.
But--
--I **fervently desire** everything I asked for before!

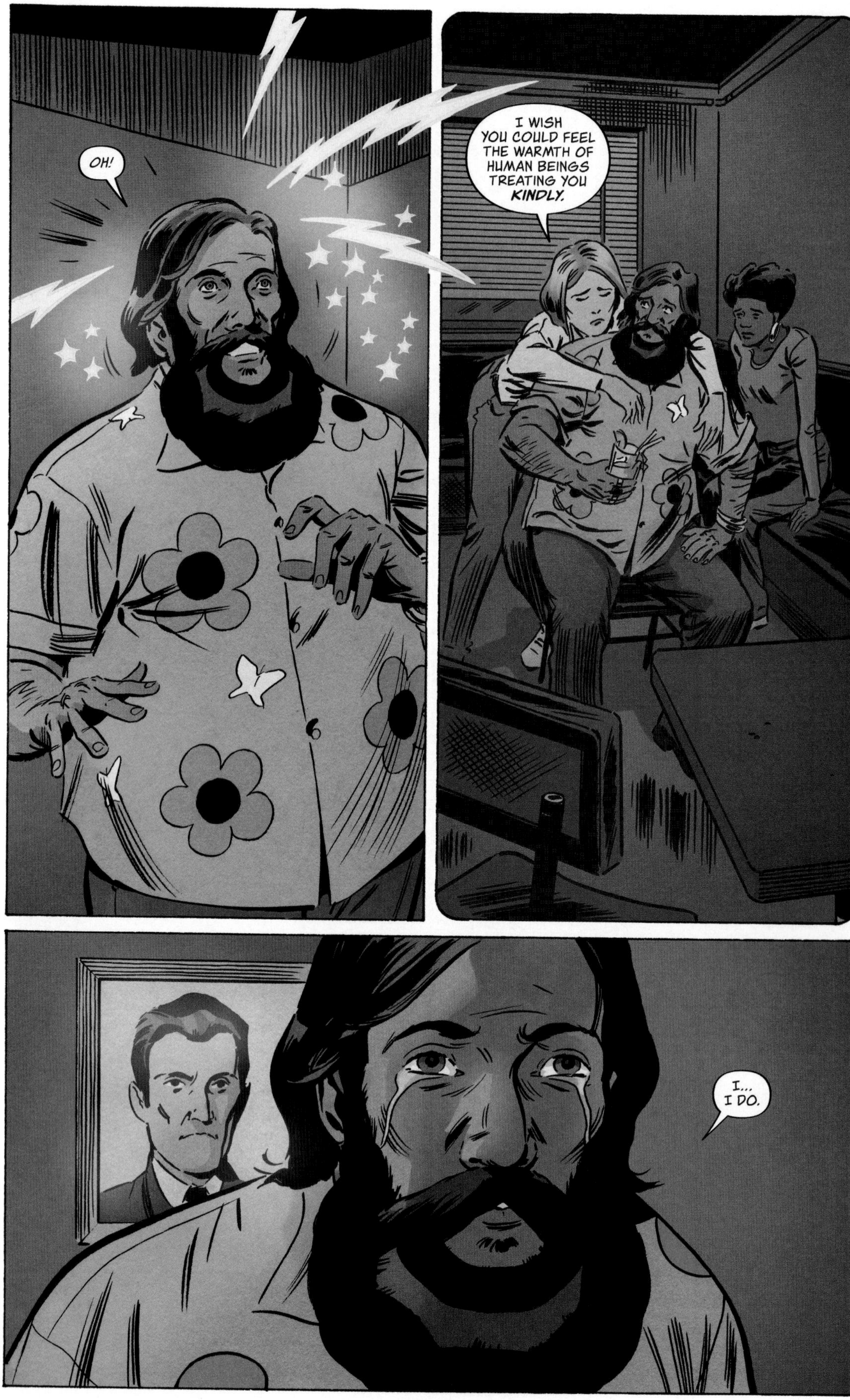
OH!
I WISH YOU COULD FEEL THE WARMTH OF HUMAN BEINGS TREATING YOU KINDLY.
I... I DO.

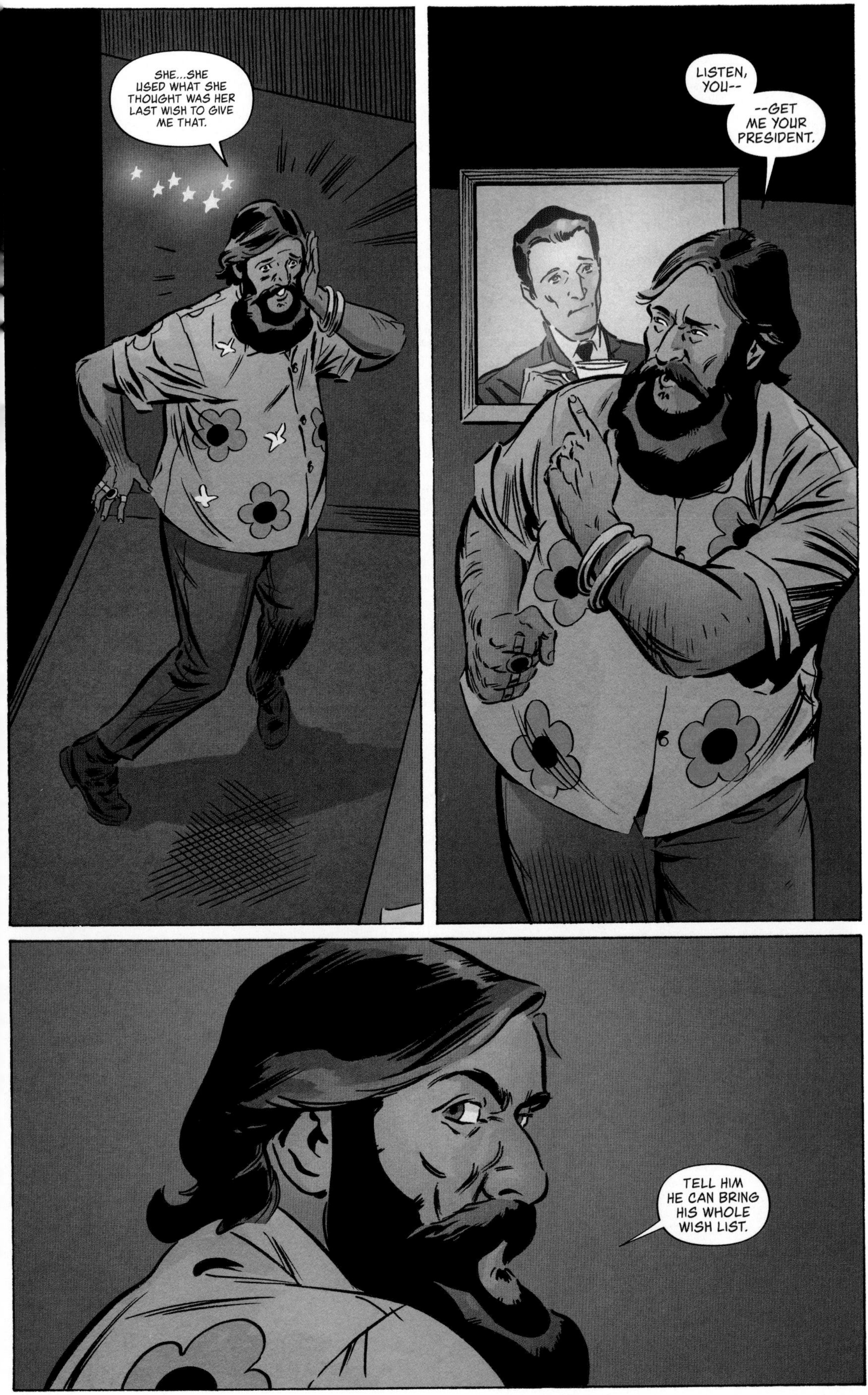
SHE...SHE USED WHAT SHE THOUGHT WAS HER LAST WISH TO GIVE ME THAT.
LISTEN, YOU--
--GET ME YOUR PRESIDENT.
TELL HIM HE CAN BRING HIS WHOLE WISH LIST.

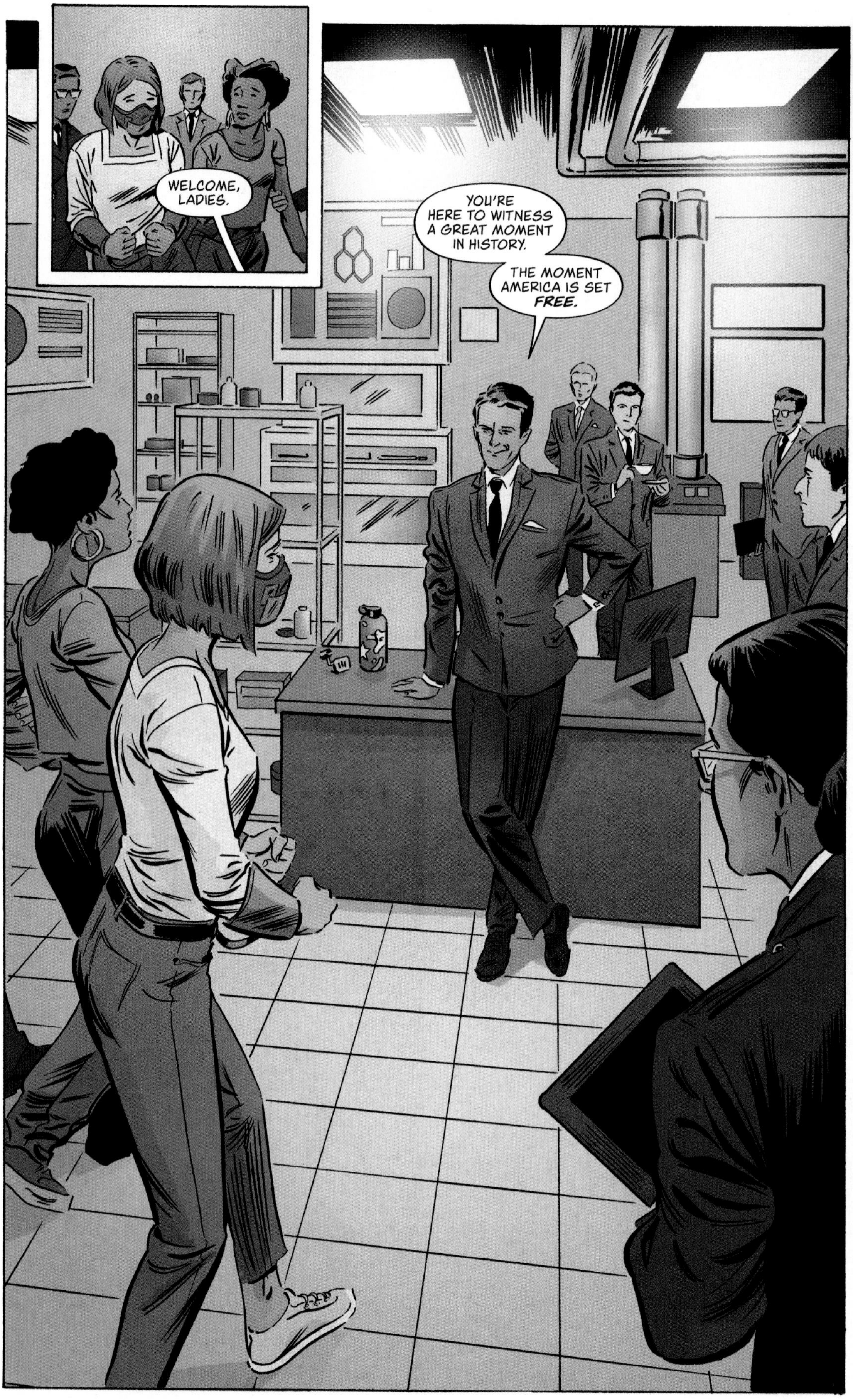
WELCOME, LADIES.
YOU'RE HERE TO WITNESS A GREAT MOMENT IN HISTORY.
THE MOMENT AMERICA IS SET *FREE.*

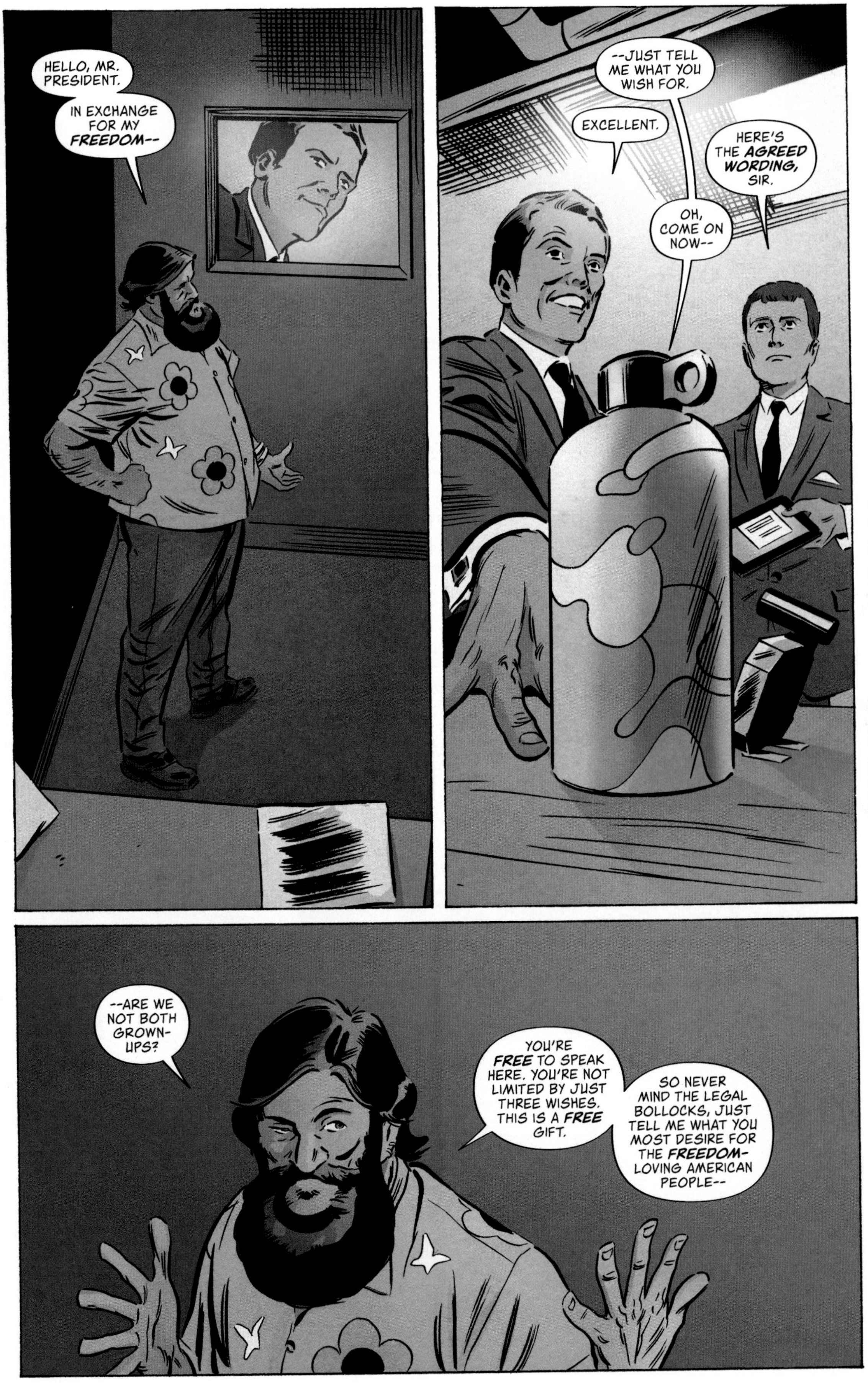
HELLO, MR. PRESIDENT.
IN EXCHANGE FOR MY *FREEDOM*--
--JUST TELL ME WHAT YOU WISH FOR.
EXCELLENT.
HERE'S THE *AGREED WORDING,* SIR.
OH, COME ON NOW--
--ARE WE NOT BOTH GROWN-UPS?
YOU'RE *FREE* TO SPEAK HERE. YOU'RE NOT LIMITED BY JUST THREE WISHES. THIS IS A *FREE* GIFT.
SO NEVER MIND THE LEGAL BOLLOCKS, JUST TELL ME WHAT YOU MOST DESIRE FOR THE *FREEDOM*-LOVING AMERICAN PEOPLE--

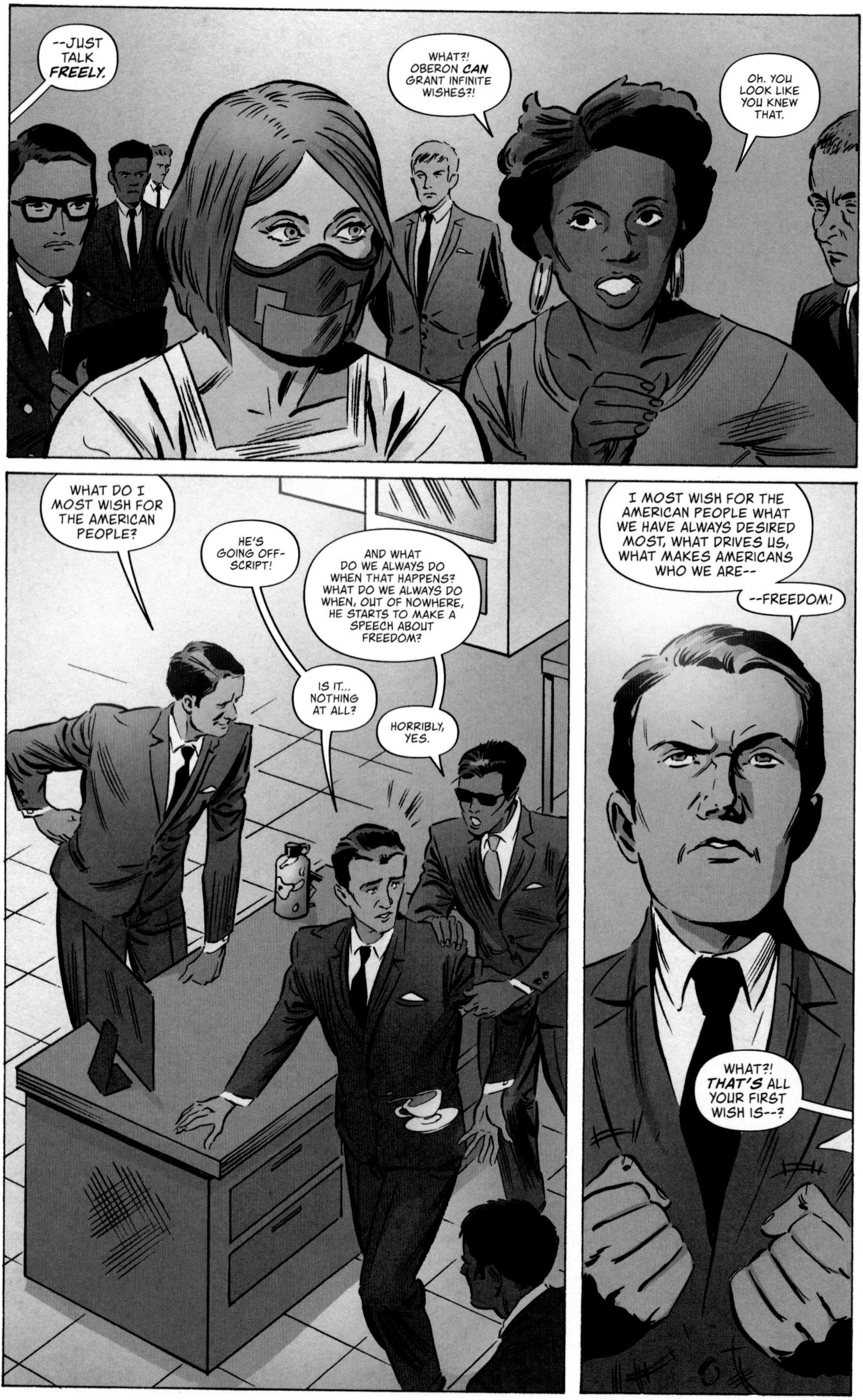
--JUST TALK *FREELY.*
WHAT?! OBERON *CAN* GRANT INFINITE WISHES?!
Oh. YOU LOOK LIKE YOU KNEW THAT.
WHAT DO I MOST WISH FOR THE AMERICAN PEOPLE?
HE'S GOING OFF-SCRIPT!
AND WHAT DO WE ALWAYS DO WHEN THAT HAPPENS? WHAT DO WE ALWAYS DO WHEN, OUT OF NOWHERE, HE STARTS TO MAKE A SPEECH ABOUT FREEDOM?
IS IT... NOTHING AT ALL?
HORRIBLY, YES.
I MOST WISH FOR THE AMERICAN PEOPLE WHAT WE HAVE ALWAYS DESIRED MOST, WHAT DRIVES US, WHAT MAKES AMERICANS WHO WE ARE--
--FREEDOM!
WHAT?! *THAT'S* ALL YOUR FIRST WISH IS--?

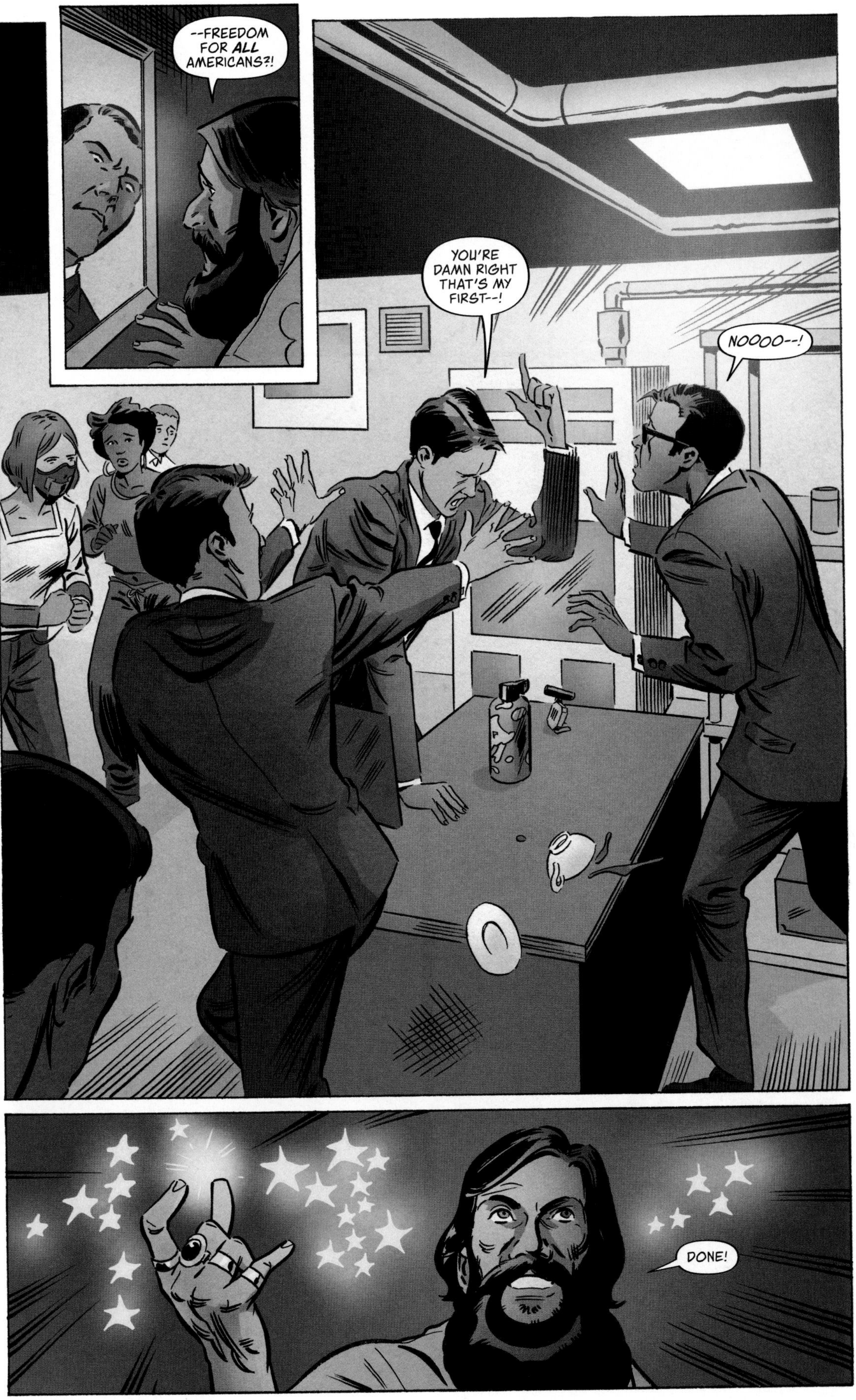
--FREEDOM FOR ALL AMERICANS?!
YOU'RE DAMN RIGHT THAT'S MY FIRST--!
NOOOO--!
DONE!

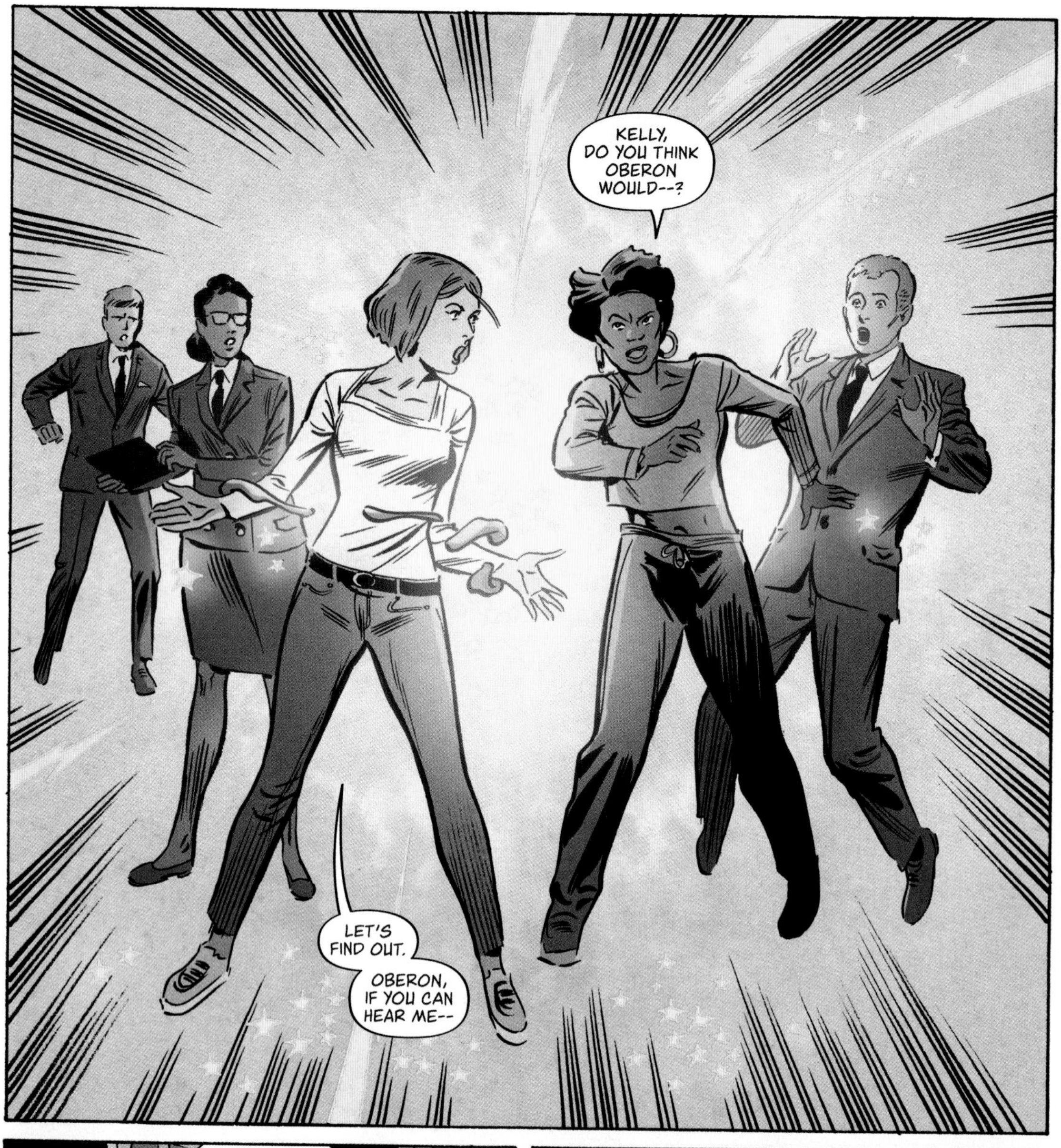
KELLY, DO YOU THINK OBERON WOULD--?
LET'S FIND OUT.
OBERON, IF YOU CAN HEAR ME--

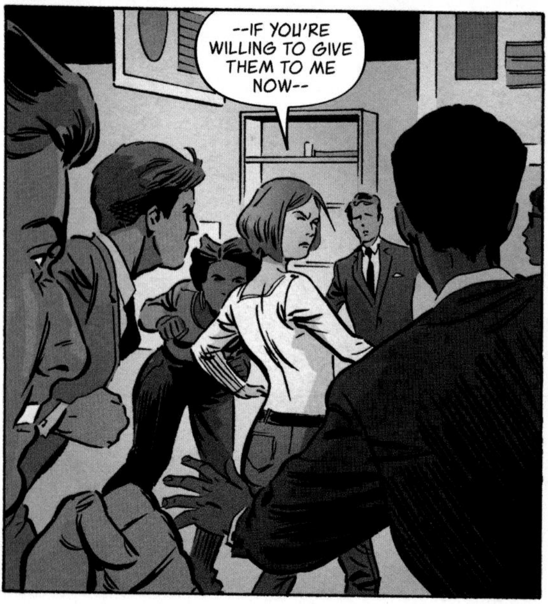
--IF YOU'RE WILLING TO GIVE THEM TO ME NOW--

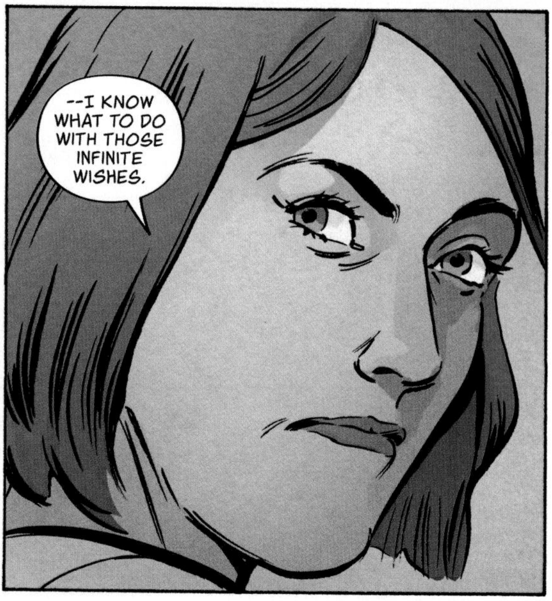
--I KNOW WHAT TO DO WITH THOSE INFINITE WISHES.

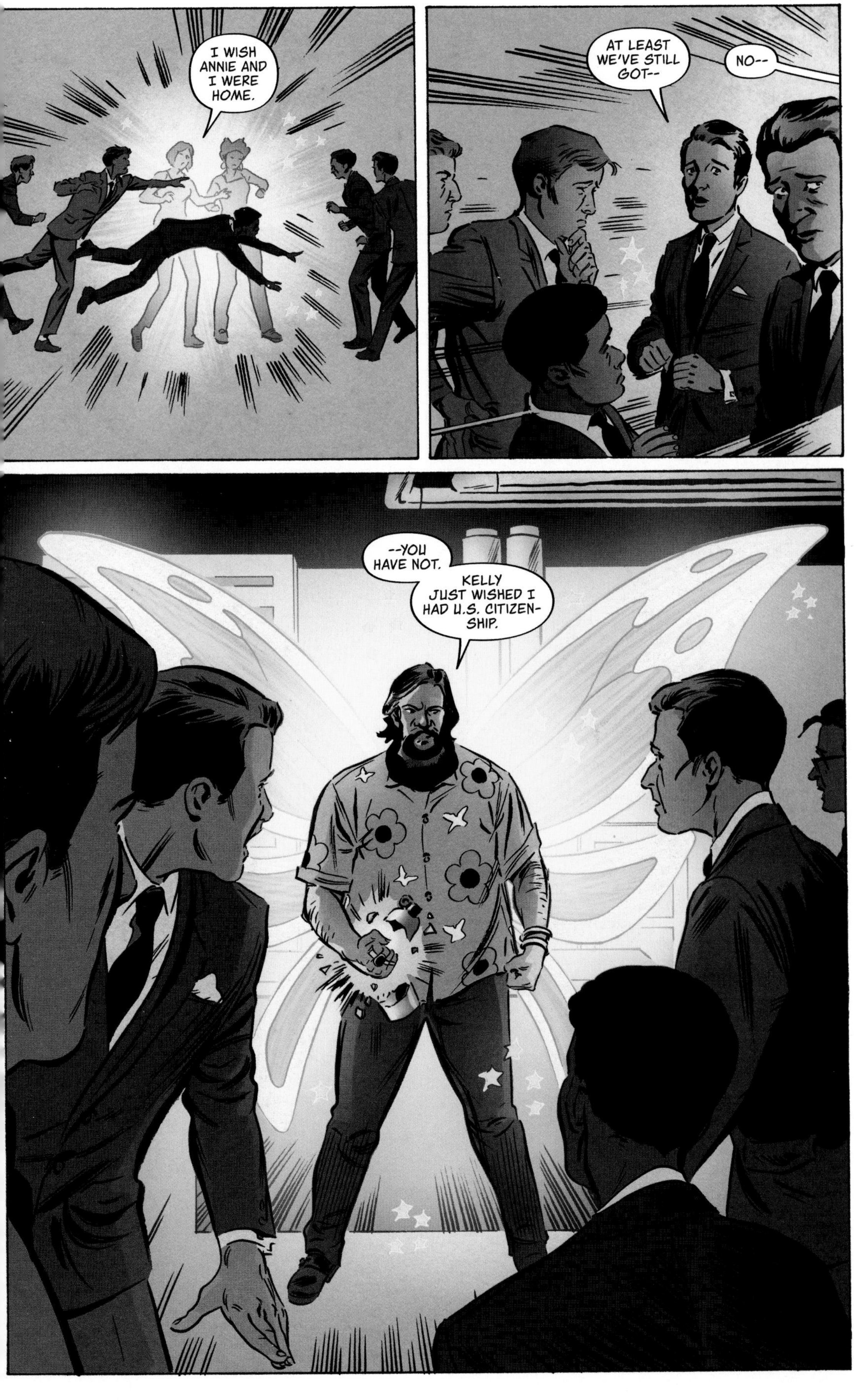
I WISH ANNIE AND I WERE HOME.
AT LEAST WE'VE STILL GOT--
NO--
--YOU HAVE NOT.
KELLY JUST WISHED I HAD U.S. CITIZEN-SHIP.

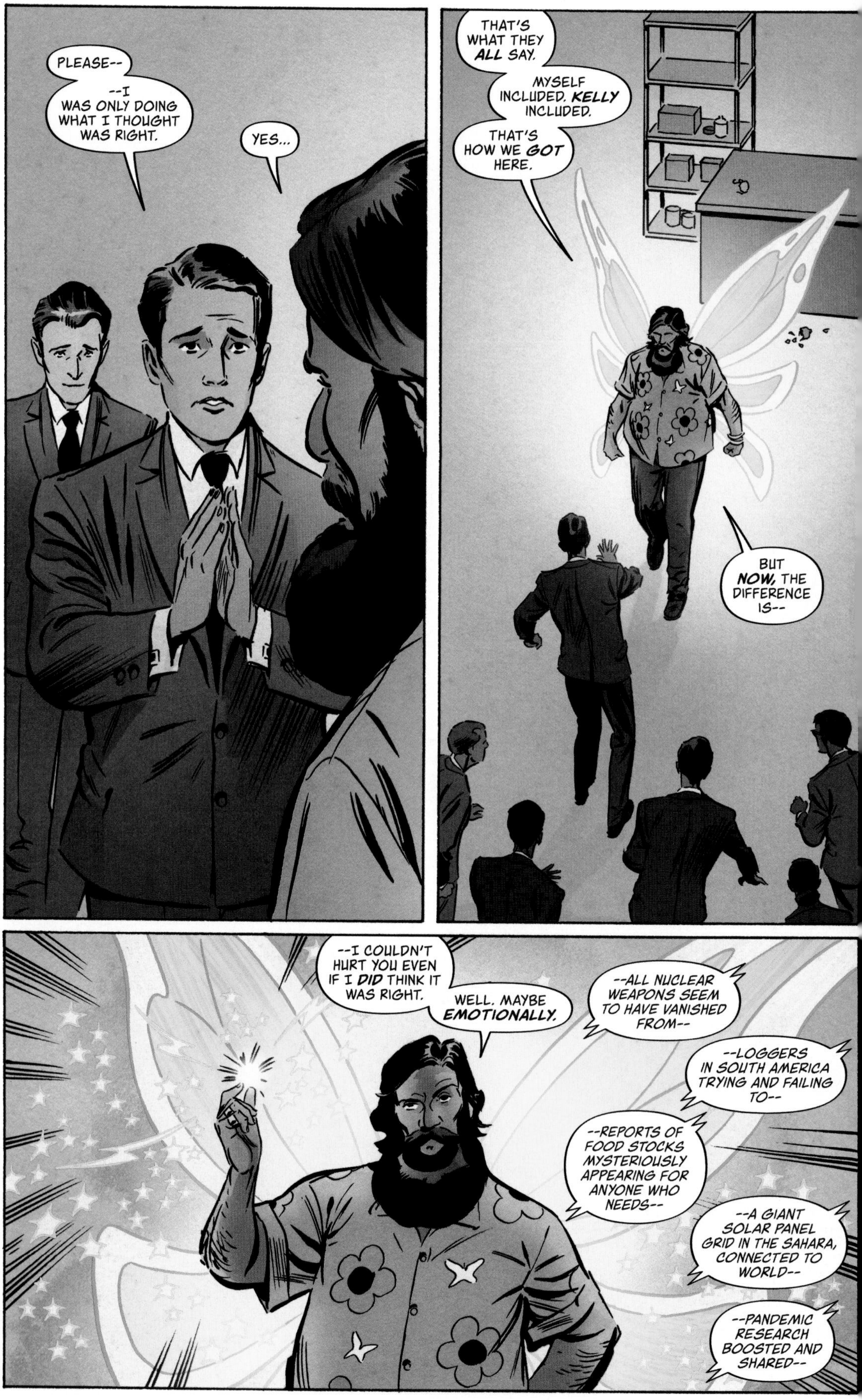

PLEASE--
--I WAS ONLY DOING WHAT I THOUGHT WAS RIGHT.
YES...
THAT'S WHAT THEY ALL SAY.
MYSELF INCLUDED. KELLY INCLUDED.
THAT'S HOW WE GOT HERE.
BUT NOW, THE DIFFERENCE IS--
--I COULDN'T HURT YOU EVEN IF I DID THINK IT WAS RIGHT.
WELL. MAYBE EMOTIONALLY.
--ALL NUCLEAR WEAPONS SEEM TO HAVE VANISHED FROM--
--LOGGERS IN SOUTH AMERICA TRYING AND FAILING TO--
--REPORTS OF FOOD STOCKS MYSTERIOUSLY APPEARING FOR ANYONE WHO NEEDS--
--A GIANT SOLAR PANEL GRID IN THE SAHARA, CONNECTED TO WORLD--
--PANDEMIC RESEARCH BOOSTED AND SHARED--

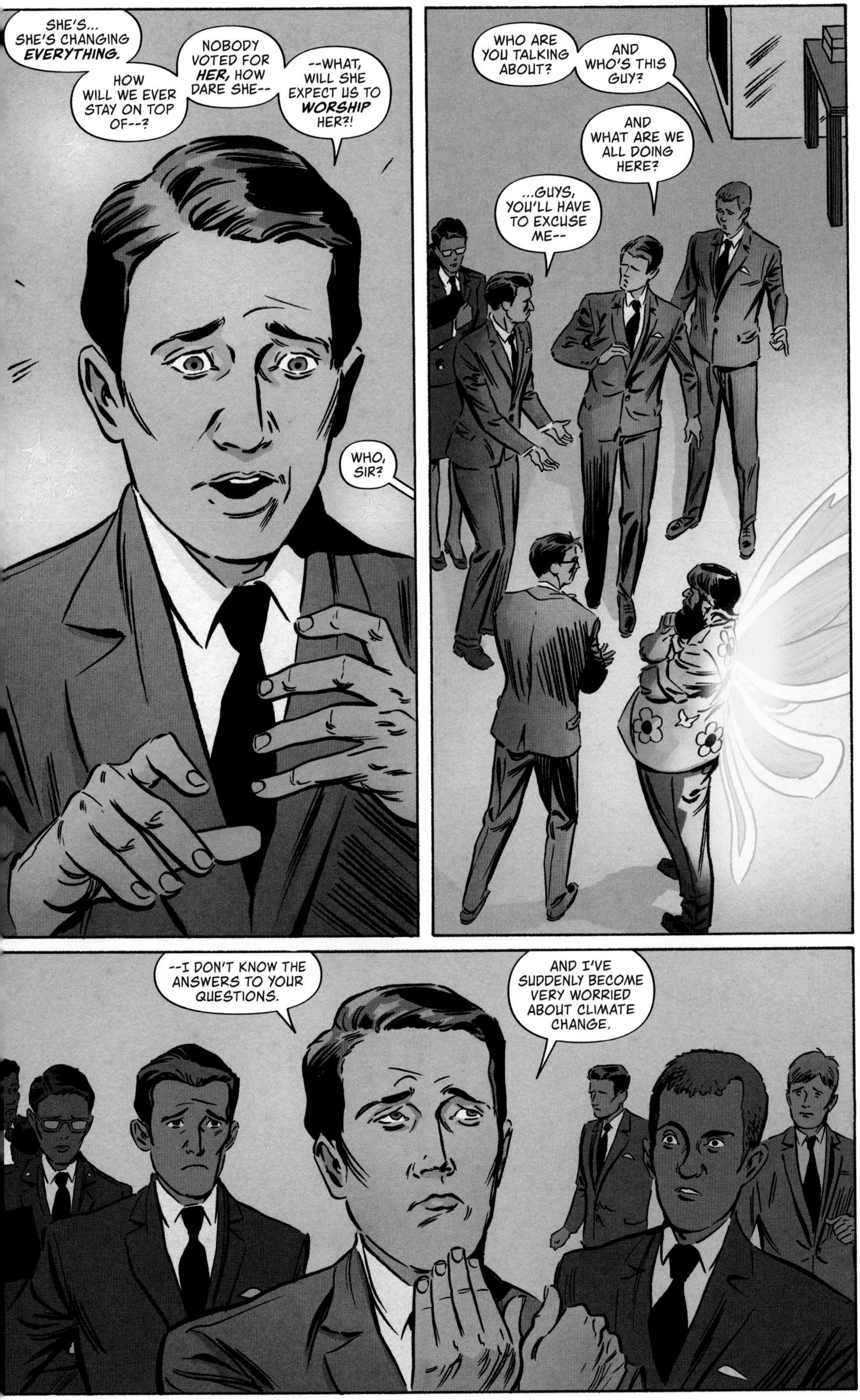

SHE'S... SHE'S CHANGING **EVERYTHING.**
HOW WILL WE EVER STAY ON TOP OF--?
NOBODY VOTED FOR **HER,** HOW DARE SHE--
--WHAT, WILL SHE EXPECT US TO **WORSHIP** HER?!
WHO, SIR?
WHO ARE YOU TALKING ABOUT?
AND WHO'S THIS GUY?
AND WHAT ARE WE ALL DOING HERE?
...GUYS, YOU'LL HAVE TO EXCUSE ME--
--I DON'T KNOW THE ANSWERS TO YOUR QUESTIONS.
AND I'VE SUDDENLY BECOME VERY WORRIED ABOUT CLIMATE CHANGE.

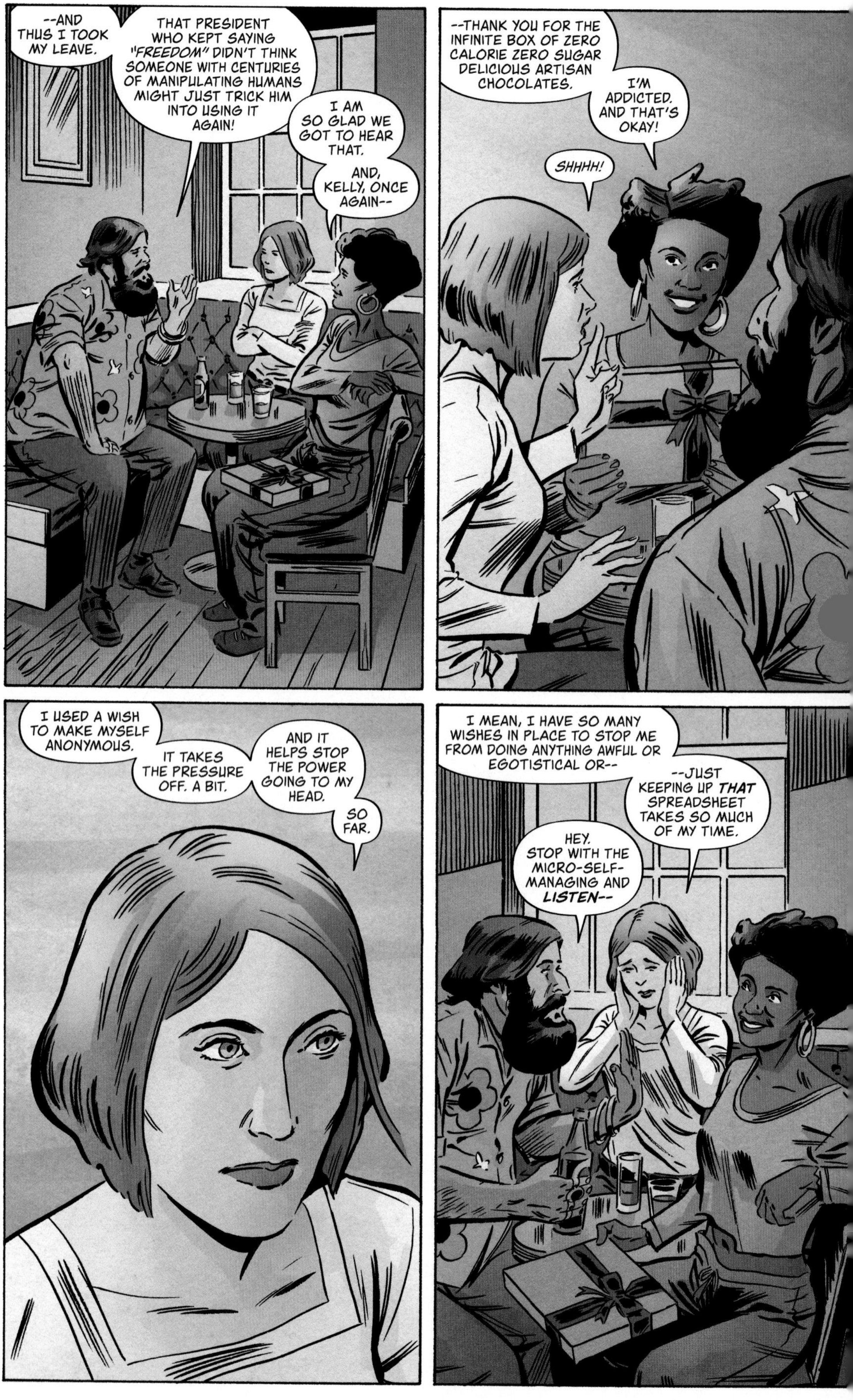
--AND THUS I TOOK MY LEAVE.
THAT PRESIDENT WHO KEPT SAYING *"FREEDOM"* DIDN'T THINK SOMEONE WITH CENTURIES OF MANIPULATING HUMANS MIGHT JUST TRICK HIM INTO USING IT AGAIN!
I AM SO GLAD WE GOT TO HEAR THAT.
AND, KELLY, ONCE AGAIN--
--THANK YOU FOR THE INFINITE BOX OF ZERO CALORIE ZERO SUGAR DELICIOUS ARTISAN CHOCOLATES.
I'M ADDICTED. AND THAT'S OKAY!
SHHHH!
I USED A WISH TO MAKE MYSELF ANONYMOUS.
IT TAKES THE PRESSURE OFF. A BIT.
AND IT HELPS STOP THE POWER GOING TO MY HEAD.
SO FAR.
I MEAN, I HAVE SO MANY WISHES IN PLACE TO STOP ME FROM DOING ANYTHING AWFUL OR EGOTISTICAL OR--
--JUST KEEPING UP ***THAT*** SPREADSHEET TAKES SO MUCH OF MY TIME.
HEY. STOP WITH THE MICRO-SELF-MANAGING AND ***LISTEN--***

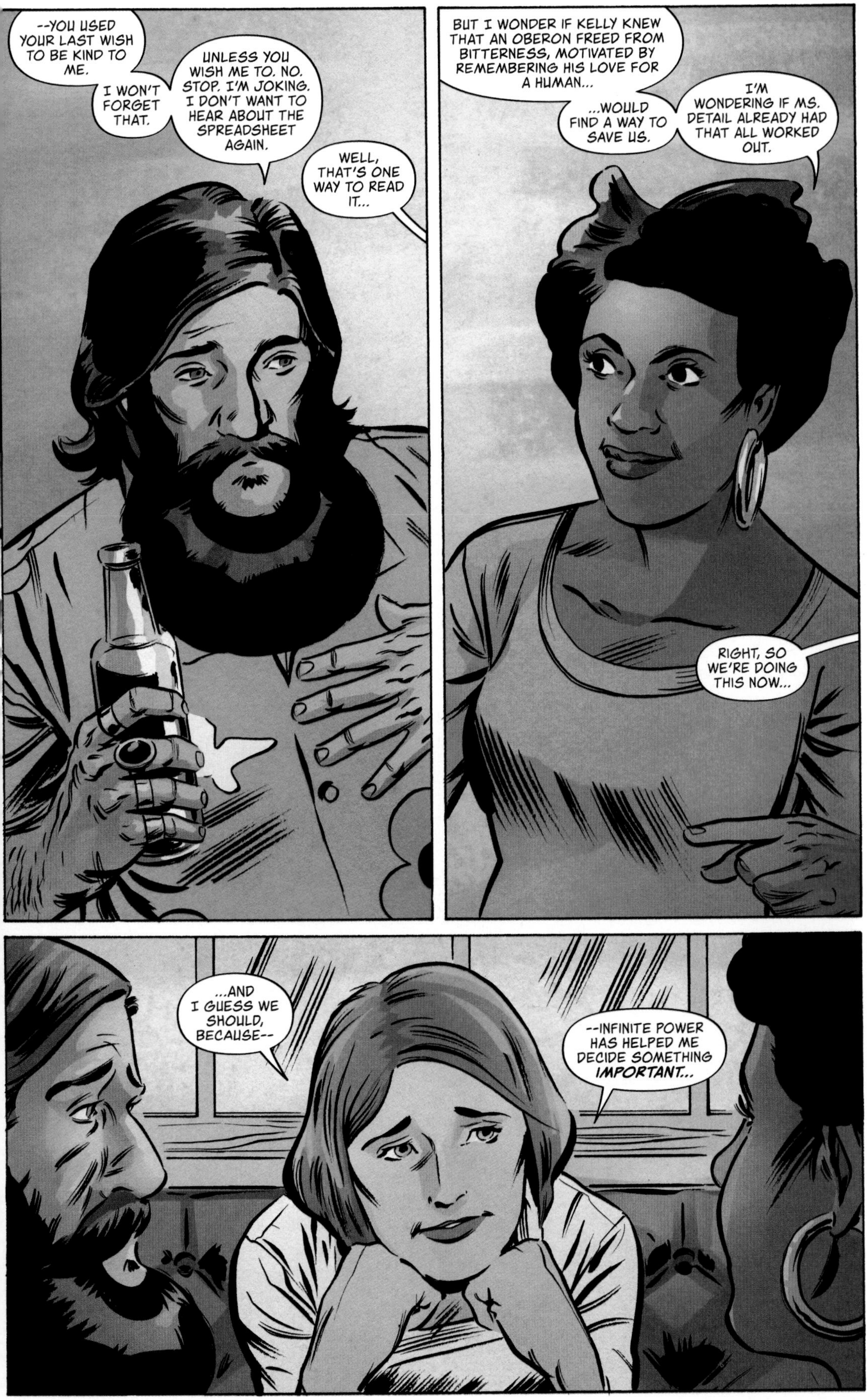
--YOU USED YOUR LAST WISH TO BE KIND TO ME.
I WON'T FORGET THAT.
UNLESS YOU WISH ME TO. NO. STOP. I'M JOKING. I DON'T WANT TO HEAR ABOUT THE SPREADSHEET AGAIN.
WELL, THAT'S ONE WAY TO READ IT...
BUT I WONDER IF KELLY KNEW THAT AN OBERON FREED FROM BITTERNESS, MOTIVATED BY REMEMBERING HIS LOVE FOR A HUMAN...
...WOULD FIND A WAY TO SAVE US.
I'M WONDERING IF MS. DETAIL ALREADY HAD THAT ALL WORKED OUT.
RIGHT, SO WE'RE DOING THIS NOW...
...AND I GUESS WE SHOULD, BECAUSE--
--INFINITE POWER HAS HELPED ME DECIDE SOMETHING IMPORTANT...

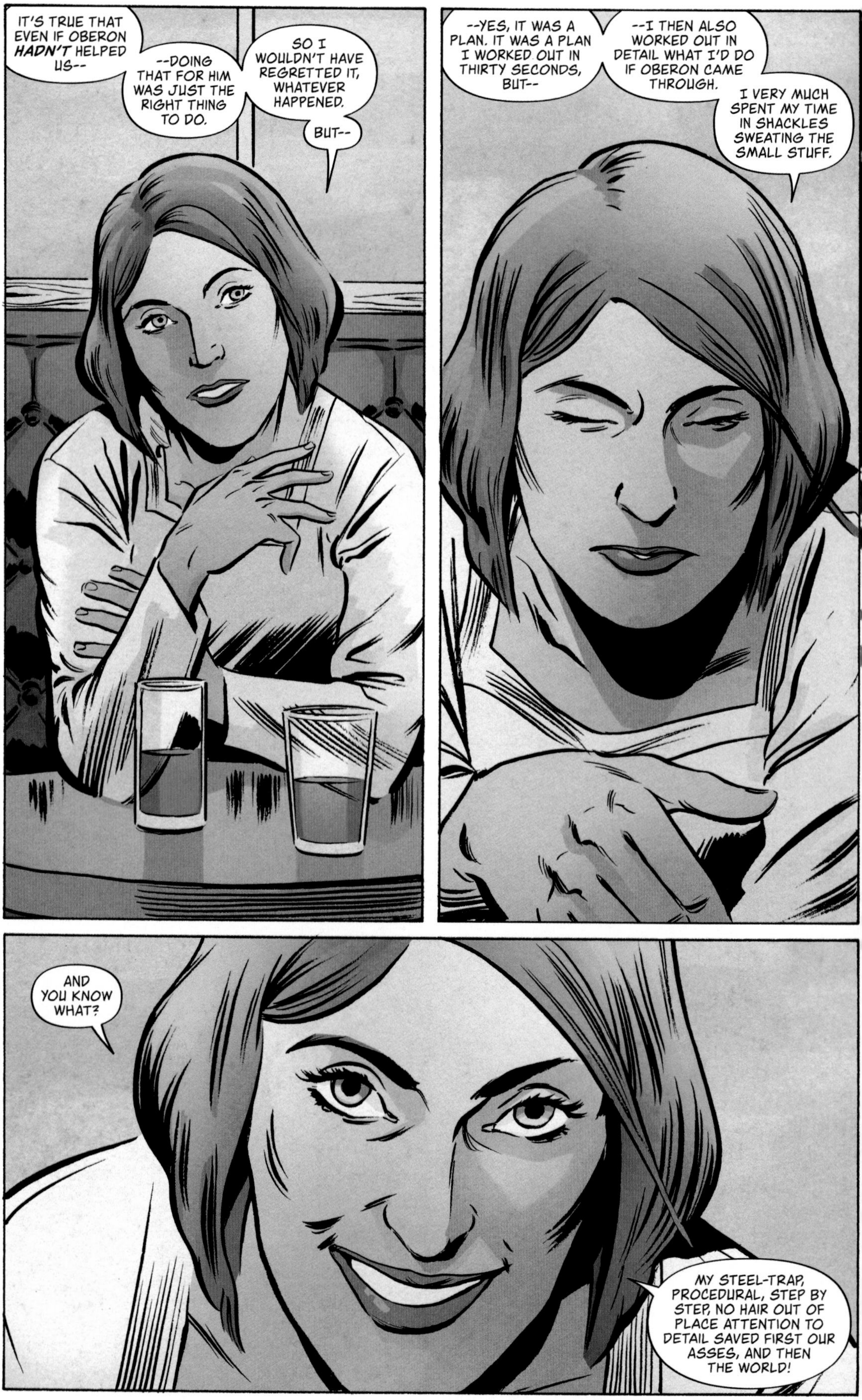
IT'S TRUE THAT EVEN IF OBERON **HADN'T** HELPED US--
--DOING THAT FOR HIM WAS JUST THE RIGHT THING TO DO.
SO I WOULDN'T HAVE REGRETTED IT, WHATEVER HAPPENED.
BUT--
--YES, IT WAS A PLAN. IT WAS A PLAN I WORKED OUT IN THIRTY SECONDS, BUT--
--I THEN ALSO WORKED OUT IN DETAIL WHAT I'D DO IF OBERON CAME THROUGH.
I VERY MUCH SPENT MY TIME IN SHACKLES SWEATING THE SMALL STUFF.
AND YOU KNOW WHAT?
MY STEEL-TRAP, PROCEDURAL, STEP BY STEP, NO HAIR OUT OF PLACE ATTENTION TO DETAIL SAVED FIRST OUR ASSES, AND THEN THE WORLD!

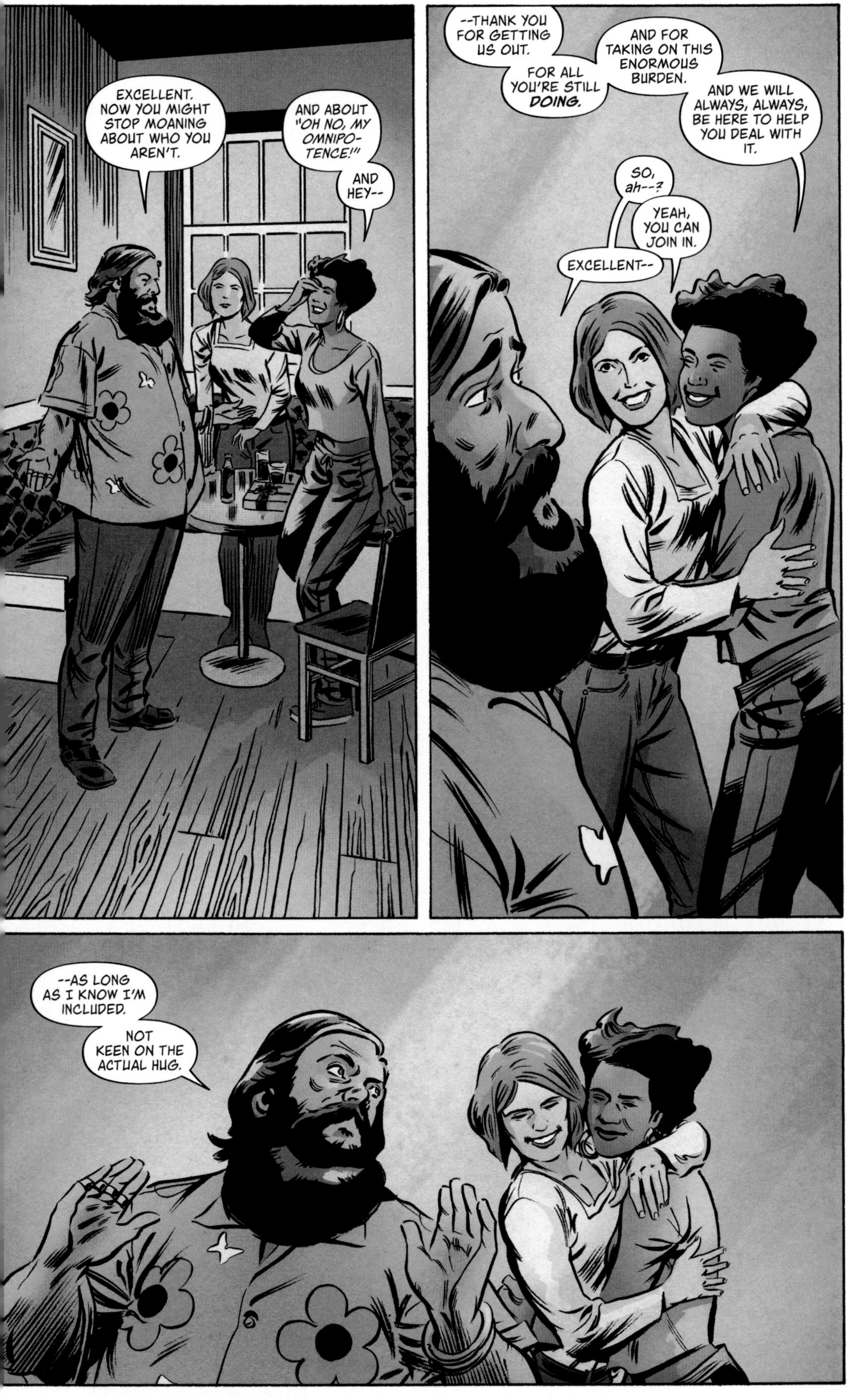
EXCELLENT. NOW YOU MIGHT STOP MOANING ABOUT WHO YOU AREN'T.
AND ABOUT "OH NO, MY OMNIPO-TENCE!"
AND HEY--
--THANK YOU FOR GETTING US OUT.
FOR ALL YOU'RE STILL DOING.
AND FOR TAKING ON THIS ENORMOUS BURDEN.
AND WE WILL ALWAYS, ALWAYS, BE HERE TO HELP YOU DEAL WITH IT.
SO, ah--?
YEAH, YOU CAN JOIN IN.
EXCELLENT--
--AS LONG AS I KNOW I'M INCLUDED.
NOT KEEN ON THE ACTUAL HUG.

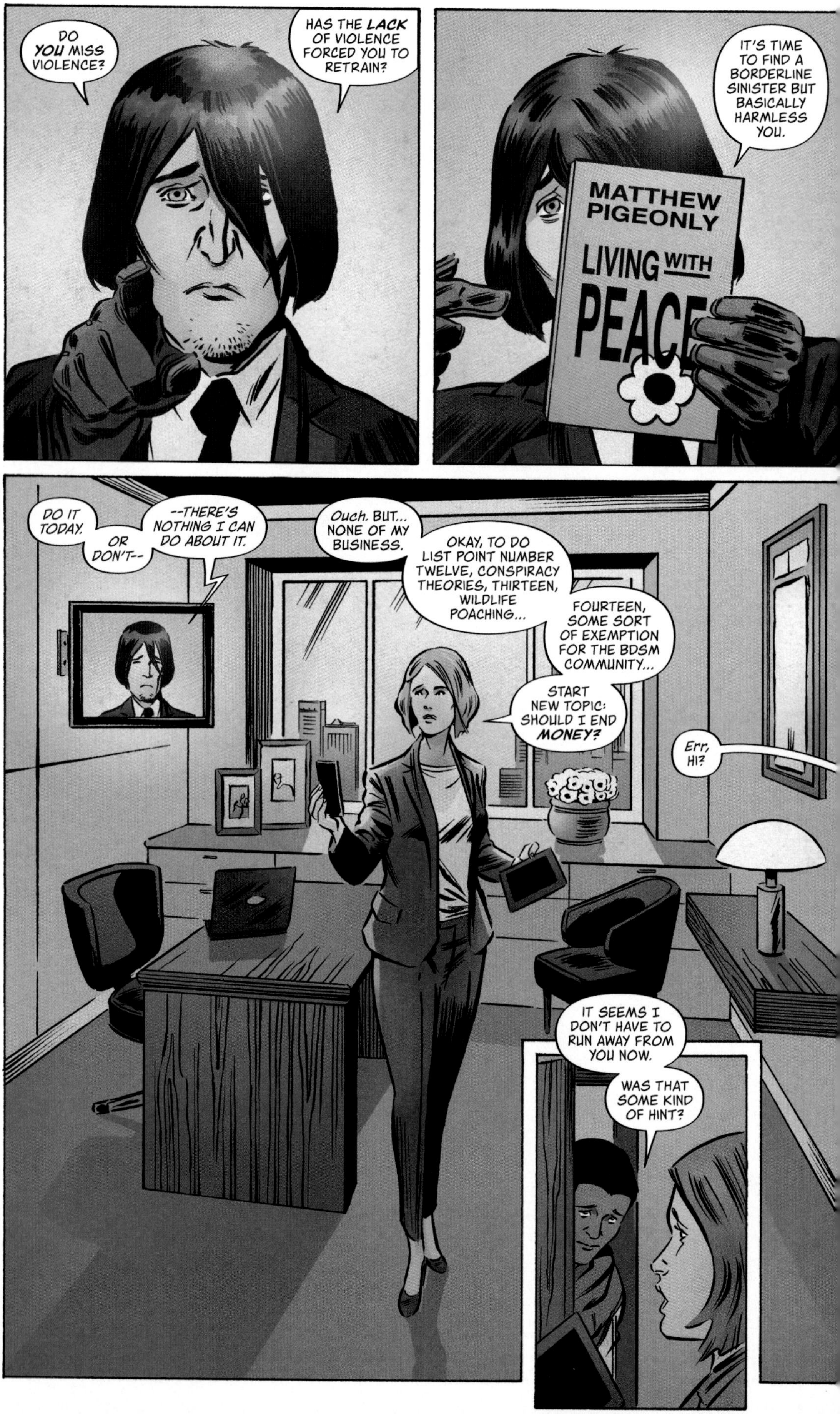
DO YOU MISS VIOLENCE?
HAS THE LACK OF VIOLENCE FORCED YOU TO RETRAIN?
IT'S TIME TO FIND A BORDERLINE SINISTER BUT BASICALLY HARMLESS YOU.
MATTHEW PIGEONLY
LIVING WITH PEACE
DO IT TODAY.
OR DON'T--
--THERE'S NOTHING I CAN DO ABOUT IT.
Ouch. BUT... NONE OF MY BUSINESS.
OKAY, TO DO LIST POINT NUMBER TWELVE, CONSPIRACY THEORIES, THIRTEEN, WILDLIFE POACHING...
FOURTEEN, SOME SORT OF EXEMPTION FOR THE BDSM COMMUNITY...
START NEW TOPIC: SHOULD I END MONEY?
Err, HI?
IT SEEMS I DON'T HAVE TO RUN AWAY FROM YOU NOW.
WAS THAT SOME KIND OF HINT?

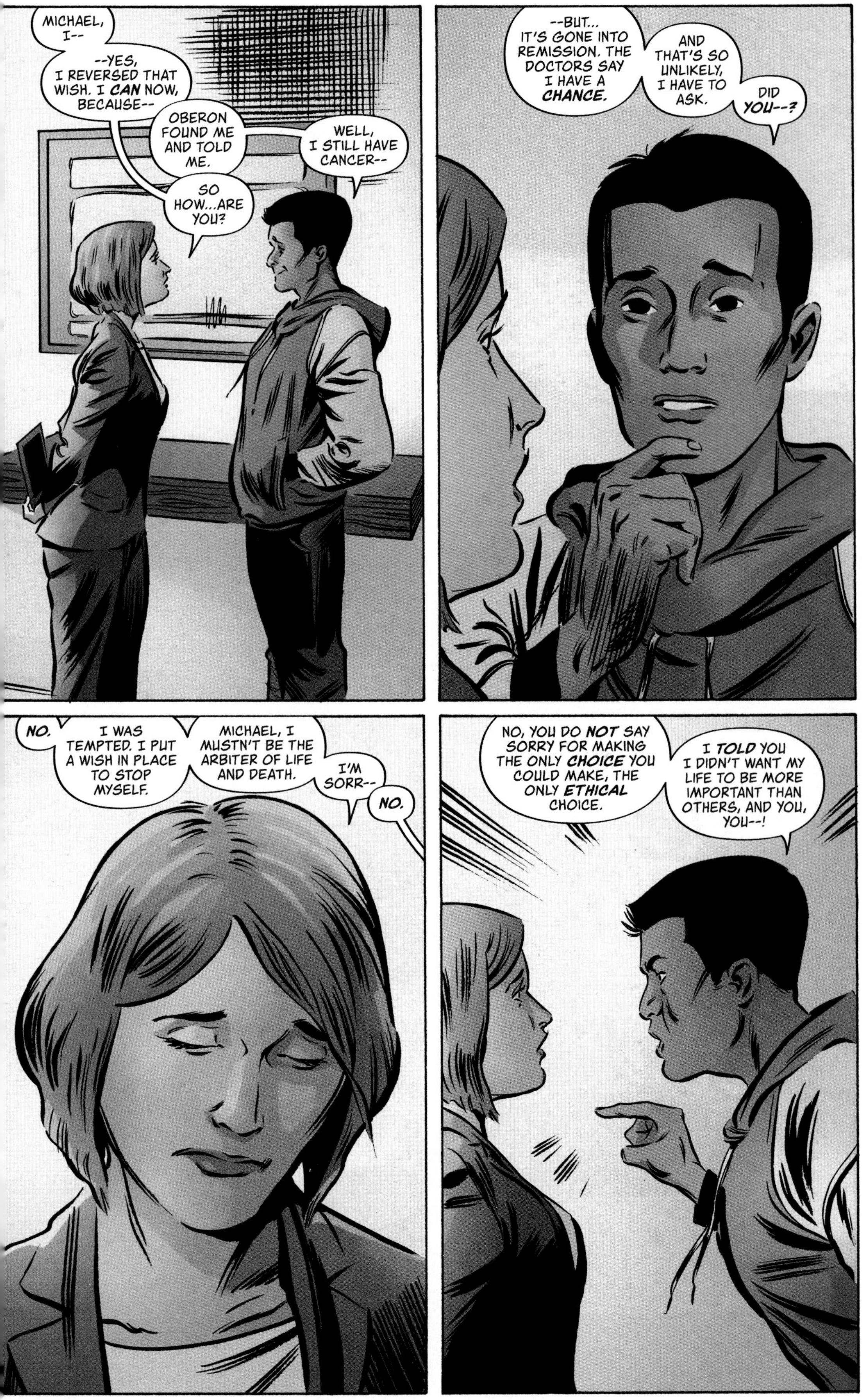
MICHAEL, I--
--YES, I REVERSED THAT WISH. I CAN NOW, BECAUSE--
OBERON FOUND ME AND TOLD ME.
WELL, I STILL HAVE CANCER--
SO HOW...ARE YOU?
--BUT... IT'S GONE INTO REMISSION. THE DOCTORS SAY I HAVE A CHANCE.
AND THAT'S SO UNLIKELY, I HAVE TO ASK.
DID YOU--?
NO.
I WAS TEMPTED. I PUT A WISH IN PLACE TO STOP MYSELF.
MICHAEL, I MUSTN'T BE THE ARBITER OF LIFE AND DEATH.
I'M SORR--
NO.
NO, YOU DO NOT SAY SORRY FOR MAKING THE ONLY CHOICE YOU COULD MAKE, THE ONLY ETHICAL CHOICE.
I TOLD YOU I DIDN'T WANT MY LIFE TO BE MORE IMPORTANT THAN OTHERS, AND YOU, YOU--!

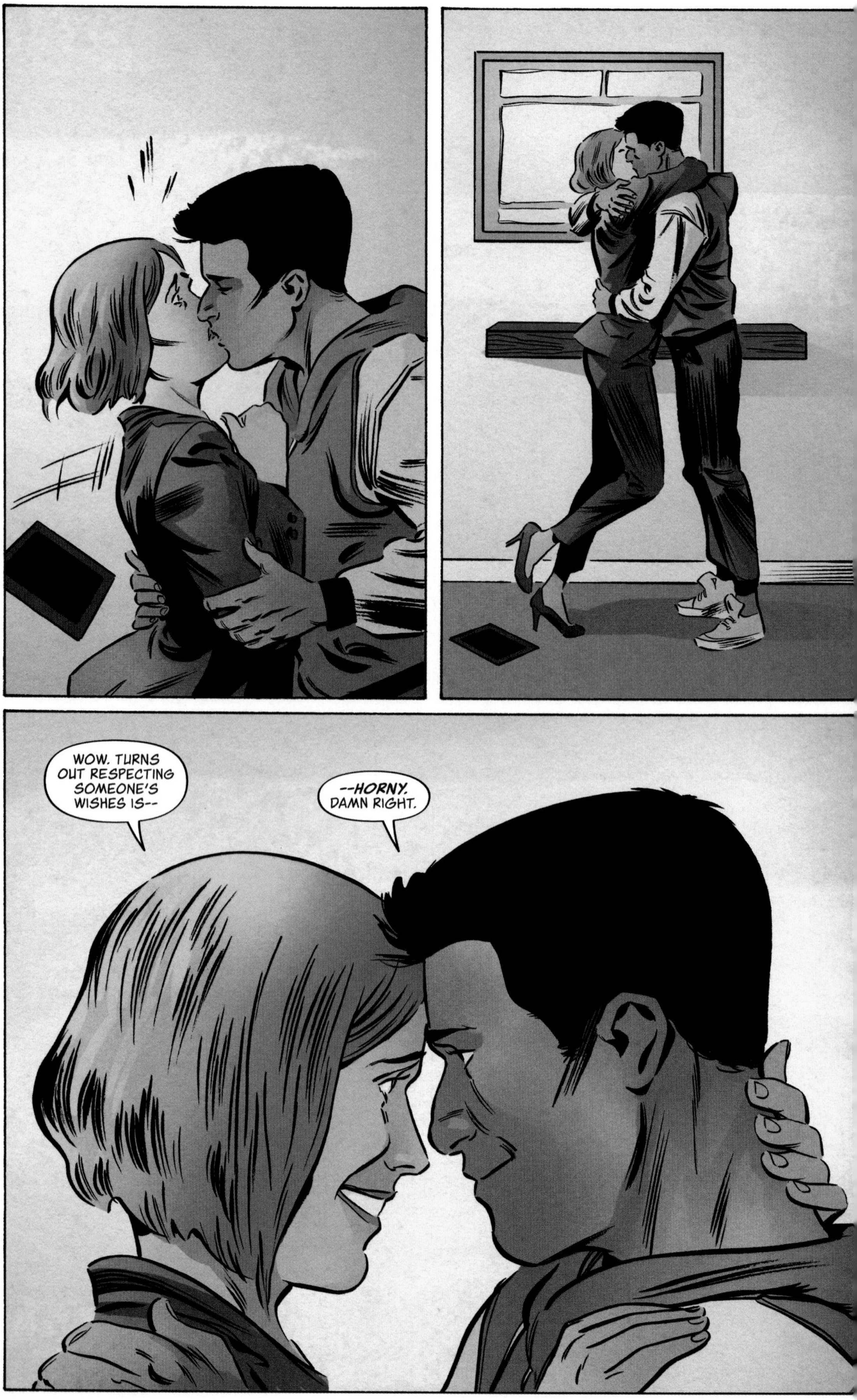
WOW. TURNS OUT RESPECTING SOMEONE'S WISHES IS--
--HORNY. DAMN RIGHT.

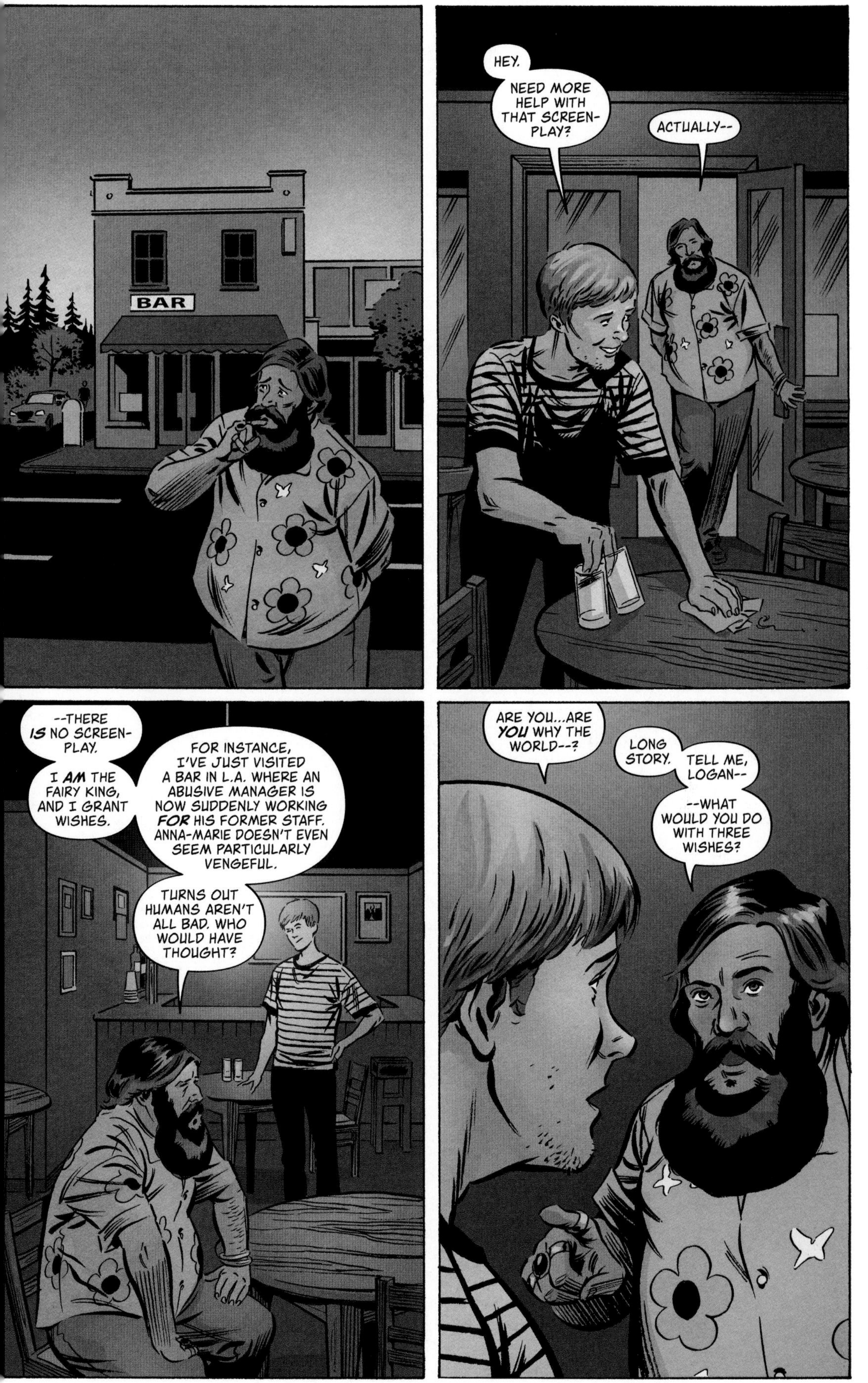
BAR
HEY.
NEED MORE HELP WITH THAT SCREEN-PLAY?
ACTUALLY--
--THERE IS NO SCREEN-PLAY.
I AM THE FAIRY KING, AND I GRANT WISHES.
FOR INSTANCE, I'VE JUST VISITED A BAR IN L.A. WHERE AN ABUSIVE MANAGER IS NOW SUDDENLY WORKING FOR HIS FORMER STAFF. ANNA-MARIE DOESN'T EVEN SEEM PARTICULARLY VENGEFUL.
TURNS OUT HUMANS AREN'T ALL BAD. WHO WOULD HAVE THOUGHT?
ARE YOU...ARE YOU WHY THE WORLD--?
LONG STORY.
TELL ME, LOGAN--
--WHAT WOULD YOU DO WITH THREE WISHES?

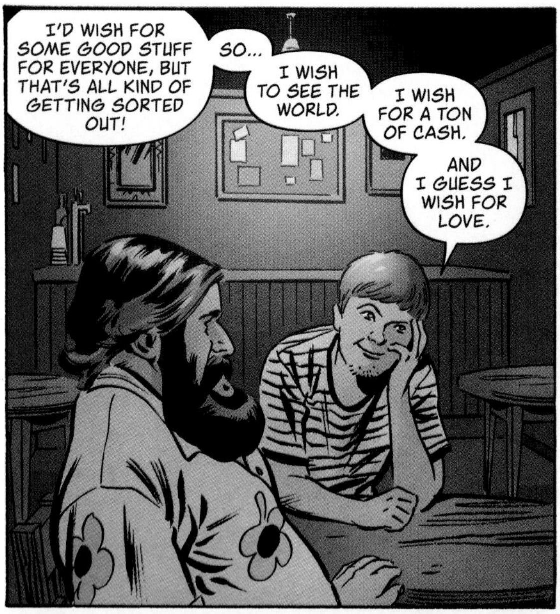
I'D WISH FOR SOME GOOD STUFF FOR EVERYONE, BUT THAT'S ALL KIND OF GETTING SORTED OUT!
SO...
I WISH TO SEE THE WORLD.
I WISH FOR A TON OF CASH.
AND I GUESS I WISH FOR LOVE.

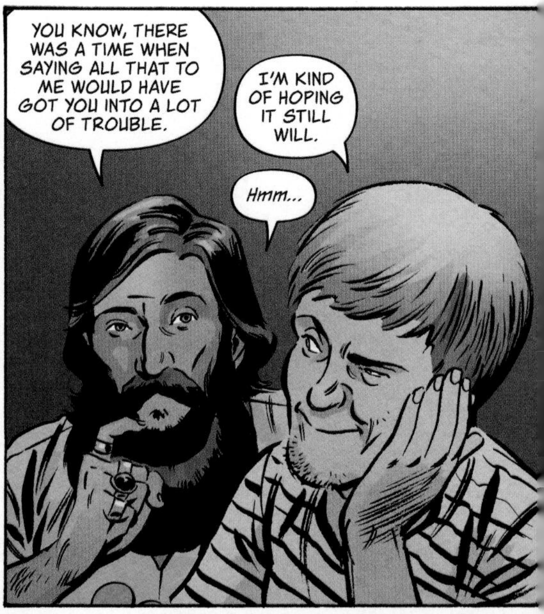
YOU KNOW, THERE WAS A TIME WHEN SAYING ALL THAT TO ME WOULD HAVE GOT YOU INTO A LOT OF TROUBLE.
I'M KIND OF HOPING IT STILL WILL.
Hmm...

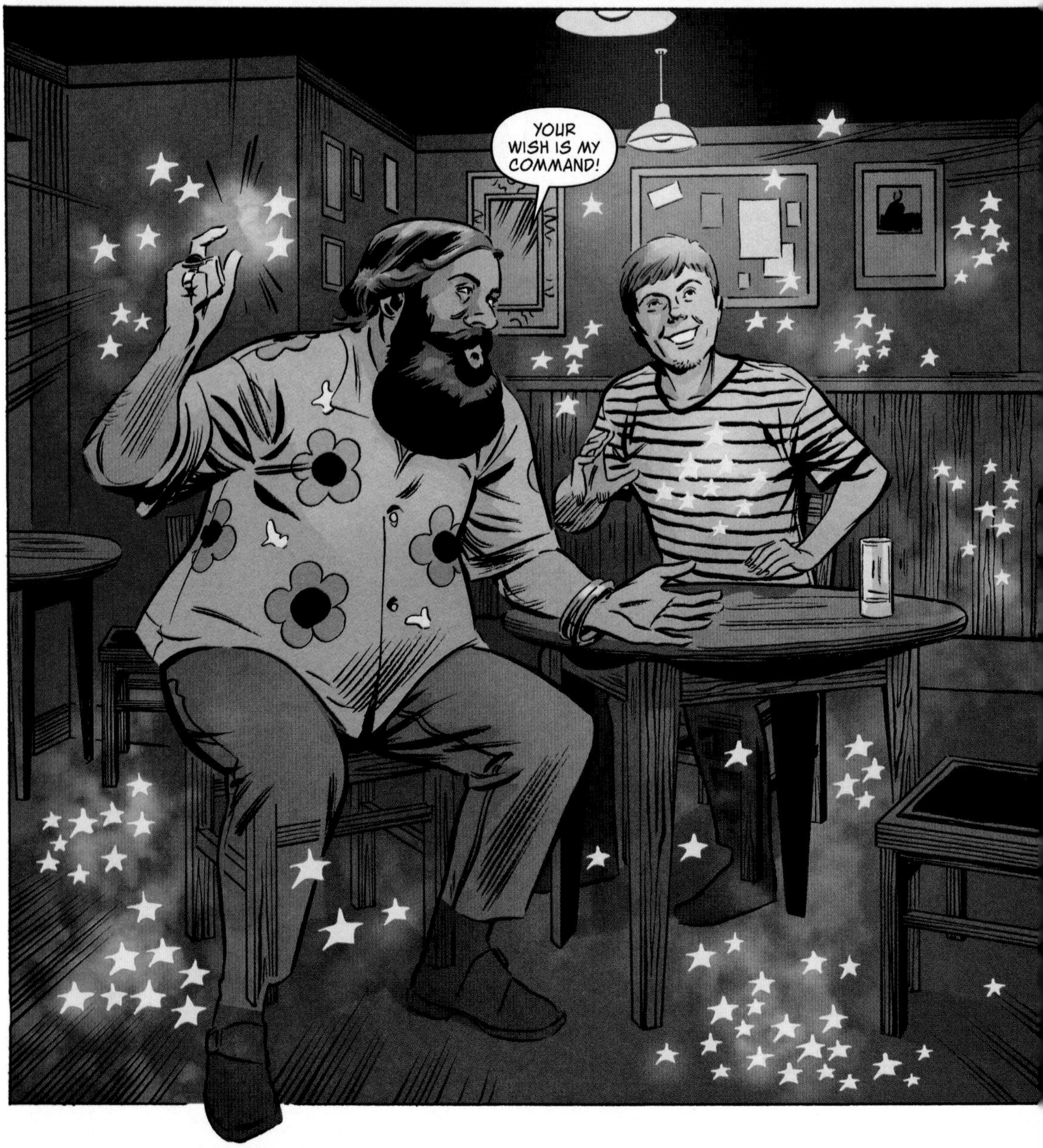
YOUR WISH IS MY COMMAND!

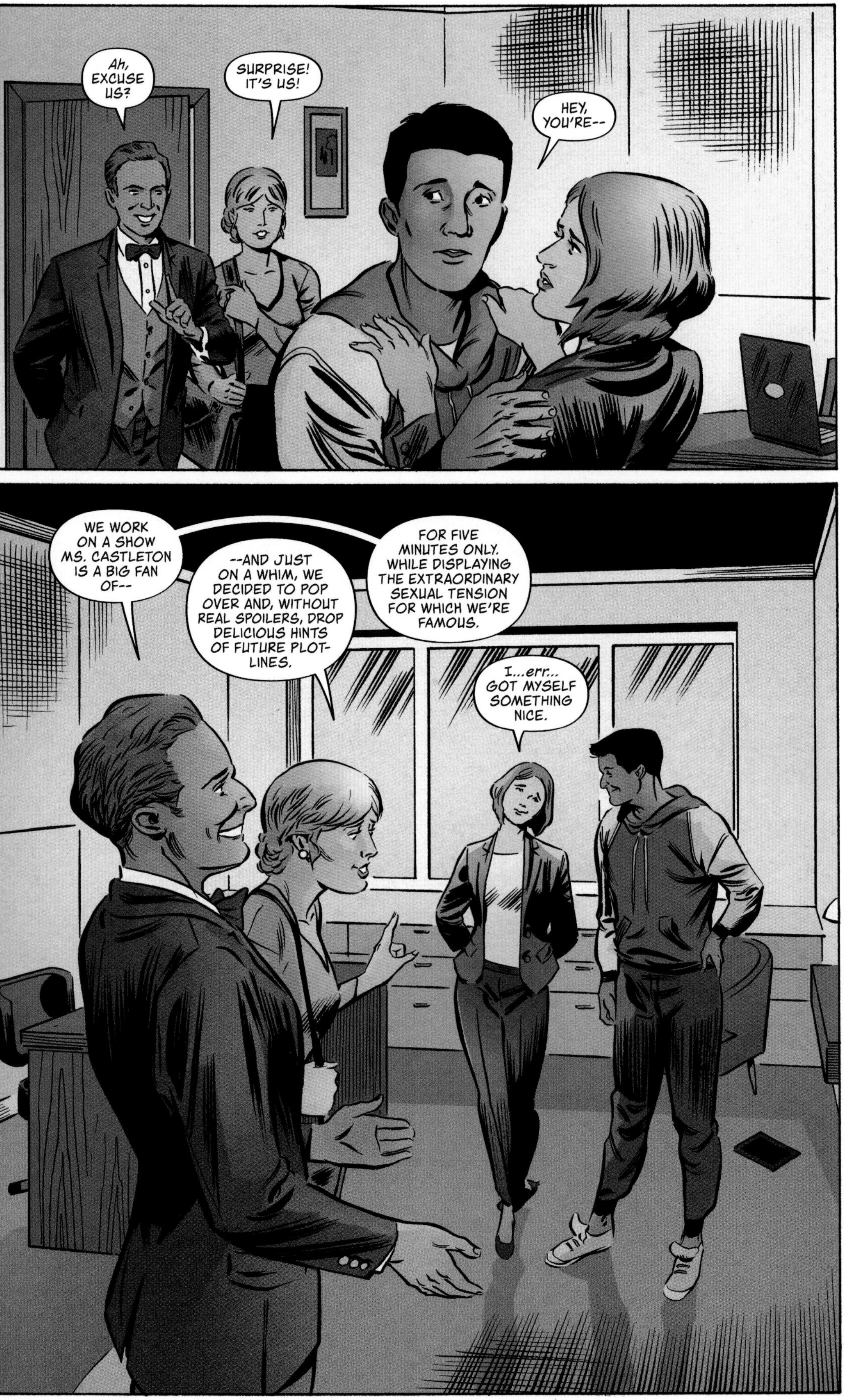
Ah, EXCUSE US?
SURPRISE! IT'S US!
HEY, YOU'RE--
WE WORK ON A SHOW MS. CASTLETON IS A BIG FAN OF--
--AND JUST ON A WHIM, WE DECIDED TO POP OVER AND, WITHOUT REAL SPOILERS, DROP DELICIOUS HINTS OF FUTURE PLOT-LINES.
FOR FIVE MINUTES ONLY. WHILE DISPLAYING THE EXTRAORDINARY SEXUAL TENSION FOR WHICH WE'RE FAMOUS.
I...err... GOT MYSELF SOMETHING NICE.

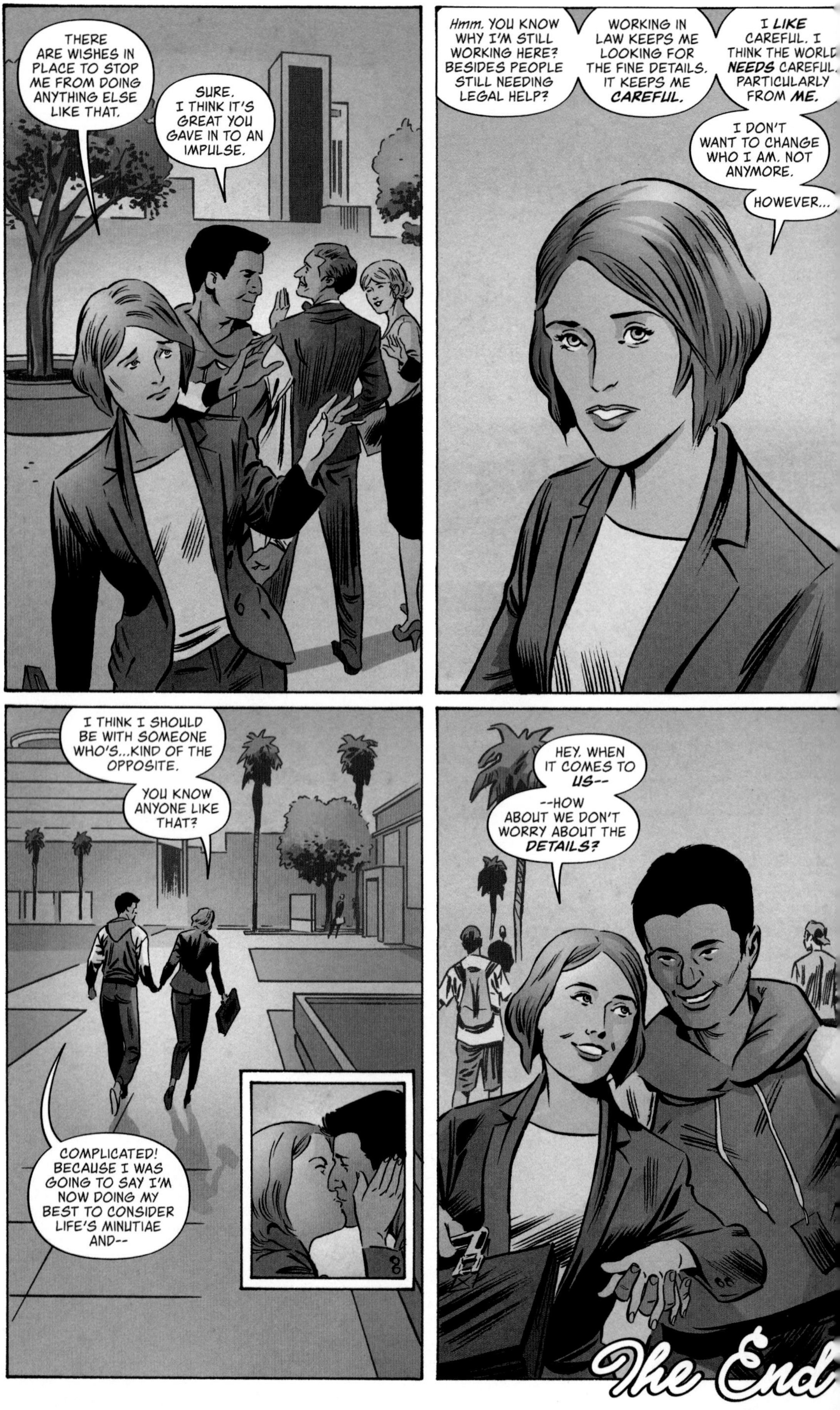
THERE ARE WISHES IN PLACE TO STOP ME FROM DOING ANYTHING ELSE LIKE THAT.
SURE. I THINK IT'S GREAT YOU GAVE IN TO AN IMPULSE.
Hmm. YOU KNOW WHY I'M STILL WORKING HERE? BESIDES PEOPLE STILL NEEDING LEGAL HELP?
WORKING IN LAW KEEPS ME LOOKING FOR THE FINE DETAILS. IT KEEPS ME ***CAREFUL.***
I ***LIKE*** CAREFUL. I THINK THE WORLD ***NEEDS*** CAREFUL. PARTICULARLY FROM ***ME.***
I DON'T WANT TO CHANGE WHO I AM. NOT ANYMORE.
HOWEVER...
I THINK I SHOULD BE WITH SOMEONE WHO'S...KIND OF THE OPPOSITE.
YOU KNOW ANYONE LIKE THAT?
COMPLICATED! BECAUSE I WAS GOING TO SAY I'M NOW DOING MY BEST TO CONSIDER LIFE'S MINUTIAE AND--
HEY. WHEN IT COMES TO ***US--***
--HOW ABOUT WE DON'T WORRY ABOUT THE ***DETAILS?***
The End

KELLY

KELLY CASTLETON is a neat, smart, slightly buttoned-up (but not to the point of caricature) white woman in her early thirties. Her conservative style is offset by her incredibly expressive face. She has wry eyebrows that are always mobile, always indicative.

OBERON is a slightly portly, slightly bumptious, very smart when he gets the chance but also very eccentric figure, luxuriously bearded like some ancient god. He's got soulful eyes, which help when he's doing bad stuff. He carries himself with great dignity, which is easily upended.

OBERON

AUG 2022

ANNIE is an African-American woman in her early thirties, as conservative as Kelly when at work, but considerably more relaxed at home. She's got style but it's offhand. She's someone who knows the world's hard, so she doesn't punish herself. A wry, humane expression.

PIGEONLY is a pale, thin goth assassin in his thirties with a sweep of hair over his face and a pained expression. He looks supremely put-upon.

MICHAEL is a gorgeous, wry-looking Japanese-American, the same age as Kelly, sporty and slim, a warm, friendly teacher. But if we look at him closely in the modern scenes, we might detect the weight loss and pain that have tested him in the last few months.

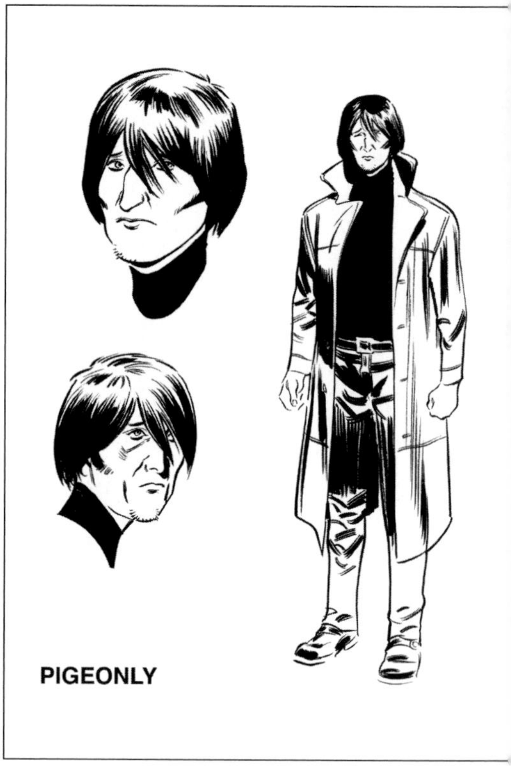
PIGEONLY

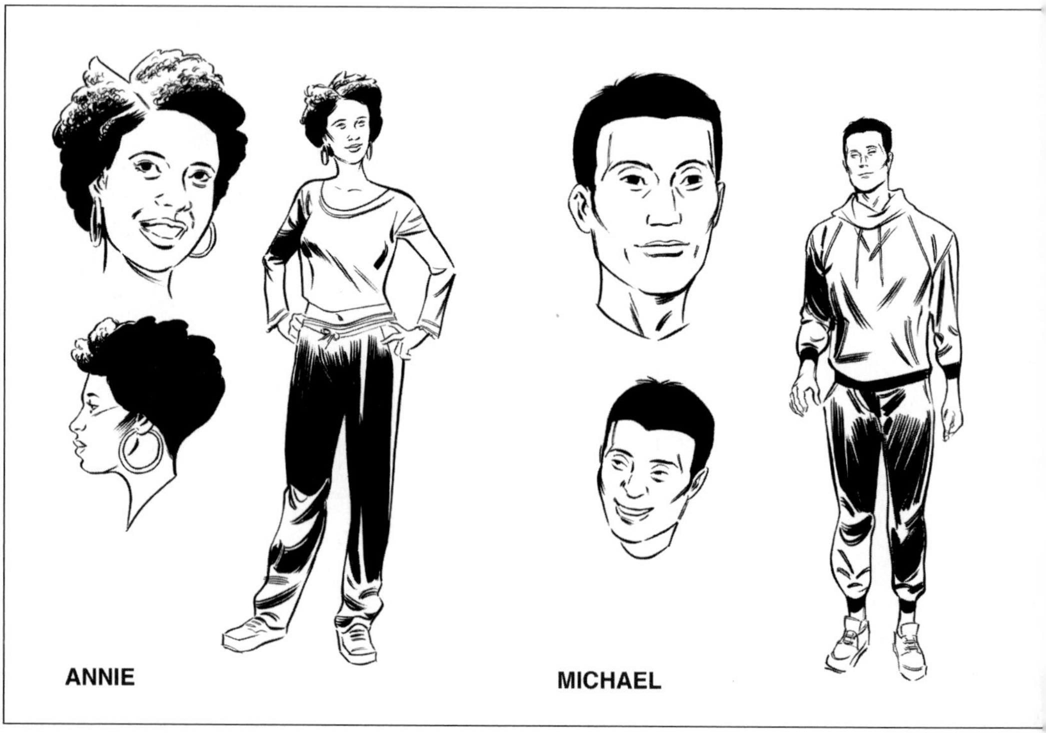
ANNIE
MICHAEL